PRISONERS OF GEOGRAPHY

TEN MAPS THAT TELL YOU EVERYTHING YOU NEED TO KNOW ABOUT GLOBAL POLITICS

TIM MARSHALL

Foreword by Sir John Scarlett

Elliott&Thompson

First published 2015 by
Elliott and Thompson Limited
2 John Street
London WC1N 2ES
www.eandtbooks.com

This paperback edition first published in 2016

ISBN: 978-1-78396-243-3

52

A catalogue record for this book is available from the British Library.

Maps: JP Map Graphics Ltd
Typesetting: Marie Doherty
Printed by CPI Group (UK) Ltd, Croydon, CR0 4YY

CONTENTS

Foreword *by Sir John Scarlett KCMG OBE* v
Introduction vii

1 Russia 1
2 China 33
3 USA 63
4 Western Europe 91
5 Africa 117
6 The Middle East 145
7 India and Pakistan 189
8 Korea and Japan 217
9 Latin America 241
10 The Arctic 269

Conclusion 288
Bibliography 293
Acknowledgements 297
Index 298

FOREWORD

IT HAS BECOME A TRUISM TO THINK, AND TO SAY, THAT we live in exceptionally unstable times. The world, we are told, has never been more unpredictable. Such statements invite a cautious, even sceptical, response. It is right to be cautious. The world has always been unstable and the future, by definition, unpredictable. Our current worries could certainly be much worse. If nothing else, the centenary of 1914 should have reminded us of that.

All that said, fundamental changes are certainly under way, and these have real meaning for our own future and that of our children, wherever we live. Economic, social and demographic change, all linked to rapid technological change, have global implications which may mark out the times we live in now from those that went before. This may be why we talk so much about 'exceptional uncertainty' and why 'geopolitical' commentary has become a growth industry.

Tim Marshall is unusually well qualified, personally and professionally, to contribute to this debate. He has participated directly in many of the most dramatic developments of the past twenty-five years. As his Introduction reminds us, he has been on the front line in the Balkans, Afghanistan and Syria. He has seen how decisions and events, international conflicts and civil wars, can only be understood by taking full account of the hopes, fears and preconceptions formed by history and how these in turn are driven by the physical surroundings – the geography – in which individuals, societies and countries have developed.

As a result, this book is full of well-judged insights of immediate relevance to our security and well-being. What has influenced Russian action in Ukraine? Did we (the West) fail to anticipate this? If so, why? How far will Moscow push now? Does China at last feel secure within what it sees as natural land borders, and how will this affect Beijing's approach to maritime power and the USA? What does this mean for other countries in the region, including India and Japan? For over 200 years the USA has benefited from highly favourable geographical circumstances and natural resource endowment. Now it has unconventional oil and gas. Will this affect its global policy? The USA has extraordinary power and resilience, so why is there so much talk of US decline? Are the deeply embedded divisions and emotions across North Africa, the Middle East and South Asia intractable, or can we detect some hope for the future? Finally, and maybe most importantly for our country, the United Kingdom, which is one of the largest and most global economies: how is Europe reacting to the uncertainties and conflicts nearby, and not so nearby? As Tim points out, over the past seventy years (and especially since 1991) Europe has become accustomed to peace and prosperity. Are we at risk now of taking this for granted? Do we still understand what is going on around us?

If you want to think about these questions, read this book.

Sir John Scarlett KCMG OBE,
Chief Secret Intelligence Service (MI6), 2004–2009

INTRODUCTION

VLADIMIR PUTIN SAYS HE IS A RELIGIOUS MAN, A GREAT supporter of the Russian Orthodox Church. If so, he may well go to bed each night, say his prayers and ask God: 'Why didn't you put some mountains in Ukraine?'

If God had built mountains in Ukraine, then the great expanse of flatland that is the North European Plain would not be such encouraging territory from which to attack Russia repeatedly. As it is, Putin has no choice: he must at least attempt to control the flatlands to the west. So it is with all nations, big or small. The landscape imprisons their leaders, giving them fewer choices and less room to manoeuvre than you might think. This was true of the Athenian Empire, the Persians, the Babylonians and before; it was true of every leader seeking high ground from which to protect their tribe.

The land on which we live has always shaped us. It has shaped the wars, the power, politics and social development of the peoples that now inhabit nearly every part of the earth. Technology may seem to overcome the distances between us in both mental and physical space, but it is easy to forget that the land where we live, work and raise our children is hugely important, and that the choices of those who lead the 7.5 billion inhabitants of this planet will to some degree always be shaped by the rivers, mountains, deserts, lakes and seas that constrain us all – as they always have.

Overall there is no one geographical factor that is more important than any other. Mountains are no more important than deserts, nor rivers than jungles. In different parts of the planet, different geographical features are among the dominant factors in determining what people can and cannot do.

Broadly speaking, geopolitics looks at the ways in which international affairs can be understood through geographical factors; not just the physical landscape – the natural barriers of mountains or connections of river networks, for example – but also climate, demographics, cultural regions and access to natural resources. Factors such as these can have an important impact on many different aspects of our civilisation, from political and military strategy to human social development, including language, trade and religion.

The physical realities that underpin national and international politics are too often disregarded both in writing about history and in contemporary reporting of world affairs. Geography is clearly a fundamental part of the 'why' as well as the 'what'. It might not be *the* determining factor, but it is certainly the most overlooked. Take, for example, China and India: two massive countries with huge populations that share a very long border but are not politically or culturally aligned. It wouldn't be surprising if these two giants had fought each other in several wars, but in fact, apart from one month-long battle in 1962, they never have. Why? Because between them is the highest mountain range in the world, and it is practically impossible to advance large military columns through or over the Himalayas. As technology becomes more sophisticated, of course, ways are emerging of overcoming this obstacle, but the physical barrier remains a deterrent, and so both countries focus their foreign policy on other regions while keeping a wary eye on each other.

Individual leaders, ideas, technology and other factors all play a role in shaping events, but they are temporary. Each new generation will still face the physical obstructions created by the Hindu Kush and the Himalayas; the challenges created by the rainy season; and the disadvantages of limited access to natural minerals or food sources.

I first became interested in this subject when covering the wars in the Balkans in the 1990s. I watched close at hand as the leaders of various peoples, be they Serbian, Croat or Bosniak, deliberately reminded their 'tribes' of the ancient divisions and, yes, ancient suspicions in a region crowded with diversity. Once they had pulled the peoples apart, it didn't take much to then push them against each other.

The River Ibar in Kosovo is a prime example. Ottoman rule over Serbia was cemented by the Battle of Kosovo Polje in 1389, fought near where the Ibar flows through the city of Mitrovica. Over the following centuries the Serb population began to withdraw behind the Ibar as Muslim Albanians gradually descended from the mountainous Malesija region into Kosovo, where they became a majority by the mid eighteenth century.

Fast-forward to the twentieth century and there was still a clear ethnic/religious division roughly marked by the river. Then in 1999, battered by NATO from the air and the Kosovo Liberation Army on the ground, the Yugoslav (Serbian) military retreated across the Ibar, quickly followed by most of the remaining Serb population. The river became the de facto border of what some countries now recognise as the independent state of Kosovo.

Mitrovica was also where the advancing NATO ground forces came to a halt. During the three-month war there had been veiled threats that NATO intended to invade all of Serbia. In truth, the restraints of both geography and politics meant the NATO leaders never really had that option. Hungary had made it clear that it would not allow an invasion from its territory, as it feared reprisals against the 350,000 ethnic Hungarians in northern Serbia. The alternative was an invasion from the south, which would have got them to the Ibar in double-quick time; but NATO would then have faced the mountains above them.

I was working with a team of Serbs in Belgrade at the time and asked what would happen if NATO came: 'We will put our cameras down, Tim, and pick up guns,' was the response. They were liberal Serbs, good friends of mine and opposed to their government, but they still pulled out the maps and showed me where the Serbs would defend their territory in the mountains, and where NATO would grind to a halt. It was some relief to be given a geography lesson in why NATO's choices were more limited than the Brussels PR machine made public.

An understanding of how crucial the physical landscape was in reporting news in the Balkans stood me in good stead in the years which followed. For example, in 2001, a few weeks after 9/11, I saw a demonstration of how, even with today's modern technology, climate still dictates the military possibilities of even the world's most powerful armies. I was in northern Afghanistan, having crossed the border river from Tajikistan on a raft, in order to link up with the Northern Alliance (NA) troops who were fighting the Taliban.

The American fighter jets and bombers were already overhead, pounding Taliban and Al Qaeda positions on the cold, dusty plains and hills east of Mazar-e-Sharif in order to pave the way for the advance on Kabul. After a few weeks it was obvious that the NA were gearing up to move south. And then the world changed colour.

The most intense sandstorm I have ever experienced blew in, turning everything a mustard-yellow colour. Even the air around us seemed to be this hue, thick as it was with sand particles. For thirty-six hours nothing moved except the sand. At the height of the storm you couldn't see more than a few yards ahead of you, and the only thing clear was that the advance would have to wait for the weather.

The Americans' satellite technology, at the cutting edge of science, was helpless, blind in the face of the climate of this wild land. Everyone, from President Bush and the Joint Chiefs of Staff to the NA troops on the ground, just had to wait. Then it rained, and the sand that had settled on everything and everyone turned into mud. The rain came down so hard that the baked-mud huts we were living in looked as if they were melting. Again it was clear that the move south was on hold until geography finished having its say. The rules of geography, which Hannibal, Sun Tzu and Alexander the Great all knew, still apply to today's leaders.

More recently, in 2012, I was given another lesson in geostrategy: as Syria descended into full-blown civil war, I was standing on a Syrian hilltop, overlooking a valley south of the city of Hama, and saw a hamlet burning in the distance. Syrian friends pointed out a much larger village about a mile away, from where they said the attack had come. They then explained that if one side could push enough people from the other faction out of the valley, then the valley could be joined onto other land that led to the country's only motorway, and as such would be useful in carving out a piece of contiguous viable territory which one day could be used to create a mini-statelet if Syria could not be put back together again. Where before I saw only a burning hamlet, I could now see its strategic importance and understand how political realities are shaped by the most basic physical realities.

Geopolitics affects every country, whether at war, as in the examples above, or at peace. There will be instances in every region you can name. In these pages I cannot explore each one: Canada, Australia and Indonesia, among others, get no more than a brief mention, although a whole book could be devoted to Australia alone and the ways in which its geography has shaped its connections with other parts of the world, both physically and culturally. Instead I have focused on the powers and regions that best illustrate the key points of the book, covering the legacy of geopolitics from the past (nation-forming); the most pressing situations we face today (the continuing troubles in Ukraine, the expanding influence of China); and looking to the future (growing competition in the Arctic).

In Russia we see the influence of the Arctic, and how its freezing climate limits Russia's ability to be a truly global power. In China we see the limitations of power without a global navy, and now the speed at which China is seeking to change this is becoming apparent. The chapter on the USA illustrates how shrewd decisions to expand its territory in key regions allowed it to achieve its modern destiny as a two-ocean superpower. Europe shows us the value of flat land and navigable rivers in connecting regions with each other and producing a culture able to kick-start the modern world, while Africa is a prime example of the effects of isolation.

The chapter on the Middle East demonstrates why drawing

lines on maps while disregarding the topography and, equally importantly, the geographical cultures in a given area is a recipe for trouble. We will continue to witness that trouble this century. The same theme surfaces in the chapters on Africa and India/Pakistan. The colonial powers drew artificial borders on paper, completely ignoring the physical realities of the region. Violent attempts are now being made to redraw them; these will continue for several years, after which the map of nation states will no longer look as it does now.

Very different from the examples of Kosovo or Syria are Japan and Korea, in that they are mostly ethnically homogeneous. But they have other problems: Japan is an island nation devoid of natural resources while the division of the Koreas is a problem still waiting to be solved. Meanwhile, Latin America is an anomaly. In its far south it is so cut off from the outside world that global trading is difficult, and its internal geography is a barrier to creating a trading bloc as successful as the EU.

Finally, we come to one of the most uninhabitable places on earth – the Arctic. For most of history humans have ignored it, but in the twentieth century we found energy there, and twenty-first-century diplomacy will determine who owns – and sells – that resource.

Seeing geography as a decisive factor in the course of human history can be construed as a bleak view of the world, which is why it is disliked in some intellectual circles. It suggests that nature is more powerful than man, and that we can only go so far in determining our own fate. However, other factors clearly have an influence on events too. Any sensible person can see that modern technology is now bending the iron rules of geography. It has found ways over, under, or through some of the barriers. The Americans can now fly a plane all the way from Missouri to Mosul on a bombing mission without needing concrete along the way on which to refuel. That, along with their partially self-sustaining great Aircraft Carrier Battle Groups, means they no longer absolutely have to have an ally or a colony in order to extend their global reach around the world. Of course, if they *do* have an airbase on the island of Diego Garcia, or permanent access to the port in Bahrain, then they have more options; but it is less essential.

So air power has changed the rules, as in a different way has the internet. But geography, and the history of how nations have established themselves within that geography, remains crucial to our understanding of the world today and our future.

The conflict in Iraq and Syria is rooted in colonial powers ignoring the rules of geography, whereas the Chinese occupation of Tibet is rooted in obeying them; America's global foreign policy is dictated by them, and even the technological genius and power projection of the last superpower standing can only mitigate the rules that nature, or God, handed down.

What are those rules? The place to begin is in the land where power is hard to defend, and so for centuries its leaders have compensated by pushing outwards. It is the land without mountains to its west: Russia.

CHAPTER 1

RUSSIA

Vast (adjective; vaster, vastest): of very great area or extent; immense.

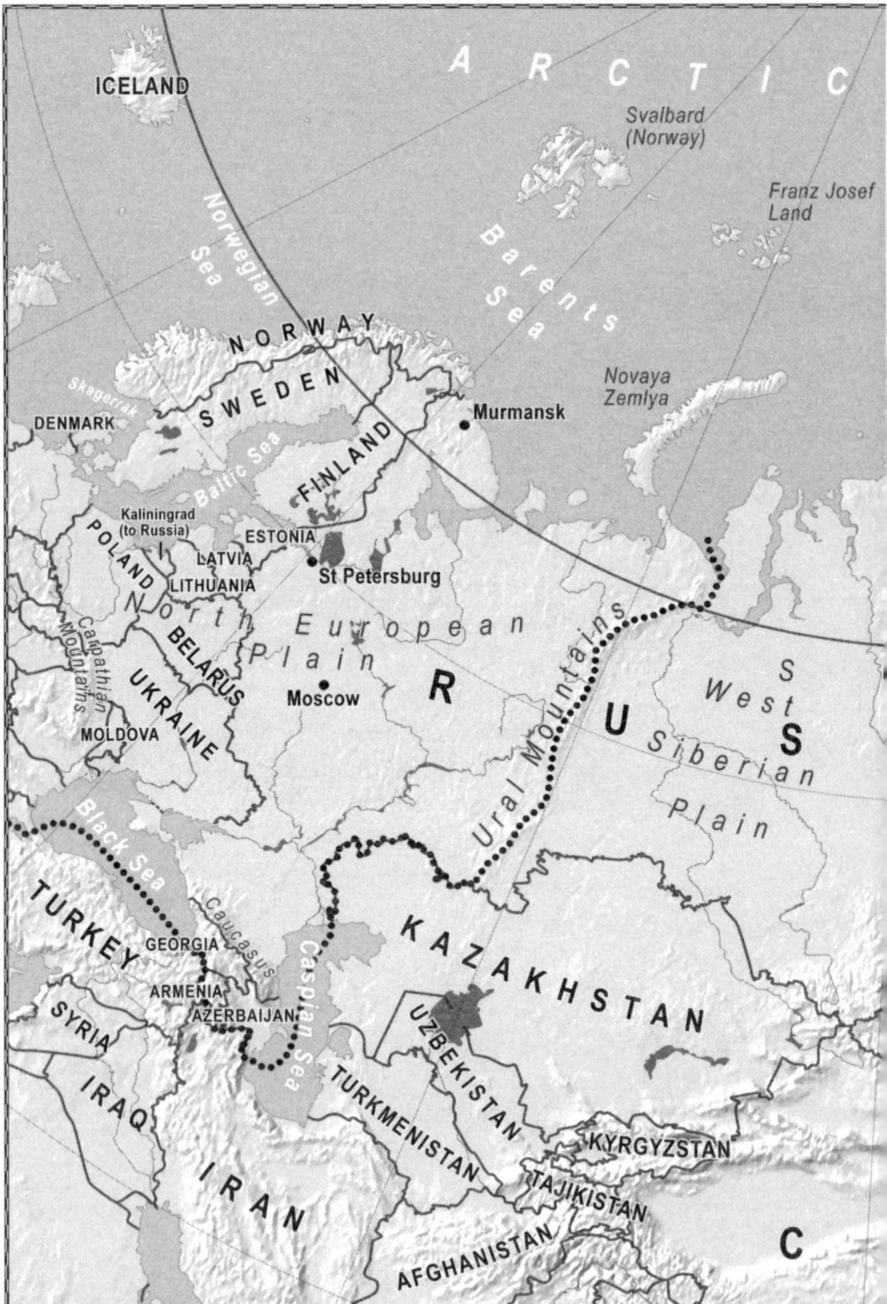
ARCTIC
ICELAND
Svalbard (Norway)
Franz Josef Land
Norwegian Sea
Barents Sea
NORWAY
SWEDEN
Skagerrak
DENMARK
Novaya Zemlya
Murmansk
Baltic Sea
FINLAND
Kaliningrad (to Russia)
POLAND
ESTONIA
LATVIA
St Petersburg
LITHUANIA
North European Plain
Carpathian Mountains
BELARUS
UKRAINE
Moscow
R
U
S
Ural Mountains
West Siberian Plain
MOLDOVA
Black Sea
TURKEY
Caucasus
GEORGIA
ARMENIA
AZERBAIJAN
Caspian Sea
KAZAKHSTAN
SYRIA
UZBEKISTAN
TURKMENISTAN
IRAQ
KYRGYZSTAN
TAJIKISTAN
IRAN
AFGHANISTAN
C

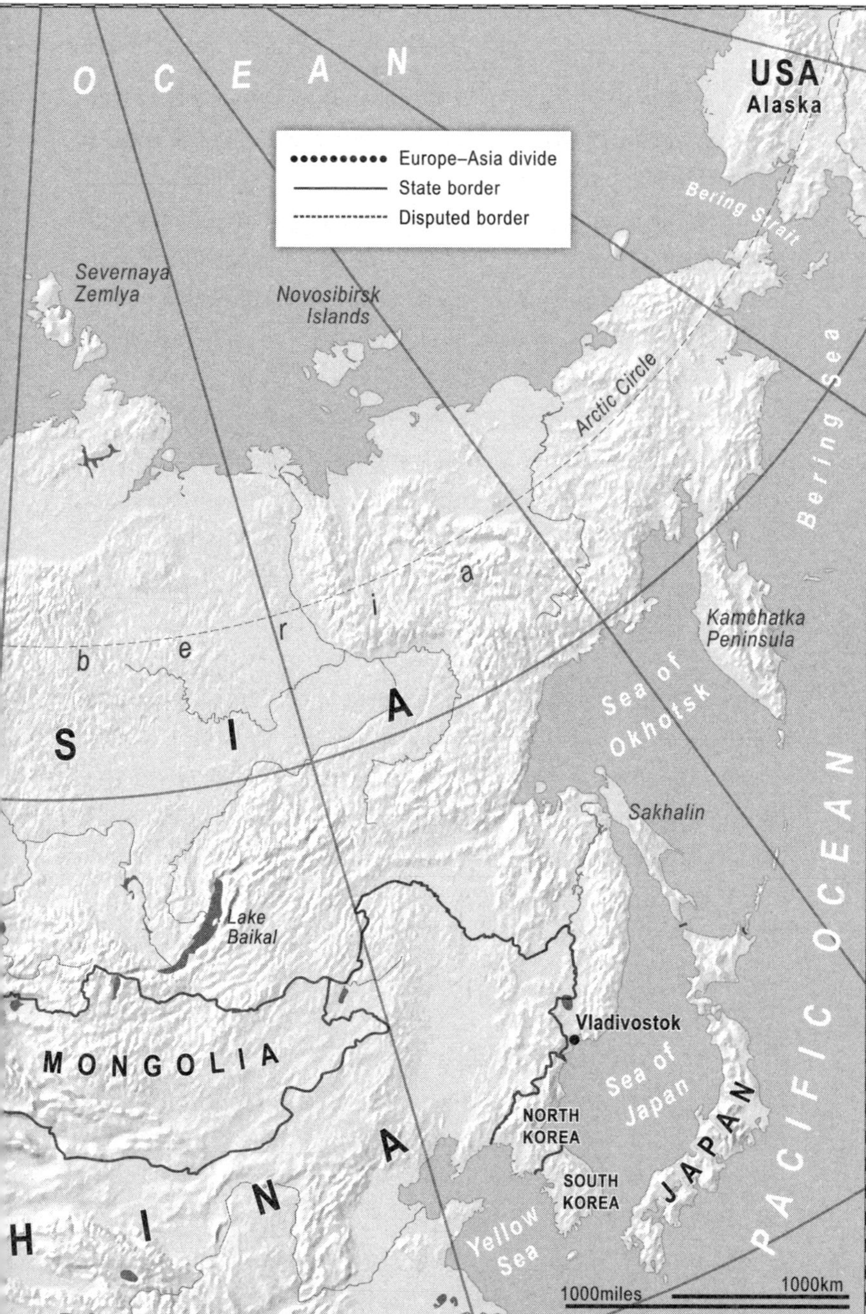

O C E A N
USA
Alaska
Europe–Asia divide
State border
Disputed border
Bering Strait
Severnaya Zemlya
Novosibirsk Islands
Arctic Circle
Bering Sea
S i b e r i a
S I A
Kamchatka Peninsula
Sea of Okhotsk
Sakhalin
PACIFIC OCEAN
Lake Baikal
Vladivostok
MONGOLIA
Sea of Japan
NORTH KOREA
SOUTH KOREA
JAPAN
H I N A
Yellow Sea
1000miles
1000km

RUSSIA IS VAST. IT IS VASTEST. IMMENSE. IT IS SIX MILLION square miles vast, eleven time zones vast; it is the largest country in the world.

Its forests, lakes, rivers, frozen tundra, steppe, taiga and mountains are all vast. This size has long seeped into our collective consciousness. Wherever we are, there is Russia, perhaps to our east or west, to our north or south – but there is the Russian Bear.

It is no coincidence that the bear is the symbol of this immense nation. There it sits, sometimes hibernating, sometimes growling, majestic, but ferocious. Bear is a Russian word, but the Russians are also wary of calling this animal by its name, fearful of conjuring up its darker side. They call it *medved*, 'the one who likes honey'.

At least 120,000 of these *medveds* live in a country which bestrides Europe and Asia. To the west of the Ural Mountains is European Russia. To their east is Siberia, stretching all the way to the Bering Sea and the Pacific Ocean. Even in the twenty-first century, to cross it by train takes six days. Russia's leaders must look across these distances, and differences, and formulate policy accordingly; for several centuries now they have looked in all directions, but concentrated mostly westward.

When writers seek to get to the heart of the bear they often use Winston Churchill's famous observation of Russia, made in 1939: 'It is a riddle wrapped in a mystery inside an enigma', but few go on to complete the sentence, which ends, 'but perhaps there is a key. That key is Russian national interest.' Seven years later he used that key to unlock his version of the answer to the riddle, asserting, 'I am convinced that there is nothing they admire so much as strength, and there is nothing for which they have less respect than for weakness, especially military weakness.'

He could have been talking about the current Russian leadership, which despite now being wrapped in the cloak of democracy, remains authoritarian in its nature with national interest still at its core.

When Vladimir Putin isn't thinking about God, and mountains, he's thinking about pizza. In particular, the shape of a slice of pizza – a wedge.

The thin end of this wedge is Poland. Here, the vast North European Plain stretching from France to the Urals (which extend 1,000 miles south to north, forming a natural boundary between Europe and Asia) is only 300 miles wide. It runs from the Baltic Sea in the north to the Carpathian Mountains in the south. The North European Plain encompasses all of western and northern France, Belgium, the Netherlands, northern Germany and nearly all of Poland.

From a Russian perspective this is a double-edged sword. Poland represents a relatively narrow corridor into which Russia could drive its armed forces if necessary and thus prevent an enemy from advancing towards Moscow. But from this point the wedge begins to broaden; by the time you get to Russia's borders it is over 2,000 miles wide, and is flat all the way to Moscow and beyond. Even with a large army you would be hard-pressed to defend in strength along this line. However, Russia has never been conquered from this direction, partially due to its strategic depth. By the time an army approaches Moscow it already has unsustainably long supply lines, a mistake that Napoleon made in 1812, and that Hitler repeated in 1941.

Likewise, in the Russian Far East it is geography that protects Russia. It is difficult to move an army from Asia up into

Asian Russia; there's not much to attack except for snow, and you could only get as far as the Urals. You would then end up holding a massive piece of territory, in difficult conditions, with long supply lines and the ever-present risk of a counter-attack.

You might think that no one is intent on invading Russia, but that is not how the Russians see it, and with good reason. In the past 500 years they have been invaded several times from the west. The Poles came across the North European Plain in 1605, followed by the Swedes under Charles XII in 1708, the French under Napoleon in 1812, and the Germans twice, in both world wars, in 1914 and 1941. Looking at it another way, if you count from Napoleon's invasion of 1812, but this time include the Crimean War of 1853–6 and the two world wars up to 1945, then the Russians were fighting on average in or around the North European Plain once every thirty-three years.

At the end of the Second World War in 1945, the Russians occupied the territory conquered from Germany in Central and Eastern Europe, some of which then became part of the USSR, as it increasingly began to resemble the old Russian Empire. In 1949 the North Atlantic Treaty Organization (NATO) was formed by an association of European and North American states, for the defence of Europe and the North Atlantic against the danger of Soviet aggression. In response, most of the Communist states of Europe – under Russian leadership – formed the Warsaw Pact in 1955, a treaty for military defence and mutual aid. The Pact was supposed to be made of iron, but with hindsight by the early 1980s was rusting, and after the fall of the Berlin Wall in 1989 it crumbled to dust.

President Putin is no fan of the last Soviet President, Mikhail Gorbachev. He blames him for undermining Russian security and has referred to the break-up of the former Soviet

Union during the 1990s as 'a major geopolitical disaster of the century'.

Since then the Russians have watched anxiously as NATO has crept steadily closer, incorporating countries which Russia claims it was promised would not be joining: the Czech Republic, Hungary and Poland in 1999, Bulgaria, Estonia, Latvia, Lithuania, Romania and Slovakia in 2004 and Albania in 2009. NATO says no such assurances were given.

Russia, like all great powers, is thinking in terms of the next 100 years and understands that in that time anything could happen. A century ago, who could have guessed that American armed forces would be stationed a few hundred miles from Moscow in Poland and the Baltic States? By 2004, just fifteen years from 1989, every single former Warsaw Pact state bar Russia was in NATO or the European Union.

The Moscow administration's mind has been concentrated by that, and by Russia's history.

Russia as a concept dates back to the ninth century and a loose federation of East Slavic tribes known as Kievan Rus', which was based in Kiev and other towns along the Dnieper River, in what is now Ukraine. The Mongols, expanding their empire, continually attacked the region from the south and east, eventually overrunning it in the thirteenth century. The fledgling Russia then relocated north-east in and around the city of Moscow. This early Russia, known as the Grand Principality of Muscovy, was indefensible. There were no mountains, no deserts and few rivers. In all directions lay flatland, and across the steppe to the south and east were the Mongols. The invader could advance at a place of his choosing, and there were few natural defensive positions to occupy.

Enter Ivan the Terrible, the first Tsar. He put into practice the concept of attack as defence – i.e., beginning your expansion by consolidating at home and then moving outwards. This led to greatness. Here was a man to give support to the theory that individuals can change history. Without his character of both utter ruthlessness and vision, Russian history would be very different.

The fledgling Russia had begun a moderate expansion under Ivan's grandfather, Ivan the Great, but that expansion accelerated after the younger Ivan was crowned Tsar and Grand Prince of all Russia in 1547. It encroached east on the Urals, south to the Caspian Sea and north towards the Arctic Circle. It gained access to the Caspian, and later the Black Sea, thus taking advantage of the Caucasus Mountains as a partial barrier between it and the Mongols. A military base was built in Chechnya to deter any would-be attackers, be they the Mongol Golden Hordes, the Ottoman Empire or the Persians.

There were setbacks, but over the next century Russia would push past the Urals and edge into Siberia, eventually incorporating all the land to the Pacific coast far to the east.

Now the Russians had a partial buffer zone and a hinterland – strategic depth – somewhere to fall back to in the case of invasion. No one was going to attack them in force from the Arctic Sea, nor fight their way over the Urals to get to them. Their land was becoming what we know now as Russia, and to get to it from the south or south-east you had to have a huge army, a very long supply line, and fight your way past defensive positions.

In the eighteenth century, Russia – under Peter the Great, who founded the Russian Empire in 1721, and then Empress Catherine the Great – looked westward, expanding the Empire to become one of the great powers of Europe, driven chiefly by trade and nationalism. A more secure and powerful Russia was now able to occupy Ukraine and reach the Carpathian Mountains. It took over most of what we now know as the Baltic States – Lithuania, Latvia and Estonia. Thus it was protected from any incursion via land that way, or from the Baltic Sea.

Now there was a huge ring around Moscow which was the heart of the country. Starting at the Arctic, it came down through the Baltic region, across Ukraine, then the Carpathians, the Black Sea, the Caucasus and the Caspian, swinging back round to the Urals, which stretched up to the Arctic Circle.

In the twentieth century Communist Russia created the Soviet Union. Behind the rhetoric of 'Workers of the World Unite', the USSR was simply the Russian Empire writ large. After the Second World War it stretched from the Pacific to Berlin, from the Arctic to the borders of Afghanistan – a superpower economically, politically and militarily, rivalled only by the USA.

Russia is the biggest country in the world, twice the size of the USA or China, five times the size of India, seventy times the size of the UK. However, it has a relatively small population of about 144 million, fewer people than Nigeria or Pakistan. Its agricultural growing season is short and it struggles to adequately distribute what is grown around the eleven time zones which Moscow governs.

Russia, up to the Urals, is a European power in so far as it borders the European land mass, but it is not an Asian power despite bordering Kazakhstan, Mongolia, China and North Korea, and having maritime borders with several countries including Japan and the USA.

Former US Vice Presidential candidate Sarah Palin was mocked when she was reported as saying, 'You can actually see Russia from land here in Alaska', a line which morphed in media coverage to 'I can see Russia from my house.' What she really said was, 'You can see Russia from land here in Alaska, from an island in Alaska.' She was right. A Russian island in the Bering Strait is two and a half miles from an American island in the Strait, Little Diomede Island, and can be seen with the naked eye. You can indeed see Russia from America.

High up in the Urals there is a cross marking the place where Europe stops and Asia starts. When the skies are clear it is a beautiful spot and you can see through the fir trees for miles towards the east. In winter it is snow-covered, as is the Siberian Plain you see below you stretching towards the city of Yekaterinburg. Tourists like to visit to put one foot in Europe and one in Asia. It is a reminder of just how big Russia is when you realise that the cross is placed merely a quarter of the way into the country. You may have travelled 1,500 miles from St Petersburg, through western Russia, to get to the Urals, but you still have another 4,500 miles to go before reaching the Bering Strait, and a possible sighting of Mrs Palin, across from Alaska in the USA.

Shortly after the fall of the Soviet Union I was in the Urals, at the point where Europe becomes Asia, accompanied by a Russian camera crew. The cameraman was a taciturn, stoic, grizzled veteran of filming, and was the son of the Red Army cameraman who had filmed a great deal of footage during the German siege of Stalingrad. I asked him, 'So, are you European or are you Asian?' He reflected on this for a few seconds, then replied, 'Neither – I am Russian.'

Whatever its European credentials, Russia is not an Asian power for many reasons. Although 75 per cent of its territory is in Asia, only 22 per cent of its population lives there. Siberia may be Russia's 'treasure chest', containing the majority of the mineral wealth, oil, and gas, but it is a harsh land, freezing for months on end, with vast forests (taiga), poor soil for farming and large stretches of swampland. Only two railway networks run west to east – the Trans-Siberian and the Baikal–Amur Mainline. There are few transport routes leading north to south and so no easy way for Russia to project power southward into modern Mongolia or China: it lacks the manpower and supply lines to do so.

China may well eventually control parts of Siberia in the long-term future, but this would be through Russia's declining birth rate and Chinese immigration moving north. Already, as far west as the swampy West Siberian Plain, between the Urals in the west and the Yenisei River 1,000 miles to the east, you can see Chinese restaurants in most of the towns and cities. Many more different businesses are coming. The empty depopulating spaces of Russia's Far East are even more likely to come under Chinese cultural, and eventually political, control.

When you move outside of the Russian heartland, much of the population in the Russian Federation is not ethnically Russian and pays little allegiance to Moscow, which results in an aggressive security system similar to the one in Soviet days. During that era Russia was effectively a colonial power ruling over nations and people who felt they had nothing in common with their masters; parts of the Russian Federation – for example, Chechnya and Dagestan in the Caucasus – still feel the same way.

Late in the last century, overstretch, spending more money than was available, the economics of the madhouse in a land not designed for people, and defeat in the mountains of Afghanistan all led to the fall of the USSR. The Russian Empire shrank back to the shape of more or less the pre-Communist era, with its European borders ending at Estonia, Latvia, Belarus, Ukraine, Georgia and Azerbaijan. The Soviet invasion of Afghanistan in 1979, in support of the Communist Afghan government against anti-Communist Muslim guerrillas, had never been about bringing the joys of Marxist-Leninism to the Afghan people. It was always about ensuring that Moscow controlled the space to prevent anyone else from doing so.

Crucially, the invasion of Afghanistan also gave hope to the great Russian dream of its army being able to 'wash their boots in the warm waters of the Indian ocean', in the words of the ultra-nationalistic Russian politician Vladimir Zhirinovsky, and thus achieve what it never had: a warm-water port where the water does not freeze in winter, with free access to the world's major trading routes. Some of the ports on the Arctic freeze for several months each year: Vladivostok, the largest Russian port on the Pacific Ocean, is ice-locked for about four months and is enclosed by the Sea of Japan, which is dominated by the Japanese. This does not just halt the flow of trade; it prevents the Russian fleet from operating as a global power. In addition, water-borne transport is much cheaper than land or airborne routes.

However, with the imposing plains of Kandahar and mountains of the Hindu Kush, no invading power has ever succeeded in Afghanistan, earning it the label of 'the Graveyard of Empires'. The Afghan experience is sometimes called 'Russia's Vietnam'; Moscow's dream of warm water open sea lanes has seeped away ever since, and is perhaps further now than it has been for 200 years.

This lack of a warm-water port with direct access to the oceans has always been Russia's Achilles heel, as strategically important to it as the North European Plain. Russia is at a geographical disadvantage, saved from being a much weaker power only because of its oil and gas. No wonder, in his will of 1725, that Peter the Great advised his descendants to 'approach as near as possible to Constantinople and India. Whoever governs there will be the true sovereign of the world. Consequently, excite continual wars, not only in Turkey, but in Persia . . . Penetrate as far as the Persian Gulf, advance as far as India.'

When the Soviet Union broke apart, it split into fifteen countries. Geography had its revenge on the ideology of the Soviets and a more logical picture reappeared on the map, one in which mountains, rivers, lakes and seas delineate where people live, are separated from each other and thus how they develop different languages and customs. The exceptions to this rule are the 'Stans', such as Tajikistan, whose borders were deliberately drawn by Stalin so as to weaken each state by ensuring it had large minorities of people from other states.

If you take the long view of history – and most diplomats and military planners do – then there is still everything to play for in each of the states which formerly made up the USSR, plus some of those previously in the Warsaw Pact military alliance. They can be divided three ways: those that are neutral, the pro-Western group and the pro-Russian camp.

The neutral countries – Uzbekistan, Azerbaijan and Turkmenistan – are those with fewer reasons to ally themselves with Russia or the West. This is because all three produce their own energy and are not beholden to either side for their security or trade.

In the pro-Russian camp are Kazakhstan, Kyrgyzstan, Tajikistan, Belarus and Armenia. Their economies are tied to Russia in the way that much of eastern Ukraine's economy is (another reason for the rebellion there). The largest of these, Kazakhstan, leans towards Russia diplomatically and its large Russian-minority population is well integrated. Of the five, all but Tajikistan have joined Russia in the new Eurasian Economic Union (a sort of poor man's EU), which celebrated its first anniversary in January 2016. And all five are in a military alliance with Russia called the Collective Security Treaty Organization. The CSTO suffers from not having a name you can boil down to one word, and from being a watered-down Warsaw Bloc. Russia maintains a military presence in Kyrgyzstan, Tajikistan and Armenia.

Then there are the pro-Western countries formerly in the Warsaw Pact but now all in NATO and/or the EU: Poland, Latvia, Lithuania, Estonia, the Czech Republic, Bulgaria, Hungary, Slovakia, Albania and Romania. By no coincidence, many are among the states which suffered most under Soviet tyranny. Add to these Georgia, Ukraine and Moldova, which would all like to join both organisations but are being held at arm's length because of their geographic proximity to Russia and because all three have Russian troops or pro-Russian militia on their soil. NATO membership of any of these three could spark a war.

All of the above explains why, in 2013, as the political battle for the direction of Ukraine heated up, Moscow concentrated hard.

As long as a pro-Russian government held sway in Kiev, the Russians could be confident that its buffer zone would remain intact and guard the North European Plain. Even a studiedly neutral Ukraine, which would promise not to join the EU or NATO and to uphold the lease Russia had on the warm-water port at Sevastopol in Crimea, would be acceptable.

That Ukraine was reliant on Russia for energy also made its increasingly neutral stance acceptable, albeit irritating. But a pro-Western Ukraine with ambitions to join the two great Western alliances, and which threw into doubt Russia's access to its Black Sea port? A Ukraine that one day might even host a NATO naval base? That could not stand.

President Viktor Yanukovych of Ukraine tried to play both sides. He flirted with the West, but paid homage to Moscow – thus Putin tolerated him. When he came close to signing a massive trade agreement with the EU, one which could lead to membership, Putin began turning the screw.

For the Russian foreign policy elite, membership of the EU is simply a stalking horse for membership of NATO, and for Russia, Ukrainian membership of NATO is a red line. Putin piled the pressure on Yanukovych, made him an offer he chose not to refuse, and the Ukrainian president scrambled out of the EU deal and made a pact with Moscow, thus sparking the protests which were eventually to overthrow him.

The Germans and Americans had backed the opposition parties, with Berlin in particular seeing former world boxing champion turned politician Vitaly Klitschko as their man. The West was pulling Ukraine intellectually and economically towards it whilst helping pro-Western Ukrainians to push it westward by training and funding some of the democratic opposition groups.

Street fighting erupted in Kiev and demonstrations across the country grew. In the east, crowds came out in support of the President, while in the west of the country, in cities such as L'viv (which used to be in Poland), they were busy trying to rid themselves of any pro-Russian influence.

By mid-February 2014 L'viv and other urban areas were no

longer controlled by the government. Then, on 22 February, after dozens of deaths in Kiev, the President, fearing for his life, fled. Anti-Russian factions, some of which were pro-Western and some pro-fascist, took over the government. From that moment the die was cast. President Putin did not have much of a choice – he had to annex Crimea, which contained not only many Russian-speaking Ukrainians but, most importantly, the port of Sevastopol.

This geographic imperative, and the whole eastward movement of NATO, is exactly what Putin had in mind when, in a speech about the annexation, he said, 'Russia found itself in a position it could not retreat from. If you compress the spring all the way to its limit, it will snap back hard. You must always remember this.'

Sevastopol is Russia's only true major warm-water port. However, access out of the Black Sea into the Mediterranean is restricted by the Montreux Convention of 1936, which gave Turkey – now a NATO member – control of the Bosporus. Russian naval ships do transit the strait, but in limited numbers, and this would not be permitted in the event of conflict. Even after crossing the Bosporus the Russians need to navigate the Aegean Sea before accessing the Mediterranean, and would still have either to cross the Gibraltar Straits to gain access to the Atlantic Ocean, or be allowed down the Suez Canal to reach the Indian Ocean.

The Russians do have a small naval presence in Tartus on Syria's Mediterranean coast (this partially explains their support for the Syrian government when fighting broke out in 2011), but it is a limited supply and replenishment base, not a major force despite being extended and modernised in 2019.

Another strategic problem is that in the event of war the

Russian navy cannot get out of the Baltic Sea either, due to the Skagerrak Strait, which connects to the North Sea. The narrow strait is controlled by NATO members Denmark and Norway; and even if the ships made it, the route to the Atlantic goes through what is known as the GIUK gap (Greenland/Iceland/UK) in the North Sea – which we will see more of when we look at Western Europe.

Having annexed Crimea, the Russians are wasting no time. Under the updated 2011 terms of their lease agreement for the port of Sevastopol Kiev had the power to block the modernisation of Russia's Black Sea Fleet. No longer – hundreds of millions of roubles are being poured into upgrading the fleet, modernising and extending the naval port in the Russian city of Novorossiysk, which, although it does not have a natural deep harbour, will give the Russians extra capacity. By 2020 eighteen new warships are expected to be operating out of the two ports with an-other eighty vessels in the pipeline. The fleet will still not be strong enough to break out of the Black Sea during wartime, but its capacity is clearly increasing.

To counter this, in the next decade we can expect to see the USA encouraging its NATO partner Romania to boost its fleet in the Black Sea whilst relying on Turkey to hold the line across the Bosporus.

Crimea was part of Russia for two centuries before being transferred to the Soviet Republic of Ukraine in 1954 by President Khrushchev at a time when it was envisaged that Soviet man would live forever and so be controlled by Moscow for ever. Now that Ukraine was no longer Soviet, or even pro-Russian, Putin knew the situation had to change. Did the Western diplomats know? If they didn't, then they were unaware of Rule A, Lesson One, in 'Diplomacy for Beginners':

when faced with what is considered an existential threat, a great power will use force. If they were aware, then they must have considered Putin's annexation of Crimea a price worth paying for pulling Ukraine into modern Europe and the Western sphere of influence.

A generous view is that the USA and the Europeans were looking forward to welcoming Ukraine into the democratic world as a full member of its liberal institutions and the rule of law, and that there wasn't much Moscow could do about it. That is a view which does not take into account the fact that geopolitics still exists in the twenty-first century, or that Russia does not play by the rule of law.

Flushed with victory, the new interim Ukrainian government had immediately made some foolish statements, not least of which was the intention to abolish Russian as the official second language in various regions. Given that these regions were the ones with the most Russian speakers and pro-Russian sentiment, and indeed included Crimea, this was bound to spark a backlash. It also gave President Putin the propaganda he needed to make the case that ethnic Russians inside Ukraine needed to be protected.

The Kremlin has a law which compels the government to protect 'ethnic Russians'. A definition of that term is, by design, hard to come by because it will be defined as Russia chooses in each of the potential crises which may erupt in the former Soviet Union. When it suits the Kremlin, ethnic Russians will be defined simply as people who speak Russian as their first language. At other times the new citizenship law will be used, which states that if your grandparents lived in Russia, and Russian is your native language, you can take Russian citizenship. Given that, as the crises arise, people will be inclined to accept Russian passports to hedge their bets, this will be a lever for Russian entry into a conflict.

Approximately 60 per cent of Crimea's population is 'ethnically Russian', so the Kremlin was pushing against an open door. Putin helped the anti-Kiev demonstrations, and stirred up so much trouble that eventually he 'had' to send his troops out of the confines of the naval base and onto the streets to protect people. The Ukrainian military in the area was in no shape to take on both the people and the Russian army, and swiftly withdrew. Crimea was once again a de facto part of Russia.

You could make the argument that President Putin did have a choice: he could have respected the territorial integrity of Ukraine. But, given that he was dealing with the geographic hand God has dealt Russia, this was never really an option. He would not be the man who 'lost Crimea', and with it the only proper warm-water port his country had access to.

No one rode to the rescue of Ukraine as it lost territory equivalent to the size of Belgium, or the US state of Maryland. Ukraine and its neighbours knew a geographic truth: that unless you are in NATO, Moscow is near, Washington DC is far away. For Russia this was an existential matter: they could not cope with losing Crimea, the West could.

The EU imposed limited sanctions – limited because several European countries, Germany among them, are reliant on Russian energy to heat their homes in winter. The pipelines run east to west and the Kremlin can turn the taps on and off.

Energy as political power will be deployed time and again in the coming years, and the concept of 'ethnic Russians' will be used to justify whatever moves Russia makes.

In a speech in 2014 President Putin briefly referred to

'Novorossiya' or 'New Russia'. The Kremlin-watchers took a deep breath. He had revived the geographic title given to what is now southern and eastern Ukraine, which Russia had won from the Ottoman Empire during the reign of Catherine the Great in the late eighteenth century. Catherine went on to settle Russians in these regions and demanded that Russian be the first language. 'Novorossiya' was only ceded to the newly formed Ukrainian Soviet Socialist Republic in 1922. 'Why?' asked Putin rhetorically, 'Let God judge them.' In his speech he listed the Ukrainian regions of Kharkiv, Luhansk, Donetsk, Kherson, Mykolaiv and Odessa before saying, 'Russia lost these territories for various reasons, but the people remained.'

Several million ethnic Russians still remain inside what was the USSR, but outside Russia.

It is no surprise that, after seizing Crimea, Russia went on to encourage the uprisings by pro-Russians in the Ukrainian eastern industrial heartlands in Luhansk and Donetsk. Russia could easily drive militarily all the way to the eastern bank of the Dnieper River in Kiev. But it does not need the headache that would bring. It is far less painful, and cheaper, to encourage unrest in the eastern borders of Ukraine and remind Kiev who controls energy supplies, to ensure that Kiev's infatuation with the flirtatious West does not turn into a marriage consummated in the chambers of the EU or NATO.

Covert support for the uprisings in eastern Ukraine was also logistically simple and had the added benefit of deniability on the international stage. Barefaced lying in the great chamber of the UN Security Council is simple if your opponent does not have concrete proof of your actions and, more importantly, doesn't want concrete proof in case he or she has to do something about it. Many politicians in the West breathed a sigh of relief and muttered quietly, 'Thank goodness Ukraine isn't in NATO or we would have had to act.'

The annexation of Crimea showed how Russia is prepared for military action to defend what it sees as its interests in what it calls its 'near abroad'. It took a rational gamble that outside powers would not intervene, and Crimea was 'doable'. It is close to Russia, could be supplied across the Black Sea and the Sea of Azov, and could rely on internal support from large sections of the population of the peninsula.

Russia has not finished with Ukraine yet, nor elsewhere. The Donbass region remains volatile and sporadic fighting continues. An outbreak of violence there in the summer of 2017 left several Ukrainian soldiers dead, leading the USA to consider upping its military assistance to Ukraine, and the Russians to conduct significant military exercises on the Ukrainian border.

In late 2018, the Russian coastguard intercepted three Ukrainian ships heading from Odessa, in the Black Sea, towards the Ukrainian base in Mariupol, in the Sea of Azov. The Russians fired on the Ukrainians, wounding three sailors, and rammed a tugboat before taking the ships and crews into custody. They then blocked access in and out of the Sea of Azov by anchoring a cargo ship under the bridge over Kerch Strait. The seized ships were not returned and six months after the incident twenty-four Ukrainian sailors were still in a Russian jail.

International condemnation followed, with NATO powers suggesting they would ensure the waterway was kept open. In April 2019, the US permanent representative to NATO, Kay Bailey Hutchison, said the alliance was working on a range of measures to 'beef up' air surveillance and that NATO would increase the number of its ships in the Black Sea to en-sure safe passage. A Crimean representative to the Russian parliament, Ruslan Balbek, responded by saying, 'No matter how much NATO beats its chest, the ships will pass through it only in accordance with Russian rules.'

Unless it feels threatened, Russia will probably not send its troops all the way into the Baltic States, or any further forward than it already is in Georgia; but it will push its power in Georgia, and in this volatile period further military action cannot be ruled out.

However, just as Russia's actions in its war with Georgia in 2008 were a warning to NATO to come no closer, so NATO's message to Russia in the summer of 2014 was, 'This far west and no further.' A handful of NATO war planes were flown to the Baltic States, military exercises were announced in Poland and the Americans began planning to 'pre-position' extra hardware as close to Russia as possible. At the same time there was a flurry of diplomatic visits by Defence and Foreign Ministers to the Baltic States, Georgia and Moldova to reassure them of support.

Some commentators poured scorn on the reaction, arguing that six RAF Eurofighter Typhoon jets flying over Baltic airspace were hardly going to deter the Russian hordes. But the reaction was about diplomatic signalling, and the signal was clear – NATO is prepared to fight. Indeed it would have to, because if it failed to react to an attack on a member state, it would instantly be obsolete. The Americans – who are already edging towards a new foreign policy in which they feel less constrained by existing structures and are prepared to forge new ones as they perceive the need arises – remain deeply unimpressed with the European countries' commitment to defence spending. As a presidential candidate, Donald Trump suggested NATO was 'obsolete'; as president he rowed back on that in the spring of 2017 but it's clear he intended to make the other NATO countries nervous and there has been a small increase in defence spending by a handful of the members.

President Trump had also failed to clarify whether the USA would automatically come to the aid of a fellow NATO ally, but again, as the realities and complexities of defence, warfare, propaganda and geopolitics became clear, he finally guaranteed NATO's Article 5 in the spring of 2017. In the case of the three Baltic States, NATO's position is clear. As they are all members of the alliance, an armed attack against any of them by Russia would trigger Article 5 of NATO's founding charter, which states: 'An armed attack against one or more [NATO member states] in Europe or North America shall be considered an attack against them all', and goes on to say NATO will come to the rescue if necessary. Article 5 was invoked after the terrorist attacks in the USA on 11 September 2001, paving the way for NATO involvement in Afghanistan.

President Putin is a student of history. He appears to have learnt the lessons of the Soviet years, in which Russia overstretched itself and was forced to contract. An overt assault on the Baltic States would likewise be overstretching and is unlikely, especially if NATO and its political masters ensure that Putin understands their signals. But in 2016, the Russian president sent his own signal. He changed the wording of Russia's overall military strategy document and went further than the naval strategy paper of 2015: for the first time, the USA was named as an 'external threat' to Russia. By 2019 NATO's fears had grown and discussions about building a permanent US military base in Poland were well advanced, with Warsaw offering to pay up to $2 billion towards the costs.

Russia does not have to send an armoured division into Latvia, Lithuania or Estonia to influence events there, but if it ever does it would justify the action by claiming that the large Russian communities there are being discriminated against. In both Estonia and Latvia approximately one in four people are ethnically Russian and in Lithuania it is 5.8 per cent. In Estonia the Russian speakers say they are under-represented in government and thousands do not have any form of citizenship. This does not mean they want to be part of Russia, but they are one of the levers Russia can pull to influence events.

The Russian-speaking populations in the Baltics can be stirred up to making life difficult. There are existing, fully formed political parties already representing many of them. Russia also controls the central heating in the homes of the Baltic people. It can set the price people pay for their heating bills each month, and, if it chooses, simply turn the heating off.

Russia will continue to push its interests in the Baltic States. They are one of the weak links in its defence since the collapse of the USSR, another breach in the wall they would prefer to see forming an arc from the Baltic Sea, south, then south-east connecting to the Urals.

This brings us to another gap in the wall and another region Moscow views as a potential buffer state. Firmly in the Kremlin's sights is Moldova.

Moldova presents a different problem for all sides. An attack on the country by Russia would necessitate crossing through Ukraine, over the Dnieper River and then over another sovereign border into Moldova. It could be done – at the cost of significant loss of life and by using Odessa as a staging post – but there would be no deniability. Although it might not trigger war with NATO (Moldova is not a member), it would provoke

A number of countries that were once members of the Soviet Union aspire to closer ties with Europe, but with certain regions, such as Transnistria in Moldova, remaining heavily pro-Russian, there is potential for future conflict.

sanctions against Moscow at a level hitherto unseen, and confirm what this writer believes to already be the case – that the cooling relationship between Russia and the West is already the New Cold War. The coming to power of Donald Trump has caused some analysts to suggest that Russia believes it may have a 'green light' to take further action in Ukraine. However, within weeks of taking office the president's defence secretary and secretary of state fired several salvoes of verbal warning shots aimed at Moscow, which suggested that although the White House might seek better relations with Russia, the realities of geopolitics mean there are limits beyond which Moscow would be wise not to venture.

Why would the Russians want Moldova? Because as the

Carpathian Mountains curve round south-west to become the Transylvanian Alps, to the south-east is a plain leading down to the Black Sea. That plain can also be thought of as a flat corridor into Russia; and, just as the Russians would prefer to control the North European Plain at its narrow point in Poland, so they would like to control the plain by the Black Sea – also known as Moldova – in the region formerly known as Bessarabia.

After the Crimean War (fought between Russia and Western European allies to protect Ottoman Turkey from Russia), the 1856 Treaty of Paris returned parts of Bessarabia to Moldova, thus cutting Russia off from the River Danube. It took Russia almost a century to regain access to it, but with the collapse of the USSR, once more Russia had to retreat eastward.

However, in effect the Russians do already control part of Moldova – a region called Transnistria, part of Moldova east of the Dniester River which borders Ukraine. Stalin, in his wisdom, settled large numbers of Russians there, just as he had in Crimea after deporting much of the Tatar population.

Modern Transnistria is now at least 50 per cent Russian- or Ukrainian-speaking, and that part of the population is pro-Russian. When Moldova became independent in 1991, the Russian-speaking population rebelled and, after a brief period of fighting, declared a breakaway Republic of Transnistria. It helped that Russia had soldiers stationed there, and it retains a force of 2,000 troops to this day.

A Russian military advance in Moldova is unlikely, but the Kremlin can and does use its economic muscle and the volatile situation in Transnistria to try to influence the Moldovan government not to join the EU or NATO.

Moldova is reliant on Russia for its energy needs, its crops go eastward and Russian imports of the excellent Moldovan wine tend to rise or fall according to the state of the relationship between the two countries.

Across the Black Sea from Moldova lies another wine-producing nation: Georgia. It is not high on Russia's list of places to control for two reasons. Firstly, the Georgia–Russian war of 2008 left large parts of the country occupied by Russian troops, who now fully control the regions of Abkhazia and South Ossetia. Secondly, it lies south of the Caucasus Mountains and Russia also has troops stationed in neighbouring Armenia. Moscow would prefer an extra layer to their buffer zone, but can live without taking the rest of Georgia. That situation could potentially change if Georgia looked close to becoming a NATO member. This is precisely why it has so far been rebuffed by the NATO governments, which are keen to avoid the inevitable conflict with Russia.

A majority of the population in Georgia would like closer ties with the EU countries, but the shock of the 2008 war, when then President Mikheil Saakashvili naively thought the Americans might ride to his rescue after he provoked the Russians, has caused many to consider that hedging their bets may be safer. In 2013 they elected a government and president, Giorgi Margvelashvili, far more conciliatory to Moscow. As in Ukraine, people instinctively know the truism everyone in the neighbourhood recognises: that Washington is far away, and Moscow is near.

Russia's most powerful weapons now, leaving to one side nuclear missiles, are not the Russian army and air force, but gas and oil. Russia is second only to the USA as the world's biggest supplier of natural gas, and of course it uses this power to its advantage. The better your relations with Russia, the less you pay for energy; for example, Finland gets a better deal than the Baltic States. This policy has been used so aggressively, and Russia has such a hold over Europe's energy needs, that moves are afoot to blunt its impact. Many countries in Europe are attempting to wean themselves off their dependency on Russian energy, not via alternative pipelines from less aggressive countries but by building ports.

On average, more than 25 per cent of Europe's gas and oil comes from Russia; but often the closer a country is to Moscow, the greater its dependency. This in turn reduces that country's foreign policy options. Latvia, Slovakia, Finland and Estonia are 100 per cent reliant on Russian gas, the Czech Republic, Bulgaria and Lithuania are 80 per cent dependent, and Greece, Austria and Hungary 60 per cent. About half of Germany's gas consumption comes from Russia, which, along with extensive trade deals, is partly why German politicians tend to be slower to criticise the Kremlin for aggressive behaviour than a country such as Britain, which not only has 13 per cent dependency, but also has its own gas-producing industry, including reserves of up to nine months' supply.

There are several major pipeline routes running east to west out of Russia, some for oil and some for gas. It is the gas lines which are the most important.

In the north, via the Baltic Sea, is the Nord Stream route, which connects directly to Germany. Below that, cutting through Belarus, is the Yamal pipeline, which feeds Poland and Germany. In the south is the Blue Stream, taking gas to Turkey via the Black Sea. Until early 2015 there was a planned project called South Stream, which was due to use the same route but branch off to Hungary, Austria, Serbia, Bulgaria and Italy. South Stream was Russia's attempt to ensure that even during disputes with Ukraine it would still have a major route to large markets in Western Europe and the Balkans. Several

EU countries put pressure on their neighbours to reject the plan, and Bulgaria effectively pulled the plug on the project by saying the pipelines would not come across its territory. President Putin reacted by reaching out to Turkey with a new proposal, sometimes known as the Turk Stream.

Russia's South Stream and Turk Stream projects to circumvent Ukraine followed the price disputes between the two states in 2005–10, which at various times cut the gas supply to eighteen countries. European nations which stood to benefit from South Stream were markedly more restrained in their criticism of Russia during the Crimea crisis of 2014. The Russians are far from finished, as the Nord Stream 2 project shows. This Gazprom-owned project under the Baltic Sea could be used to reduce gas shipments through Ukraine, thus denying it an important source of revenue. It also undermines the EU's efforts to diversify its energy sources, offering a source of cheap gas that may tempt some member states.

Enter the Americans, with a win-win strategy for the USA and Europe. Noting that Europe wants gas, and not wanting to be seen to be weak in the face of Russian foreign policy, the Americans believe they have the answer. The massive boom in shale gas production in the USA is not only enabling it to be self-sufficient in energy, but also to sell its surplus to one of the great energy consumers – Europe.

To do this, the gas needs to be liquefied and shipped across the Atlantic. This in turn requires liquefied natural gas (LNG) terminals and ports to be built along the European coastlines to receive the cargo and turn it back into gas. Washington is already approving licences for export facilities, and Europe is beginning a long-term project to build more LNG terminals. Poland and Lithuania are constructing LNG terminals; other countries such as the Czech Republic want to build pipelines connecting to those terminals, knowing they could then benefit not just from American liquefied gas, but also supplies from North Africa and the Middle East. The Kremlin would no longer be able to turn the taps off.

The EU now has about thirty LNG import terminals, which include huge storage capacities and are set to grow. It also has the ability to reverse the direction of gas through its LNG pipe-lines, which usually flows east to west and north to south, so if Russia did cut the supply of gas into one EU country, other countries could pump LNG back up the pipe to supply them instead.

The Russians, seeing the long-term danger, point out that piped gas is cheaper than LNG, and President Putin, with a 'what did I ever do wrong' expression on his face, says that Europe already has a reliable and cheaper source of gas coming from his country. LNG is unlikely to completely replace Russian gas, but it will strengthen what is a weak European hand in both price negotiation and foreign policy. To prepare for a potential reduction in revenue Russia is planning pipelines heading south-east and hopes to increase sales to China.

This is an economic battle based on geography and one of the modern examples where technology is being utilised in an attempt to beat the geographic restraints of earlier eras.

A lot was made of the economic pain Russia suffered in 2014 when the price of oil fell below $50 a barrel, and lower still in 2015. Moscow's 2016 budget and predicted spending for 2017 was based on prices of $50, and even though Russia began pumping record levels of oil, it knows it cannot balance the books. Russia loses about $2 billion in revenue for each dollar drop in the oil price and the Russian economy duly took the hit, bringing great hardship to many ordinary people, but predictions of the collapse of the state were wide of the mark. Russia will struggle to fund its huge increase in military spending, but despite the difficulties it faces, the World Bank predicts that in the second half of this decade the economy will grow slightly. If the new discoveries of vast amounts of oil in the Arctic's Kara Sea can be brought to shore, that growth will be healthier.

Away from the heartland Russia does have a global political reach and uses its influence, notably in Latin America, where it buddies up to whichever South American country has the least friendly relationship with the United States, for example Venezuela. In the spring of 2019, Russia flew in 100 troops, thought to be Special Forces and cyber experts, at a time when there was media speculation about a US military intervention to overthrow President Maduro. While 100 Russian troops might not have been able to pre-vent that, they certainly could have complicated matters. Russia also tries to check American moves in the Middle East, or at least ensure it has a say in matters, it is spending massively on its Arctic military forces, and it consistently takes an interest in Greenland to maintain its territorial claims. Since the fall of Communism it has focused less on Africa, but maintains what influence it can there, albeit in a losing battle with China.

Competitors they may be, but the two giants also cooperate on various levels. Moscow, knowing that the Europeans have a long-term ambition to wean themselves off dependency on Russian energy, is looking to China as an alternative customer. China has the upper hand in what is a buyers' market, but the lines of communication are cordial and well used. From 2020 Russia will supply China with huge amounts of gas, rising to 38 billion cubic metres of gas a year by 2025 in a $400 billion thirty-year deal.

The days when Russia was considered a military threat to China have passed, and the idea of Russian troops occupying Manchuria, as they did 1945, is inconceivable, although they do keep a wary eye on each other in places each would like to be the dominant power, such as Kazakhstan. However, they are not in competition for the ideological leadership of global Communism and this has freed each side to cooperate at a military level where their interests coincide. What seems like an odd example came in May 2015 when they conducted joint military live fire exercises in the Mediterranean. Beijing's push into a sea 9,000 miles from home was part of its attempt to extend its naval reach around the globe, while Moscow has designs on the gas fields found in the Mediterranean, is courting Greece, and wants to protect its small naval port on the Syrian coast. In addition, both sides are quite happy to annoy the NATO powers in the region, including the American 6th Fleet based in Naples.

At home, Russia is facing many challenges, not least of which is demographic. The sharp decline in population growth may have been arrested, but it remains a problem. The average lifespan for a Russian man is below sixty-five, ranking Russia in the bottom half of the world's 193 UN member states, and there are now only 144 million Russians (excluding Crimea).

From the Grand Principality of Muscovy, through Peter the Great, Stalin and now Putin, each Russian leader has been confronted by the same problems. It doesn't matter if the ideology of those in control is tsarist, Communist or crony capitalist – the ports still freeze, and the North European Plain is still flat.

Strip out the lines of nation states, and the map Ivan the Terrible confronted is the same one Vladimir Putin is faced with to this day.

CHAPTER 2

CHINA

'China is a civilisation pretending to be a nation.'

Lucian Pye, political scientist

R U S
KAZAKHSTAN
MONGO
KYRGYZSTAN
Ürümqi
TAJIKISTAN
Xinjiang
AFGHANISTAN
G
In
PAKISTAN
Karakoram
Kunlun Shan
Aksai Chin
Himalayas
Tibetan Plateau
C H I N
Tibet
Lhasa
NEPAL
BHUTAN
INDIA
BANGLADESH
Mekong River
BURMA
LAOS
VIETNA
Bay of Bengal
THAILAND
State border
Administrative border
Disputed border
Great Wall

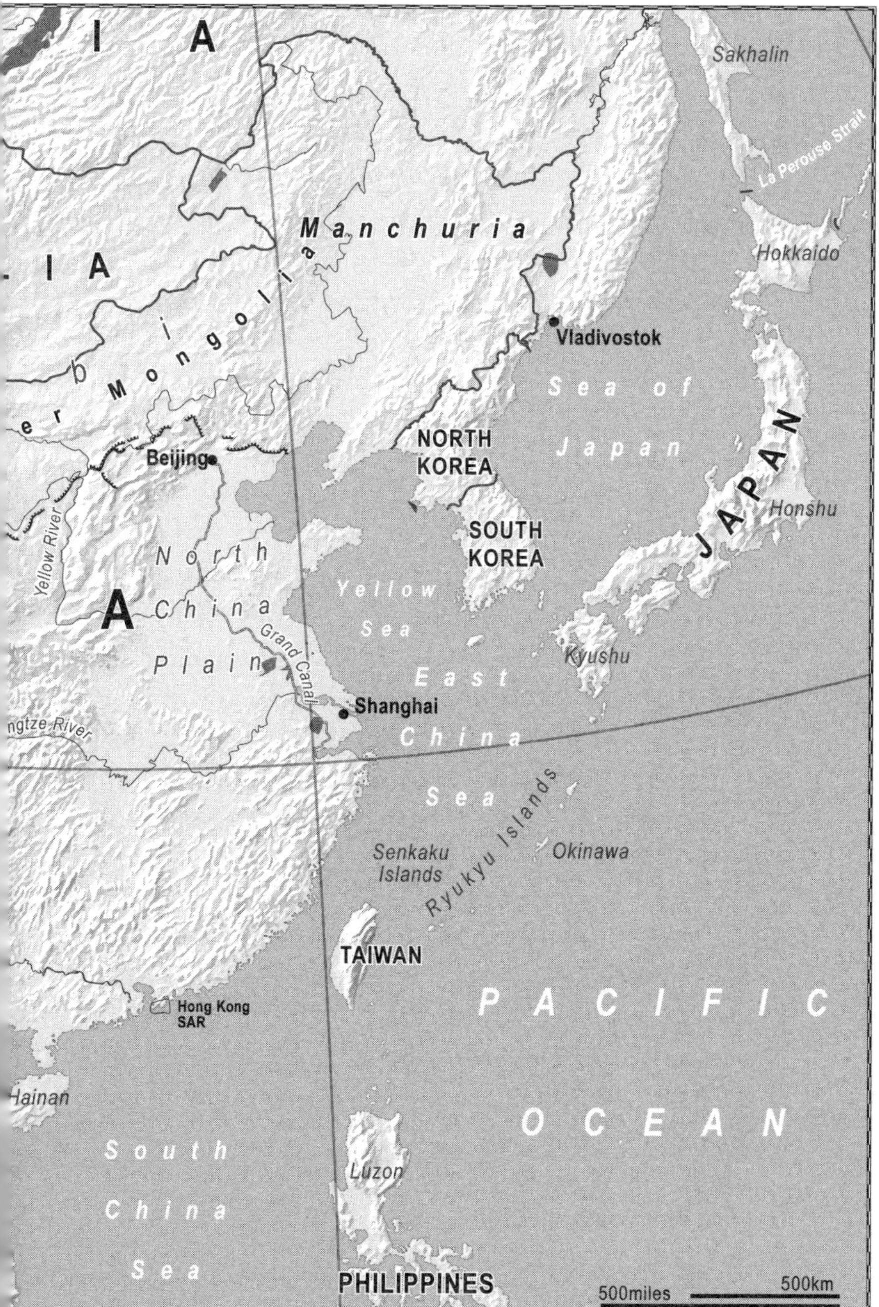

I A
I A
Manchuria
Inner Mongolia
Beijing
Yellow River
North China Plain
A
Grand Canal
Shanghai
Yangtze River
Sakhalin
La Perouse Strait
Hokkaido
Vladivostok
Sea of Japan
NORTH KOREA
SOUTH KOREA
JAPAN
Honshu
Yellow Sea
Kyushu
East China Sea
Ryukyu Islands
Senkaku Islands
Okinawa
TAIWAN
Hong Kong SAR
PACIFIC OCEAN
Hainan
South China Sea
Luzon
PHILIPPINES
500miles
500km

IN OCTOBER 2006, A US NAVAL SUPERCARRIER GROUP LED by the 1,000-foot USS *Kitty Hawk* was confidently sailing through the East China Sea between southern Japan and Taiwan, minding everyone's business, when, without warning, a Chinese navy submarine surfaced in the middle of the group.

An American aircraft carrier of that size is surrounded by about twelve other warships, with air cover above and submarine cover below. The Chinese vessel, a Song-class attack submarine, may well be very quiet when running on electric power but, still, this was the equivalent to Pepsi-Cola's management popping up in a Coca-Cola board meeting after listening under the table for half an hour.

The Americans were amazed and angry in equal measure. Amazed because they had no idea a Chinese sub could do that without being noticed, angry because they hadn't noticed and because they regarded the move as provocative, especially as the sub was within torpedo range of the *Kitty Hawk* itself. They protested, perhaps too much, and the Chinese said: 'Oh! What a coincidence, us surfacing in the middle of your battle group which is off our coast, we had no idea.'

This was twenty-first-century reverse gunboat diplomacy; whereas the British used to heave a man-of-war off the coast of some minor power to signal intent, the Chinese hove into view off their own coast with a clear message: 'We are now a maritime power, this is our time, and this is our sea.' It has taken 4,000 years, but the Chinese are coming to a port – and a shipping lane – near you.

Until now China has never been a naval power – with its large land mass, multiple borders and short sea routes to trading partners, it had no need to be, and it was rarely ideologically expansive. Its merchants have long sailed the oceans to trade goods, but its navy did not seek territory beyond its region, and the difficulty of patrolling the great sea lanes of the Pacific, Atlantic and Indian Oceans was not worth the effort. It was always a land power, with a lot of land and a lot of people – now nearly 1.4 billion.

The concept of China as an inhabited entity began almost 4,000 years ago. The birthplace of Chinese civilisation is the region known as the North China Plain, which the Chinese refer to as the Central Plain. A large, low-lying tract of nearly 160,000 square miles, it is situated below Inner Mongolia, south of Manchuria, in and around the Yellow River Basin and down past the Yangtze River, which both run west to east. It is now one of the most densely populated areas in the world.

The Yellow River basin is subject to frequent and devastating floods, earning the river the unenviable sobriquet of 'Scourge of the Sons of Han'. The industrialisation of the region began in earnest in the 1950s and has been rapidly accelerating in the last three decades. The terribly polluted river is now so clogged with toxic waste that it sometimes struggles even to reach the sea. Nevertheless the Yellow River is to China what the Nile is to Egypt – the cradle of its civilisation, where its people learnt to farm, to make paper and gunpowder.

To the north of this proto-China were the harsh lands of the Gobi Desert in what is now Mongolia. To the west the land gradually rises until it becomes the Tibetan Plateau, reaching to the Himalayas. To the south-east and south lies the sea.

The heartland, as the North China Plain is known, was and is a large, fertile plain with two main rivers and a climate that allows rice and soy beans to be harvested twice a season (double-cropping), which encouraged rapid population growth. By 1500 BCE in this heartland, out of hundreds of mini city-states, many warring with each other, emerged the earliest version of a Chinese state – the Shang dynasty. This is where what became known as the Han people emerged, protecting the heartland and creating a buffer zone around them.

The Han now make up over 90 per cent of China's population and they dominate Chinese politics and business. They are differentiated by Mandarin, Cantonese and many other regional languages, but united by ethnicity and at a political level by the geopolitical impulsion to protect the heartland. Mandarin, which originated in the northern part of the region, is by far the dominant language and is the medium of government, national state television and education. Mandarin is similar to Cantonese and many other languages when written, but very different when spoken.

The heartland is the political, cultural, demographic and – crucially – the agricultural centre of gravity. About a billion people live in this part of China, despite it being just half the size of the United States, which has a population of 327 million. Because the terrain of the heartland lent itself to settlement and an agrarian lifestyle, the early dynasties felt threatened by the non-Han regions which surrounded them, especially Mongolia with its nomadic bands of violent warriors.

China chose the same strategy as Russia: attack as defence, leading to power. As we shall see, there were natural barriers which – if the Han could reach them and establish control – would protect them. It was a struggle over millennia, only fully realised with the annexation of Tibet in 1951.

By the time of the famous Chinese philosopher Confucius (551–479 BCE) there was a strong feeling of Chinese identity and of a divide between civilised China and the 'barbarous' regions which surrounded it. This was a sense of identity shared by 60 million or so people.

By 200 BCE China had expanded towards, but not reached, Tibet in the south-west, north to the grasslands of Central Asia and south all the way down to the South China Sea. The Great Wall (known as the Long Wall in China) had been first built by the Qin dynasty (221–207 BCE), and on the map China was beginning to take on what we now recognise as its modern form. It would be more than 2,000 years before today's borders were fixed, however.

Between 605 and 609 CE the Grand Canal, centuries in the making and today the world's longest man-made waterway, was extended and finally linked the Yellow River to the Yangtze. The Sui dynasty (581–618 CE) had harnessed the vast numbers of workers under its control and used them to connect existing natural tributaries into a navigable waterway between the two great rivers. This tied the northern and southern Han to each other more closely than ever before. It took several million slaves five years to do the work, but the ancient problem of how to move supplies south to north had been solved – but not the problem which exists to this day, that of flooding.

The Han still warred with each other, but increasingly less so, and by the early eleventh century CE they were forced to concentrate their attention on the waves of Mongols pouring down from the north. The Mongols defeated whichever dynasty, north or south, they came up against and by 1279 their leader Kublai Khan became the first foreigner to rule all of the country as Emperor of the Mongol (Yuan) dynasty. It would be almost ninety years before the Han took charge of their own affairs with the establishment of the Ming dynasty.

By now there was increasing contact with traders and

emissaries from the emerging nation states of Europe, such as Spain and Portugal. The Chinese leaders were against any sort of permanent European presence, but increasingly opened up the coastal regions to trade. It remains a feature of China to this day that when China opens up, the coastland regions prosper but the inland areas are neglected. The prosperity engendered by trade has made coastal cities such as Shanghai wealthy, but that wealth has not been reaching the countryside. This has added to the massive influx of people into urban areas and accentuated regional differences.

In the eighteenth century China reached into parts of Myanmar (previously known as Burma) and Indo-China to the south, and Xinjiang in the north-west was conquered, becoming the country's biggest province. An area of rugged mountains and vast desert basins, Xinjiang is 642,820 square miles, twice the size of Texas – or, to put it another way, you could fit the UK, France, Germany, Austria, Switzerland, the Netherlands and Belgium into it and still have room for Luxembourg. And Liechtenstein.

But, in adding to its size, China also added to its problems. Xinjiang, a region populated by Muslims, was a perennial source of instability, indeed insurrection, as were other regions; but for the Han the buffer was worth the trouble, even more so after the fate which befell the country in the nineteenth and twentieth centuries with the coming of the Europeans.

The imperial powers arrived, the British among them, and carved the country up into spheres of influence. It was, and is, the greatest humiliation the Chinese suffered since the Mongol invasions. This is a narrative the Communist Party uses frequently; it is in part true, but it is also useful to cover up the Party's own failures and repressive policies.

Later the Japanese – expanding their territory as an emerging world power – invaded, attacking first in 1931 and then again in 1937, after which they occupied most of the heartland as well as Manchuria and Inner Mongolia. Japan's unconditional surrender to the Americans at the end of the Second World War in 1945 led to the withdrawal of Japanese troops, although in Manchuria they were replaced by the advancing Soviet army, which then withdrew in 1946.

A few outside observers thought the post-war years might bring liberal democracy to China. It was wishful thinking akin to the naive nonsense Westerners wrote during the early days of the recent 'Arab Spring', which, as with China, was based on a lack of understanding of the internal dynamics of the people, politics and geography of the region.

Instead, nationalist forces under Chiang Kai-shek and Communist armies under Mao Zedong battled for supremacy until 1949, when the Communists emerged victorious and the Nationalists withdrew to Taiwan. That same year Radio Beijing announced: 'The People's Liberation Army must liberate all Chinese territories, including Tibet, Xinjiang, Hainan and Taiwan.'

Mao centralised power to an extent never seen in previous dynasties. He blocked Russian influence in Inner Mongolia and extended Beijing's influence into Mongolia. In 1951 China completed its annexation of Tibet (another vast non-Han territory), and by then Chinese school textbook maps were beginning to depict China as stretching even into the Central Asian republics. The country had been put back together; Mao would spend the rest of his life ensuring it stayed that way and consolidating Communist Party control in every facet of life, but turning away from much of the outside world. The country remained desperately poor, especially away from the coastal areas, but unified.

Mao's successors tried to turn his Long March to victory into an economic march towards prosperity. In the early 1980s the Chinese leader Deng Xiaoping coined the term 'Socialism with Chinese Characteristics', which appears to translate as 'Total control for the Communist Party in a Capitalist Economy'. China was becoming a major trading power and a rising military giant. By the end of the 1990s it had recovered from the shock of the Tiananmen Square massacre of 1989, regained Hong Kong and Macau from the British and Portuguese respectively, and could look around its borders, assess its security and plan ahead for its great move out into the world.

If we look at China's modern borders we see a great power now confident that it is secured by its geographical features, which lend themselves to effective defence and trade. In China the points of the compass are always listed in the order east–south–west–north, but let's start in the north and move clockwise.

In the north we see the 2,906-mile-long border with Mongolia. Straddling this border is the Gobi Desert. Nomadic warriors from ancient times might have been able to attack south across it, but a modern army would be spotted massing there weeks before it was ready to advance, and it would need incredibly long supply lines running across inhospitable terrain before it got into Inner Mongolia (part of China) and close to the heartland. There are few roads fit to move heavy armour, and few habitable areas. The Gobi Desert is a massive early warning system-cum-defensive line. Any Chinese expansion northward will come not via the military, but from trade deals as China attempts to hoover up Mongolia's natural resources, primarily minerals. This will bring with it increased migration of the Han into Mongolia.

Next door, to the east, is China's border with Russia, which runs all the way to the Pacific Ocean – or at least the Sea of Japan subdivision of it. Above this is the mountainous Russian Far East, a huge, inhospitable territory with a tiny population. Below it is Manchuria, which the Russians would have to push through if they wanted to reach the Chinese heartland. The population of Manchuria is 100 million and growing; in contrast, the Russian Far East has fewer than seven million people and no indications of population growth. Large-scale migration south to north can be expected, which will in turn give China more leverage in its relations with Russia. From a military perspective the best place to cross would be near the Russian Pacific port of Vladivostok, but there are few reasons, and no current intentions, to so do. Indeed, the recent Western sanctions against Russia due to the crisis in Ukraine have driven Russia into massive economic deals with China on terms which help keep Russia afloat, but are favourable to the Chinese. Russia is the junior partner in this relationship.

Below the Russian Far East, along the coast, are China's Yellow, East China and South China seas which lead to the Pacific and Indian Oceans, have many good harbours and have always been used for trade. But across the waves lie several island-sized problems – one shaped like Japan, which we shall come to shortly.

Continuing clockwise, we come to the next land borders: Vietnam, Laos and Myanmar. Vietnam is an irritation for China. For centuries the two have squabbled over territory, and unfortunately for both this is the one area to the south which has a border an army can get across without too much trouble – which partially explains the 1,000-year domination and occupation of Vietnam by China from 111 BCE to 938 CE and their brief cross-border war of 1979. However, as China's military prowess grows, Vietnam will be less inclined to get drawn into a shooting match and will either cosy up even closer to the Americans for protection or quietly begin shifting diplomatically to become friends with Beijing. That both countries are nominally ideologically Communist has little to do with the state of their relationship: it is their shared geography that has defined relations. Viewed from Beijing, Vietnam is only a minor threat and a problem that can be managed.

The border with Laos is hilly jungle terrain, difficult for traders to cross – and even more complicated for the military. As they move clockwise to Myanmar, the jungle hills become mountains until at the western extreme they are approaching 20,000 feet and beginning to merge into the Himalayas.

This brings us to Tibet and its importance to China. The Himalayas run the length of the Chinese–Indian border before descending to become the Karakorum Range bordering Pakistan, Afghanistan and Tajikistan. This is nature's version of a Great Wall of China, or – looking at it from New Delhi's side – the Great Wall of India. It cuts the two most populous countries on the planet off from each other both militarily and economically.

They have their disputes: China claims the Indian province of Arunachal Pradesh, India says China is occupying Aksai Chin; but despite pointing their artillery at each other high up on this natural wall, both sides have better things to do than reignite the shooting match which broke out in 1962, when a series of violent border disputes culminated in vicious large-scale mountain fighting. Nevertheless, the tension is ever-present and each side needs to handle the situation with care.

Very little trade has moved between China and India over the centuries, and that is unlikely to change soon. Of course the border is really the Tibetan–Indian border – and that is precisely why China has always wanted to control it.

This is the geopolitics of fear. If China did not control Tibet, it would always be possible that India might attempt to do so. This would give India the commanding heights of the Tibetan Plateau and a base from which to push into the Chinese heartland, as well as control of the Tibetan sources of three of China's great rivers, the Yellow, Yangtze and Mekong, which is why Tibet is known as 'China's Water Tower'. China, a country with approximately the same volume of water usage as the USA, but with a population five times as large, will clearly not allow that.

It matters not whether India wants to cut off China's river supply, only that it would have the power to do so. For centuries China has tried to ensure that it could never happen. The actor Richard Gere and the Free Tibet movement will continue to speak out against the injustices of the occupation, and now settlement, of Tibet by Han Chinese; but in a battle between the Dalai Lama, the Tibetan independence movement, Hollywood stars and the Chinese Communist Party – which rules the world's second-largest economy – there is only going to be one winner.

When Westerners, be they Mr Gere or former President Obama, talk about Tibet, the Chinese find it deeply irritating. Not dangerous, not subversive – just irritating. They see it not through the prism of human rights, but that of geopolitical security, and can only believe that the Westerners are trying to undermine their security. However, Chinese security has not been undermined and it will not be, even if there are further uprisings against the Han. Demographics and geopolitics oppose Tibetan independence.

The Chinese are building 'facts on the ground' on the 'roof of the world'. In the 1950s the Chinese Communist People's Army began building roads into Tibet, and since then they have helped to bring the modern world to the ancient kingdom; but the roads, and now railways, also bring the Han.

It was long said to be impossible to build a railway through the permafrost, the mountains and the valleys of Tibet. Europe's best engineers, who had cut through the Alps, said it could not be done. As late as 1988 the travel writer Paul Theroux wrote in his book *Riding the Iron Rooster*: 'The Kunlun Range is a guarantee that the railway will never get to Lhasa.' The Kunlun separated Xinjiang province from Tibet, for which Theroux gave thanks: 'That is probably a good thing. I thought I liked railways until I saw Tibet, and then I realised that I liked wilderness much more.' But the Chinese built it. Perhaps only they could have done. The line into the Tibetan capital, Lhasa, was opened in 2006 by the then Chinese President Hu Jintao. Now passenger and goods trains arrive from as far away as Shanghai and Beijing, four times a day, every day.

They bring with them many things, such as consumer goods from across China, computers, colour televisions and mobile phones. They bring tourists who support the local economy, they bring modernity to an ancient and impoverished land, a huge improvement in living standards and healthcare, and they bring the potential to carry Tibetan goods out to the wider world. But they have also brought several million Han Chinese settlers.

The true figures are hard to come by: the Free Tibet movement claims that in the wider cultural Tibetan region Tibetans are now a minority, but the Chinese government says that in the official Tibetan Autonomous Region more than 90 per cent of people are Tibetan. Both sides are exaggerating, but the evidence suggests the government is the one with the greater degree of exaggeration. Its figures do not include Han migrants who are not registered as residents, but the casual observer can see that Han neighbourhoods now dominate the Tibetan urban areas.

Once, the majority of the population of Manchuria, Inner Mongolia and Xinjiang were ethnically Manchurian, Mongolian and Uighur; now all three are majority Han Chinese, or approaching the majority. So it will be with Tibet.

This means that resentment of the Han will continue to manifest itself in rioting such as that of 2008, when anti-Chinese Tibetan protestors in Lhasa burnt and looted Han properties, twenty-one people died and hundreds were injured. The authorities' crackdown will continue, the Free Tibet movement will continue, monks will continue to set themselves on fire to bring the plight of the Tibetans to the world's attention – and the Han will keep coming.

China's massive population, mostly crammed into the heartland, is looking for ways to expand. Just as the Americans looked west, so do the Chinese, and just as the Iron Horse brought the European settlers to the lands of the Comanche and the Navajo, so the modern Iron Roosters are bringing the Han to the Tibetans.

They also now bring the Red Army all the way to the Indian border area. The path beaten and built over the past decade has taken the military to the Doklam plateau. The roads are now capable of taking the weight of heavy armour and so for the first time in history the Chinese can project serious force across the Himalayas. This has spooked the Indian military and in 2018 there was a tense stand-off between the two sides on the plateau.

The Indians fear that the Chinese could make a lightning dash down into India, cutting off what is known as Chicken's Neck, a relatively narrow stretch of land above Bangladesh that joins West India to East. Cut that and you divide one from the other – which would be a nightmare for India.

Finally the clock hand moves round past the borders with Pakistan, Tajikistan and Kyrgyzstan (all mountainous) before reaching the border with Kazakhstan, which leads back round north to Mongolia. This is the ancient Silk Route, the trade land bridge from the Middle Kingdom to the world. Theoretically it's a weak spot in China's defence, a gap between the mountains and desert; but it is far from the heartland, the Kazakhs are in no position to threaten China, and Russia is several hundred miles distant.

South-east of this Kazakh border is the restive 'semi-autonomous' Chinese province of Xinjiang and its native Muslim population of the Uighur people, who speak a language related to Turkish. Xinjiang borders eight countries: Russia, Mongolia, Kazakhstan, Kyrgyzstan, Tajikistan, Afghanistan, Pakistan and India.

There was, is and always will be trouble in Xinjiang. The Uighurs have twice declared an independent state of 'East Turkestan', in the 1930s and 1940s. They watched the collapse of the Russian Empire result in their former Soviet neighbours in the 'Stans' becoming sovereign states, were inspired by the Tibetan independence movement, and many are now again calling to break away from China.

Inter-ethnic rioting erupted in 2009, leading to over 200 deaths. Beijing responded in three ways: it ruthlessly suppressed dissent, it poured money into the region, and it continued to pour in Han Chinese workers. For China, Xinjiang is too strategically important to allow an independence movement to get off the ground: it not only borders eight countries, thus buffering the heartland, but it also has oil, and is home to China's nuclear weapons testing sites. The territory is also key to the Chinese economic strategy of 'One Belt, One Road'. The road is, oddly enough, a sea route – the creation of an ocean-going highway for goods; the belt is the 'Silk Road Economic Belt' – a land-based route formed from the old Silk Route, which goes straight through Xinjiang and will in turn connect down southwards to the massive deep-water port China is building in Gwadar, Pakistan. In late 2015 China signed a forty-year lease on the port. This is part of the way in which 'the belt and the road' will be connected.

Most of the new towns and cities springing up across Xinjiang are overwhelmingly populated by Han Chinese attracted by work in the new factories in which the central government invests. A classic example is the city of Shihezi, 85 miles north-west of the capital, Ürümqi. Of its population of 650,000, it is thought that at least 620,000 are Han. Overall, Xinjiang is reckoned to be 40 per cent Han, at a conservative estimate – and even Ürümqi itself may now be majority Han, although official figures are difficult to obtain and not always reliable due to their political sensitivity.

There is a 'World Uighur Congress' based in Germany, and the 'East Turkestan Liberation Movement' set up in Turkey; but Uighur separatists lack a Dalai Lama-type figure upon whom foreign media can fix, and until recently their cause was almost unknown around the world. China tries to keep it that way, ensuring it stays on good terms with as many border countries as possible in order to prevent any organised independence movement from having supply lines or somewhere to which it could fall back. Beijing also paints separatists as Islamist terrorists. Al Qaeda and other groups, which have a foothold in places like Tajikistan, are indeed attempting to forge links with the Uighur separatists, but the movement is nationalist first, Islamic second. However, gun, bomb and knife attacks in the region against state and/or Han targets over the past few years do look as if they will continue, and could escalate into a full-blown uprising.

Beijing's response has been to incarcerate huge numbers of Ui-ghurs in 're-education camps'. How many people are being held is known only to the Chinese authorities, but estimates range from 150,000 to 1 million. It is alleged that inmates are banned from pray-ing or growing beards as part of a policy designed to strip the Uighurs of their religious beliefs. In April 2019 China denied the allegations, called the camps 'boarding schools' and said it had arrested about 13,000 terrorists and 'broken up hundreds of terrorist gangs'.

In 2016, local government officials said that the de-radicalisation effort had 'markedly weakened' the nascent Islamist movement. However, given that the Turkish Army said it had arrested 324 suspected jihadists from Xinjiang en route to Syria in 2015, that seems unlikely. The routing of Islamic State in Iraq and parts of Syria in 2017 has also increased the dan-gers of foreign fighters returning home but not retiring.

China will not cede this territory and, as in Tibet, the window for independence is closing. Both are buffer zones, one is a major land trade route, and – crucially – both offer markets (albeit with a limited income) for an economy which must keep producing and selling goods if it is to continue to grow and to prevent mass unemployment. Failure to so do would likely lead to widespread civil disorder, threatening the control of the Communist Party and the unity of China.

There are similar reasons for the Party's resistance to democracy and individual rights. If the population were to be given a free vote, the unity of the Han might begin to crack or, more likely, the countryside and urban areas would come into conflict. That in turn would embolden the people of the buffer zones, further weakening China. It is only a century since the most recent humiliation of the rape of China by foreign powers; for Beijing, unity and economic progress are priorities well ahead of democratic principles.

The Chinese look at society very differently from the West. Western thought is infused with the rights of the individual; Chinese thought prizes the collective above the individual. What the West thinks of as the rights of man, the Chinese leadership thinks of as dangerous theories endangering the majority, and much of the population accepts that, at the least, the extended family comes before the individual.

I once took a Chinese ambassador in London to a high-end French restaurant in the hope they would repeat Prime Minister Zhou Enlai's much-quoted answer to Richard Nixon's question 'What is the impact of the French Revolution?', to which the prime minister replied 'It's too soon to tell.' Sadly this was not forthcoming, but I was treated to a stern lecture about how the full imposition of 'what you call human rights' in China would lead to widespread violence and death and was then asked, 'Why do you think your values would work in a culture you don't understand?'

The deal between the Party leaders and the people has been, for a generation now, 'We'll make you better off – you will follow our orders.' So long as the economy keeps growing, that grand bargain may last. If it stops, or goes into reverse, the deal is off. The current level of demonstrations and anger against corruption and inefficiency are testament to what would happen if the deal breaks.

Another growing problem for the Party is its ability to feed the population. More than 40 per cent of arable land is now either polluted or has thinning topsoil, according to their Ministry of Agriculture.

China is caught in a catch-22. It needs to keep industrialising as it modernises and raises standards of living, but that very process threatens food production. If it cannot solve this problem there will be unrest.

There are now around 500 mostly peaceful protests a day across China over a variety of issues. If you introduce mass unemployment, or mass hunger, that tally will explode in both number and the degree of force used by both sides.

So, on the economic side China now also has a grand bargain with the world – 'We'll make the stuff for cheap – you buy it for cheap.'

Leave to one side the fact that already labour costs are rising in China and it is being rivalled by Thailand and Indonesia, for price if not volume. What would happen if the resources required to make the stuff dried up, if someone else got them first, or if there was a naval blockade of your goods – in and out? Well, for that, you'd need a navy.

The Chinese were great sea voyagers, especially in the fifteenth century, when they roamed the Indian Ocean; Admiral Zheng He's expedition ventured as far as Kenya. But these were money-making exercises, not power projections, and they were not designed to create forward bases that could be used to support military operations.

Having spent 4,000 turbulent years consolidating its land mass, China is now building a Blue Water navy. A Green Water navy patrols its maritime borders, a Blue Water navy patrols the oceans. It will take another thirty years (assuming economic progression) for China to build naval capacity to seriously challenge the most powerful seaborne force the world has ever seen – the US navy. But in the medium to short term, as it builds, and trains, and learns, the Chinese navy will bump up against its rivals on the seas; and how those bumps are managed – especially the Sino–American ones – will define great power politics in this century.

The young seamen now training on the second-hand aircraft carrier (the *Liaoning*) China salvaged from a Ukrainian rust yard will be the ones who, if they make it to the rank of admiral, may have learnt enough to know how to take a twelve-ship carrier group across the world and back – and if necessary fight a war along the way. As some of the richer Arab nations came to realise, you cannot buy an efficient military off the shelf.

In the summer of 2017 the Chinese sailed the *Liaoning* into Hong Kong harbour accompanied by two guided-missile destroyers, a guided-missile frigate and two corvettes. It was timed to honour the visit of President Xi – but it was also meant as a reminder to Hong Kong, and the rest of the world, of who controls Hong Kong, and who intends one day to control the South China Sea.

A few months earlier China had launched its second aircraft carrier. It was seaworthy, but not yet combat ready. A third carrier is supposed to be launched in 2021. It is doubtful it will be nuclear powered, and it will lack the capabilities of US carriers; nevertheless, it will give China more reach and more options. In early 2019 Chinese naval experts were confident enough to brief that the country would have six aircraft carrier groups by 2035, with four of them available for active duty at any one time.

Gradually the Chinese will put more and more vessels into the seas off their coast, and into the Pacific. Each time one is launched there will be less space for the Americans in the China Seas. The Americans know this, and know the Chinese are working towards a land-based anti-ship missile system to double the reasons why the US navy, or any of its allies, might one day want to think hard about sailing through the South China Sea. Or indeed, any other 'China' sea. China's increasingly long-distance shore-to-ship artillery firepower will allow its growing navy to venture further from its coastline because the navy will become less vital for defence. There was a hint of this in September 2015 when the Chinese (lawfully) sailed five vessels through American territorial waters off the coast of Alaska. That this took place just before President Xi's visit to the United States was not a coincidence. The Bering Strait is the quickest way for Chinese vessels to reach the Arctic Ocean, and we will see more of them off the Alaskan coast in the coming years. And all the while, the developing Chinese space project will be watching every move the Americans make, and those of its allies.

So, having gone clockwise around the land borders, we now look east, south and south-west towards the sea.

Between China and the Pacific is the archipelago that Beijing calls the 'First Island Chain'. There is also the 'Nine Dash Line', more recently turned into ten dashes in 2013 to include Taiwan, which China says marks its territory. This dispute over ownership of more than 200 tiny islands and reefs is poisoning China's

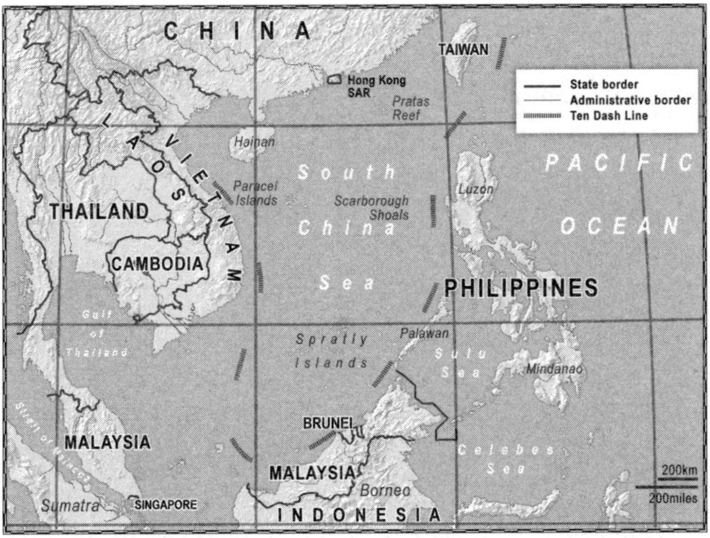

The South China Sea is a hotly contested area between China and its neighbours, leading to disputes over ownership of islands, natural resources and control of the seas and shipping lanes.

relations with its neighbours. National pride means China wants to control the passageways through the Chain; geopolitics dictates it has to. It provides access to the world's most important shipping lanes in the South China Sea. In peacetime the route is open in various places, but in wartime they could very easily be blocked, thus blockading China. All great nations spend peacetime preparing for the day war breaks out.

Free access to the Pacific is firstly hindered by Japan. Chinese vessels emerging from the Yellow Sea and rounding the Korean Peninsula would have to go through the Sea of Japan and up through La Perouse Strait above Hokkaido and into the Pacific. Much of this is Japanese or Russian territorial waters and at a time of great tension, or even hostilities, would be inaccessible to China. Even if they made it they would still have to navigate through the Kuril Islands north-east of Hokkaido, which are controlled by Russia but claimed by Japan.

Japan is also in dispute with China over the uninhabited island chain it calls Senkaku and the Chinese know as Diaoyu, north-east of Taiwan. This is the most contentious of all territorial claims between the two countries. If, instead, Chinese ships pass through, or indeed set off from, the East China Sea off Shanghai and go in a straight line towards the Pacific, they must pass the Ryukyu Islands, which include Okinawa – upon which there is not only a huge American military base, but as many shore-to-ship missiles as the Japanese can pile up at the tip of the island. The message from Tokyo is: 'We know you're going out there, but don't mess with us on the way out.'

Another potential flare-up with Japan centres on the East China Sea's gas deposits. Beijing has declared an 'Air Defence Identification Zone' over most of the sea, requiring prior notice before anyone else flies through it. The Americans and Japanese are trying to ignore it, but it will become a hot issue at a time of their choosing or due to an accident which is mismanaged.

Below Okinawa is Taiwan, which sits off the Chinese coast and separates the East China Sea from the South China Sea. China claims Taiwan as its twenty-third province, but it is currently an American ally with a navy and air force armed to the teeth by Washington. It came under Chinese control in the seventeenth century but has only been ruled by China for five years in the last century (from 1945 to 1949).

Taiwan's official name is the Republic of China (ROC) to differentiate it from the People's Republic of China, although both sides believe they should have jurisdiction over both territories. This is a name Beijing can live with as it does not state that Taiwan is a separate state. The Americans are committed to defending Taiwan in the event of a Chinese invasion under the Taiwan Relations Act of 1979. However, if Taiwan declares full independence from China, which China would consider an act of war, the USA is not bound to come to its rescue, as the declaration would be considered provocative.

The two governments vie for recognition for themselves and non-recognition of the other in every single country in the world, and in most cases Beijing wins. When you can offer a potential market of 1.4 billion people as opposed to 23 million, most countries don't need long to consider. However, there are twenty-two countries (mostly developing states such as Swaziland, Burkina Faso and the islands of São Tomé and Príncipe) which do opt for Taiwan, and which are usually handsomely rewarded.

The Chinese are determined to have Taiwan but are nowhere near being able to challenge for it militarily. Instead they are using soft power by increasing trade and tourism between the two states. China wants to woo Taiwan back into its arms. During the 2014 student protests in Hong Kong, one of the reasons the authorities did not quickly batter them off the streets – as they would have done in, for example, Ürümqi – was that the world's cameras were there and would have captured the violence. In China much of this footage would be blocked, but in Taiwan people would see what the rest of the world saw and ask themselves how close a relationship they wanted with such a power. Beijing hesitated; it is playing the long game.

The soft-power approach is to persuade the people of Taiwan they have nothing to fear in rejoining the 'Motherland'. The Air Defence Identification Zone, the surfacing near US ships and the build-up of a navy are part of a long-term plan to weaken American resolve to defend an island 140 miles off the coast of mainland China, but 6,400 miles from the west coast of the USA.

From the South China Sea Chinese ships would still have problems, whether they headed towards the Pacific or the Indian Ocean – which is the world's waterway for the gas and oil without which China would collapse.

To go westward towards the energy-producing states of the Gulf they must pass Vietnam, which, as we have noted, has recently been making overtures to the Americans. They must go near the Philippines, a US ally, before trying to get through the Strait of Malacca between Malaysia, Singapore and Indonesia, all of which are diplomatically and militarily linked to the USA. The Strait is approximately 500 miles long and at its narrowest is less than two miles wide. It has always been a choke point – and the Chinese remain vulnerable to being choked. All of the states along the Strait and near its approaches are anxious about Chinese dominance, and most have territorial disputes with Beijing.

China claims almost the entire South China Sea, and the energy supplies believed to be beneath it, as its own. However, Malaysia, Taiwan, Vietnam, the Philippines and Brunei also have territorial claims against China and each other. For example, the Philippines and China argue bitterly over the Mischief Islands, a large reef in the Spratly Islands in the South China Sea, which one day could live up to their name. Every one of the hundreds of disputed atolls, and sometimes just rocks poking out of the water, could be turned into a diplomatic crisis, as surrounding each rock is a potential dispute about fishing zones, exploration rights and sovereignty.

To further its aims, China is using dredging and land reclamations methods to begin turning a series of reefs and atolls in disputed territory into islands. For example, one in the Spratly Islands (whose name, Fiery Cross Reef, aptly described it) is now an island complete with a port and a runway that could host fighter jets, giving China far more control of the skies over the region than it currently has. Another reef has had artillery units stationed on it.

Speaking in the summer of 2015, US Defense Secretary Ash Carter said, 'Turning an underwater rock into an airfield simply does not afford the rights of sovereignty or permit restrictions on international air or maritime transit.' This was shortly after China announced it was switching its military posture in the region from defence to both offence and defence. The move underlines China's intention to be the rule maker in the region and for that it will both court and threaten its neighbours.

China must secure the routes through the South China Sea, both for its goods to get to market, and for the items required to make those goods – oil, gas and precious metals among them – to get into China. It cannot afford to be blockaded. Diplomacy is one solution; the ever-growing navy is another; but the best guarantees are pipelines, roads and ports.

Diplomatically, China will attempt to pull the South-East Asian nations away from the USA using both carrot and stick. Too much stick, and the countries will tie themselves ever closer into defence treaties with Washington; too much carrot, and they may not bend to Beijing's will. At the moment they still look across the Pacific for protection.

The maps of the region that the Chinese now print show almost the whole of the South China Sea as theirs. This is a statement of intent, backed by aggressive naval patrols and official statements. Beijing intends to change its neighbours' ways of thinking and to change America's way of thinking and behaving – pushing and pushing an agenda until its competitors back off. At stake here is the concept of international waters and free passage in peacetime; it is not something which will easily be given up by the other powers.

With this in mind, the British announced in the summer of 2017 that one of the first missions to be conducted by their two new aircraft carriers would be a 'freedom of navigation' operation through the South China Sea. Beijing took a very dim view of this, which it would deem a provocative act. However, the following year a British amphibious assault ship, HMS *Albion*, sailed close to the disputed Paracel Islands, claimed by China, and in early 2019 the then defence secretary Gavin Williamson con-firmed that a carrier would sail through the South China Sea in 2020, complete with warplanes aboard.

The geopolitical writer Robert Kaplan expounds the theory that the South China Sea is to the Chinese in the twenty-first century what the Caribbean was to the USA at the beginning of the twentieth century. The Americans, having consolidated their land mass, had become a two-ocean power (Atlantic and Pacific), and then moved to control the seas around them, pushing the Spanish out of Cuba.

China also intends to become a two-ocean power (Pacific and Indian). To achieve this China is investing in deep-water ports in Myanmar, Bangladesh, Pakistan and Sri Lanka – an investment which buys it good relations, the potential for its future navy to have friendly bases to visit or reside in, and trade links back home. A good example came in 2017. Sri Lanka had repeatedly asked China for loan after loan to build the Hambantota port, to which the Chinese had repeatedly said 'yes'. A Chinese state-owned company built the port, despite feasibility studies suggesting it wouldn't be successful.

It wasn't. The Sri Lankan government found it couldn't make the debt repayments and so handed over the port, along with 15,000 acres of land surrounding it and a ninety-nine-year lease. At a stroke, China had acquired a naval base a few hundred miles away from one of its main strategic rivals – India.

The Indian Ocean and Bay of Bengal ports are part of an even bigger plan to secure China's future. Its lease on the new deep-water port at Gwadar, Pakistan, will be key (if the Pakistan region of Baluchistan is stable enough) to creating an alternative land route up to China. From Myanmar's west coastline China has built natural gas and oil pipelines linking the Bay of Bengal up into south-west China – China's way of reducing its nervous reliance on the Strait of Malacca, through which almost 80 per cent of its energy supplies pass. This partially explains why, when the Burmese Junta began to slowly open up to the outside world in 2010, it wasn't just the Chinese who beat a path to their door. The Americans and Japanese were quick to establish better relations, with both President Obama and Prime Minister Abe of Japan going to pay their respects in person. The Trump administration has since said it doesn't want to get entangled in foreign adventures, but the game in Myanmar is not an adventure, it is a long-term strategy. If the USA can influence Myanmar, it can help check China. So far, the Chinese are winning this particular game on the global chessboard, but the Americans may be able to outmuscle them as long as the Burmese government is confident Washington will stand by it.

The Chinese are also building ports in Kenya, railway lines in Angola, and a hydroelectric dam in Ethiopia. They are scouring the length and breadth of the whole of Africa for minerals and precious metals.

Chinese companies and workers are spread out across the

world; slowly China's military will follow. With great power comes great responsibility. China will not leave the sea lanes in its neighbourhood to be policed by the Americans. There will be events which require the Chinese to act out of region. A natural disaster or a terrorist/hostage incident involving large numbers of Chinese workers would require China to take action, and that entails forward bases, or at least agreements from other states that China could pass through their territory. There are now tens of millions of Chinese around the world, in some cases housed in huge complexes for workers in parts of Africa.

China will struggle to become agile over the next decade. It could barely manoeuvre the People's Army's equipment to help in the aftermath of the devastating 2008 earthquake in Sichuan. It mobilised the army, but not their *materiel*; moving abroad at speed would be an even greater challenge.

This will change. China is not weighed down or motivated diplomatically or economically by human rights in its dealings with the world. It is secure in its borders, straining against the bonds of the First Island Chain, and now moving around the globe with confidence. If it can avoid a serious conflict with Japan or the USA, then the only real danger to China is itself.

There are 1.4 billion reasons why China may succeed, and 1.4 billion reasons why it may not surpass America as the greatest power in the world. A great depression like that of the 1930s could set it back decades. China has locked itself into the global economy. If we don't buy, they don't make. And if they don't make there will be mass unemployment. If there is mass and long-term unemployment, in an age when the Chinese are a people packed into urban areas, the inevitable social unrest could be – like everything else in modern China – on a scale hitherto unseen.

CHAPTER 3

USA

'Reports of my death have been greatly exaggerated.'

Mark Twain

CANADA
Washington
Oregon
Idaho
Montana
Wyoming
North Dakota
South Dakota
Nebraska
Nevada
Utah
Colorado
Kansas
California
Arizona
New Mexico
Oklah
Texas
Rocky Mountains
Great Plains
Sierra Nevada
PACIFIC OCEAN
Rio Grande
MEXICO
500miles
500km
State border
Administrative border
Mississippi basin

A D A
Great Lakes
Maine
Vermont
New Hampshire
Massachusetts
Rhode Island
Connecticut
New York
New Jersey
Minnesota
Michigan
Wisconsin
Iowa
Missouri
Pennsyl-vania
Ohio
Maryland
Delaware
Illinois
Indiana
West Virginia
Washington D.C.
Appalachian Mountains
Virginia
Ohio
Missouri
Kentucky
North Carolina
Mississippi
Tennessee
Arkansas
South Carolina
Mississippi
Alabama
East Coast Plain
Georgia
ATLANTIC OCEAN
Louisiana
New Orleans
Florida
Gulf of Mexico
BAHAMAS
CUBA

LOCATION, LOCATION, LOCATION. IF YOU WON THE LOTTERY, and were looking to buy a country to live in, the first one the estate agent would show you would be the United States of America.

Twain was referring to the erroneous reporting of his death, but he could have been talking about the over-reporting of the demise of the USA.

It's in a wonderful neighbourhood, the views are marvellous and there are some terrific water features, the transport links are excellent; and the neighbours? The neighbours are great, no trouble at all.

If you broke this living space up into numerous sections it would considerably lower its value – especially if the tenants did not all speak the same language and paid the rent in different currencies – but as one home, for one family, it can't be bettered.

There are fifty American states, but they add up to one nation in a way the twenty-eight sovereign states of the European Union never can. Most of the EU states have a national identity far stronger, more defined, than any American state. It is easy to find a French person who is French first, European second, or one who pays little allegiance to the idea of Europe, but an American identifies with their Union in a way few Europeans do theirs. This is explained by geography, and by the history of the unification of the USA.

Painting this vast country in bold, broad brushstrokes from east to west, you can divide it into three parts.

First there is the East Coast Plain leading to the Appalachian Mountains, an area well watered by short but navigable rivers and with fertile soil. Then, heading further west, you have the Great Plains stretching all the way to the Rocky Mountains, and within this section lies the Mississippi basin with its network of huge, navigable rivers flowing into the Mississippi River all the way down to the Gulf of Mexico, which is sheltered by the peninsula of Florida and several islands. Once over the massive mountain range that is the Rockies you get to the desert, the Sierra Nevada Mountains, a narrow coastal plain, and finally to the shores of the Pacific Ocean.

To the north, above the Great Lakes, lies the Canadian Shield, the world's largest area of Precambrian rock, much of which forms a barrier to human settlement. To the south-west – desert. Geography had determined that if a political entity could get to and then control the land 'from sea to shining sea', it would be a great power, the greatest history has known. Once that power was achieved, the Union would become almost impossible to invade. As we saw with Russia, there is 'strategic depth' for a defending force to fall back to. The size of Canada, (and to a lesser extent Mexico) is also an asset, as any hostile power attempting to invade by going through these countries would have incredibly long supply lines.

Equally important, in modern times, is that anyone stupid enough to contemplate invading America would soon be forced to reflect on the fact that it contains hundreds of millions of guns, readily available to a population that takes its life, liberty and pursuit of happiness very seriously. In addition to the formidable US Armed Forces, there is the National Guard, state police and, as we saw on various occasions in 2015, an urban police force that can quickly resemble a military unit. In the event of an invasion, every US Folsum, Fairfax, and Farmerville would quickly resemble an Iraqi Fallujah.

But to achieve this rare geographical position of near invulnerability from conventional attack, first the space had to be acquired and unified, which, considering the continent is 3,000 miles from coast to coast, was achieved astonishingly quickly.

When the Europeans first began to land and stay in the early seventeenth century, they quickly realised that the east coast of this 'virgin' territory was packed with natural harbours and fertile soil. Here was a place where they could live and, unlike their home countries, a place where they hoped they could live freely. Their descendants would go on to deny the native inhabitants their freedom, but that was not the intention of the first settlers. Geography pulled them across the Atlantic in ever greater numbers.

The last of the original thirteen colonies to be established was Georgia in 1732. The thirteen became increasingly independently minded all the way up to the American Revolutionary War (1775–83). At the beginning of this period the colonies, which gradually began to connect to each other, stretched 1,000 miles from Massachusetts in the north, down to Georgia, and had an estimated combined population of about 2.5 million people. They were bounded by the Atlantic to their east, and the Appalachian Mountains to their west. The Appalachians, 1,500 miles long, are impressive, but compared to the Rockies, not particularly high. Nevertheless, they still formed a formidable barrier to westward movement for the early settlers, who were busy consolidating what territory they had subdued and preparing to govern it themselves. The colonists had another barrier, this one political. The British government forbade settlement west of the Appalachians as it wanted to ensure that trade, and taxes, remained on the Eastern seaboard.

The Declaration of Independence (1776) states: 'When in the course of human events, it becomes necessary for one people to dissolve the political bands which have connected them with another, and to assume the Powers of the earth, the separate and equal station to which the Laws of Nature and of Nature's God entitle them, a decent respect to the opinions of mankind requires that they should declare the causes which impel them to the separation.' It goes on to outline at some length those causes, and to state (with no hint of slave-owning irony) that it was self-evident that all men were created equal. These noble sentiments helped to fuel the victory in the War of Independence, which in turn gave birth to a new nation state.

In the early 1800s this new country's leadership still had little idea that it was thousands of miles from the 'South Sea' or Pacific. Using Indian trails, a few explorers, for whom the word intrepid could have been coined, had pushed through the Appalachians and reached the Mississippi. There they thought they might find a waterway leading to the ocean and thus joining up with the vast tracts of lands the Spanish had explored across the south-western and Pacific coastal regions, including what are now Texas and California.

At this point the fledgling USA was far from secure, and if it had been restricted to its then boundaries, would have struggled to become a great power. Its citizens already had access to the Ohio River, just west of the Appalachians, but that led to the Mississippi, whose western bank was controlled by the French all the way down to the city of New Orleans. This gave the French command of American trade heading out to the Old World from the Gulf of Mexico, as well as the vast territory to the west in what is now the American heartland. In 1802, a year after Thomas Jefferson assumed the presidency, he wrote: 'There is on the globe one single spot, the possessor of which is our natural and habitual enemy. It is New Orleans.'

So France was the possessor and the problem; but the solution, unusually, was not warfare.

In 1803 the United States simply bought control of the entire Louisiana Territory from France. The land stretched from the Gulf of Mexico north-west up to the headwaters of the tributaries of the Mississippi River in the Rocky Mountains. It was an area equivalent in size to modern-day Spain, Italy, France, the UK and Germany combined. With it came the Mississippi basin, from which flowed America's route to greatness.

At the stroke of a pen, and the handing over of $15 million, the Louisiana Purchase of 1803 doubled the size of the USA and gave it mastery over the greatest inland water transport route in the world. As the American historian Henry Adams wrote, 'Never did the United States get so much for so little.'

The greater Mississippi basin has more miles of navigable inland waterways than the rest of the world put together. Nowhere else are there so many rivers whose source is not in high land, and whose waters run smoothly all the way to the ocean across vast distances. The Mississippi, fed by much of the basin river system, begins near Minneapolis and ends 1,800 miles away in the Gulf of Mexico. So the rivers were the natural conduit for ever-increasing trade, leading to a great port and all using waterborne craft which was, and is, many times cheaper than road travel.

The Americans now had strategic geographical depth, a massive fertile land and an alternative to the Atlantic ports with which to conduct business. They also had ever-expanding routes east to west linking the East Coast to the new territory, and then the river systems flowing north to south to connect the then sparsely populated lands with each other, thus encouraging America to form as a single entity.

There was now a sense that the nation would become a colossus, a continental power. They pushed onwards, ever westwards, but with an eye on the south and the security of the jewel in the crown – the Mississippi.

By 1814 the British had gone, and the French had given up on Louisiana. The trick now was to get the Spanish to go. It wasn't too difficult. The Spanish were exhausted by the war in Europe against Napoleon; the Americans were pushing the Seminole Indian nation into Spanish Florida, and Madrid knew that waves of settlers would be following. In 1819 the Spanish ceded Florida to the USA and with it a massive amount of territory.

The Louisiana Purchase had given the USA the heartland, but the Transcontinental Treaty of 1819 gave them something almost as valuable. The Spanish accepted that the USA would have jurisdiction in the far west above the 42nd parallel, on what is now the border of California and Oregon, while Spain would control what lay below, west of the American territories. The USA had reached the Pacific.

At the time most Americans thought the great victory of 1819 was getting Florida, but Secretary of State John Quincy Adams wrote in his diary: 'The acquisition of a definite line of boundary to the [Pacific] forms a great epoch in our history.'

But there was another Spanish-speaking problem – Mexico.

Because the Louisiana Purchase doubled the size of the USA, when Mexico became independent of Spain in 1821 its border was just 200 miles from the port of New Orleans. In the twenty-first century Mexico poses no territorial threat to the USA, although its proximity causes America problems, as it feeds its northern neighbour's appetite for illegal labour and drugs.

In 1821 that was different. Mexico controlled land all the way up to northern California, which the USA could live with, but it also stretched out east, including what is now Texas which, then as now, borders Louisiana. Mexico's population at the time was 6.2 million, the USA's 9.6 million. The US army may have been able to see off the mighty British, but they had been fighting 3,000 miles from home with supply lines across an ocean. The Mexicans were next door.

Quietly, Washington encouraged Americans and new arrivals to begin to settle on both sides of the US–Mexican border. Waves of immigrants came and spread west and south-west. There was little chance of them putting down roots in the region we now know as modern Mexico, thus assimilating, and boosting the population numbers there. Mexico is not blessed in the American way. It has poor-quality agricultural land, no river system to use for transport, and was wholly undemocratic, with new arrivals having little chance of ever being granted land.

While the infiltration of Texas was going on, Washington issued the 'Monroe Doctrine' (named after President James Monroe) in 1823. This boiled down to warning the European powers that they could no longer seek land in the Western Hemisphere, and that if they lost any parts of their existing territory they could not reclaim them. Or else.

By the mid-1830s there were enough white settlers in Texas to force the Mexican issue. The Mexican, Catholic, Spanish-speaking population numbered in the low thousands, but there were about 20,000 white Protestant settlers. The Texas Revolution of 1835–6 drove the Mexicans out, but it was a close-run thing, and had the settlers lost then the Mexican army would have been in a position to march on New Orleans and control the southern end of the Mississippi. It is one of the great 'what ifs' of modern history.

However, history turned the other way and Texas became independent via American money, arms and ideas. The territory went on to join the Union in 1845 and together they fought the 1846–8 Mexican War, in which they crushed their southern neighbour, which was required to accept that Mexico ended in the sands of the southern bank of the Rio Grande.

With California, New Mexico and land which is now Arizona, Nevada, Utah and part of Colorado included, the borders of continental USA then looked similar to those of today, and they are in many ways natural borders. In the south, the Rio Grande runs through desert; to the north are great lakes and rocky land with few people close to the border, especially in the eastern half of the continent; and to the east and west – the great oceans. However, in the twenty-first century, in the south-west the cultural historical memory of the region as Hispanic land is likely to resurface, as the demographics are changing rapidly and Hispanics will be the majority population within a few decades.

But back to 1848. The Europeans had gone, the Mississippi basin was secure from land attack, the Pacific was reached and it was obvious that the remaining Indian nations would be subdued: there was no threat to the USA. It was time to make some money, and then venture out across the seas to secure the approaches to the three coastlines of the superpower-to-be.

The California Gold Rush of 1848–9 helped, but the immigrants were heading west anyway. After all, there was a continental empire to build, and as it developed, more immigrants followed. The Homestead Act of 1862 awarded 160 acres of federally owned land to anyone who farmed it for five years and paid a small fee. If you were a poor man from Germany, Scandinavia, or Italy, why go to Latin America and be a serf, when you could go to the USA and be a free land-owning man?

In 1867 Alaska was bought from Russia. At the time it was known as 'Seward's folly' after the Secretary of State, William Seward, who agreed the deal. He paid $7.2 million, or 2 cents an acre. The press accused him of purchasing snow, but minds were changed with the discovery of major gold deposits in 1896. Decades later huge reserves of oil were also found.

Two years on, in 1869, came the opening of the transcontinental railroad. Now you could cross the country in a week, whereas it had previously taken several hazardous months.

As the country grew, and grew wealthy, it began to develop a Blue Water navy. For most of the nineteenth century foreign policy was dominated by expanding trade and avoiding entanglements outside the neighbourhood, but it was time to push out and protect the approaches to the coastlines. The only real threat was from Spain – it may have been persuaded to leave the mainland but it still controlled the islands of Cuba, Puerto Rico and part of what is now the Dominican Republic.

Cuba in particular kept American presidents awake at night, as it would again in 1962 during the Cuban Missile Crisis. The island sits just off Florida, giving it access to and potential control of the Florida Straits and the Yucatan Channel in the Gulf of Mexico. This is the exit and entry route for the port of New Orleans.

Spain's power may have been diminishing towards the end of the nineteenth century, but it was still a formidable military force. In 1898 the USA declared war on Spain, routed its military and gained control of Cuba, with Puerto Rico, Guam and the Philippines thrown in for good measure. They would all come in useful, but Guam in particular is a vital strategic asset and Cuba a strategic threat if controlled by a major power.

In 1898 that threat was removed by war with Spain. In 1962 it was removed by the threat of war with the Soviet Union after they blinked first. Today no great power sponsors Cuba and it appears destined to come under the cultural, and probably political, influence of the USA again.

America was moving quickly. In the same year it secured Cuba, the Florida Straits and to a great extent the Caribbean, it also annexed the Pacific island of Hawaii, thus protecting the approaches to its own west coast. In 1903 America signed a treaty leasing it exclusive rights to the Panama Canal. Trade was booming.

The time was right for the USA to show it had more than arrived on the world stage, and what better way to demonstrate that than a show of force circumnavigating the globe.

President Theodore Roosevelt was speaking relatively softly – but in essence he sailed a large stick around the world. Sixteen navy battleships from the Atlantic force set out from the USA in December 1907. Their hulls were painted white, the Navy's peacetime colour, and this impressive example of diplomatic signalling became known as 'the Great White Fleet'. Over the following fourteen months the fleet called in on twenty ports, including ones in Brazil, Chile, Mexico, New Zealand, Australia, the Philippines, Japan, China, Italy and Egypt. Of these the most important was Japan, which was put on notice that, in extremis, America's Atlantic fleet could be deployed to the Pacific. The voyage, a mixture of hard and soft power, preceded the military term 'force projection' but that is what it was, and it was duly noted by every major power in the world.

Most subsequent presidents bore in mind George Washington's advice in his farewell address in 1796 not to get involved in 'inveterate antipathies against particular nations, and passionate attachments for others', and to 'steer clear of permanent alliances with any portion of the foreign world'.

Apart from a late – albeit crucial – entry into the First World War, twentieth-century America did manage, mostly, to avoid entanglements and alliances until 1941.

The Second World War changed everything. The USA was attacked by an increasingly militaristic Japan after Washington imposed economic sanctions on Tokyo which would have brought the country to its knees. The Americans came out swinging. They projected their now vast power around the world, and in order to keep things that way, this time they didn't go home.

As the world's greatest economic and military post-war power, America now needed to control the world's sea lanes, to keep the peace and get the goods to market.

They were the 'last man standing'. The Europeans had exhausted themselves, and their economies, like their towns and cities, were in ruins. The Japanese were crushed, the Chinese devastated and at war with each other, the Russians weren't even in the capitalist game.

A century earlier, the British had learnt they needed forward bases and coaling stations from which to project and protect their naval power. Now, with Britain in decline, the Americans looked lasciviously at the British assets and said, 'Nice bases – we'll have them.'

The price was right. In the autumn of 1940 the British had desperately needed more warships. The Americans had fifty spare and so, with what was called the 'Destroyers for Bases

Agreement', the British swapped their ability to be a global power for help in remaining in the war. Almost every British naval base in the Western Hemisphere was handed over.

This was, and is still, for all countries, about concrete. Concrete in the building of ports, runways, hardened aircraft hangars, fuel depots, dry docks and Special Forces training areas. In the East, after the defeat of Japan, America seized the opportunity to build these all over the Pacific. Guam, halfway across, they already had; now they had bases right up to the Japanese island of Okinawa in the East China Sea.

The Americans also looked to the land. If they were going to pay to reconstruct Europe through the Marshall Plan of 1948–51, they had to ensure that the Soviet Union wouldn't wreck the place and reach the Atlantic coast. The Doughboys didn't go home. Instead they set up shop in Germany and faced down the Red Army across the North European Plain.

In 1949 Washington led the formation of NATO and with it effectively assumed command of the Western world's surviving military might. The civilian head of NATO might well be a Belgian one year, a Brit the next, but the military commander is always an American, and by far the greatest firepower within NATO is American.

No matter what the treaty says, NATO's Supreme Commander ultimately answers to Washington. The UK and France would learn to their cost during the Suez Crisis of 1956, when they were compelled by American pressure to cease their occupation of the canal zone, losing most of their influence in the Middle East as a result, that a NATO country does not hold a strategic naval policy without first asking Washington.

With Iceland, Norway, Britain and Italy (all founding members of NATO) having granted the USA access and rights to their bases, it now dominated the North Atlantic and the Mediterranean as well as the Pacific. In 1951 it extended its domination there down to the south by forming an alliance with Australia and New Zealand, and also to the north following the Korean War of 1950–53.

There were now two maps of the United States: the familiar one stretching diagonally down from Seattle on the Pacific coast to the panhandle in the Sargasso Sea, and the one demonstrating America's geopolitical power footprint. This latter map showed the bases, ports and runways – the real things you could mark on the page. But it was also a conceptual map, one which told you that in the event of situation A happening in region B, country C could be relied on to be a US ally and vice versa. If a major power wanted to play anywhere in the world, it knew that if the USA chose to, it could have dog in the fight. A superpower had arrived. In the 1960s the USA's failure in Vietnam damaged its confidence, and made it more cautious about foreign entanglements. However, what was effectively a defeat did not substantially alter America's global strategy.

There were now only three places from which a challenge to American hegemony could come: a united Europe, Russia and China. All would grow stronger, but two would reach their limits.

The dream of some Europeans of an EU with 'ever closer union' and a common foreign and defence policy is dying slowly before our eyes, and even if it were not, the EU countries spend so little on defence that ultimately they remain reliant on the USA. The economic crash of 2008 has left the European powers reduced in capacity and with little appetite for foreign adventures, especially after seeing how badly the intervention in Libya ended, when the French and British, with the Americans 'leading from behind', enabled the overthrow of the Gaddafi regime. In 2013 the then UK Prime Minister David Cameron visited Tripoli and told the Libyan people that the lesson learned in Afghanistan and Iraq was: 'helping other counties, intervening in other countries, is not simply about military intervention.' To cries of 'Allahu Akbar' he pledged: 'In building a new Libya you will have no greater friend than the United Kingdom. We will stand with you every step of the way.' But then, as the country plunged into chaos, with numerous militia battling for control, the Europeans walked away, leaving a broken state, a desperate people and a new route opening up for illegal immigration into the continent.

In 1991 the Russian threat had been seen off due to Russia's own staggering economic incompetence, military overstretch and failure to persuade the subjected masses in its empire that gulags and the over-production of state-funded tractors was the way ahead. The recent push-back by Putin's Russia is a thorn in America's side, but not a serious threat to America's dominance. When President Obama described Russia as 'no more than a regional power' in 2014 he may have been needlessly provocative, but he wasn't wrong. The bars of Russia's geographical prison, as seen in Chapter One, are still in place: they still lack a warm-water port with access to the global sea lanes and still lack the military capacity in wartime to reach the Atlantic via the Baltic and North seas, or the Black Sea and the Mediterranean.

The USA was partially behind the change of government in Ukraine in 2014. It wanted to extend democracy in the world, and it wanted to pull Ukraine away from Russian influence and thus weaken President Putin. Washington knows that during the last decade, as America was distracted in Iraq and Afghanistan, the Russians took advantage in what they call their 'near abroad', regaining a solid footing in places such as Kazakhstan and seizing territory in Georgia. Belatedly, and somewhat half-heartedly, the Americans have been trying to roll back Russian gains. President Trump has made overtures to Moscow and sought a personal relationship with Putin, but the differences between the two countries are greater than the bond between their leaders.

Americans care about Europe, they care about NATO, they will sometimes act (if it is in the American interest), but Russia is now, for the Americans, mostly a European problem, albeit one they keep an eye on.

That leaves China, and China is rising.

Most analysis written over the past decade assumes that by the middle of the twenty-first century China will overtake the USA and become the leading superpower. For reasons partially discussed in Chapter Two, I am not convinced. It may take a century.

Economically the Chinese are on their way to matching the Americans and that buys them a lot of influence and a place at the top table, but militarily and strategically they are decades behind. The USA will spend those decades attempting to ensure it stays that way, but it feels inevitable that the gap will close.

The concrete costs a lot. Not just to mix and pour, but to be allowed to mix and pour it where you want to. As we saw with the 'Destroyers for Bases Agreement', American assistance to other governments is not always entirely altruistic. Economic and, equally importantly, military assistance buys permission to pour the concrete, but much more as well, even if there is also an added cost.

For example, in 2017 Washington expressed outrage at human rights abuses in Syria (a hostile state); following a gas attack by the regime, President Trump even ordered a cruise missile strike. However, its outrage at abuses in Bahrain might be somewhat more difficult to hear, muffled as they have been by the engines of the US 5th Fleet which is based in Bahrain as the guest of the Bahraini government. On the other hand, assistance does buy the ability to suggest to government B (say Myanmar) that it might want to resist the overtures of government C (say China). In that particular example the USA is behind the curve because the Burmese government only recently began to open up to most of the outside world and Beijing has a head start.

However, when it comes to Japan, Thailand, Vietnam, South Korea, Singapore, Malaysia, Indonesia and others, the Americans are pushing at a door already open due to those countries' anxiety about their giant neighbour and keenness to engage with Washington. They may all have issues with each other, but those issues are dwarfed by the knowledge that if they do not stand together they will be picked off one by one and eventually fall under Chinese hegemony.

The USA's famous 'pivot to Asia' under the Obama administration was taken by some to mean the abandonment of Europe; but a pivot towards one place does not mean the abandonment of another. It is more a case of how much weight you put on which foot. Even before President Trump came to power the Americans were already hedging their bets. There was never a mad rush to get out of Europe – indeed US military hardware has been built up in Eastern Europe. Team Trump are balancing fairly evenly, although it is safe to say it is developments in Asia that are likely to keep them awake at night, rather than Europe or Russia.

Many US government foreign policy strategists are persuaded that the history of the twenty-first century will be written in Asia and the Pacific. Half of the world's population lives there, and if India is included it is expected to account for half of global economic output by 2050.

Hence we will see the USA increasingly investing time and money in East Asia to establish its presence and intentions in the region. For example, in Northern Australia the Americans have set up a base for the US Marine Corps. But in order to exert real influence, they may also have to invest in limited military action to reassure their allies that they will come to their rescue in the event of hostilities. For example, if China begins shelling a Japanese destroyer and it looks as if they might take further military action, the US Navy may have to fire warning shots towards the Chinese navy, or even fire directly, to signal that it is willing to go to war over the incident. Equally, when North Korea fires at South Korea, the south fires back, but currently the US does not. Instead it puts forces on alert in a public manner to send a signal. If the situation escalated it would then fire warning shots at a North Korean target, and finally, direct shots. It's a way of escalating without declaring war – and this is when things get dangerous.

The USA is seeking to demonstrate to the whole region that it is in their best interests to side with Washington – China is doing the opposite. So when challenged, each side must react, because for each challenge it ducks, its allies' confidence, and competitors' fear, slowly drains away until eventually there is an event which persuades a state to switch sides.

Cold War, and neither side is looking for conflict. The Chinese can accept America guarding most of the sea lanes which deliver Chinese goods to the world, so long as the Americans accept that there will be limits to just how close to China that control extends.

There will be arguments, and nationalism will be used to ensure the unity of the Chinese people from time to time, but each side will be seeking compromise. The danger comes if they misread each other and/or gamble too much.

There are flashpoints. The Americans have a treaty with Taiwan which states that if the Chinese invade what they regard as their 23rd province, the USA will go to war. A red line for China, which could spark an invasion, is formal recognition of Taiwan by the USA, or a declaration of independence by Taiwan. However, there is no sign of that, and a Chinese invasion cannot be seen on this side of the horizon.

As China's thirst for foreign oil and gas grows, so that of the United States declines. This will have a huge impact on its foreign relations, especially in the Middle East, with knock-on effects for other countries.

Due to offshore drilling in US coastal waters, and underground fracking across huge regions of the country, America looks destined to become not just self-sufficient in energy, but a net exporter of energy by 2020. This will mean that its focus on ensuring a flow of oil and gas from the Gulf region will diminish. It will still have strategic interests there, but the focus will no longer be so intense. If American attention wanes, the Gulf nations will seek new alliances. One candidate will be Iran, another China, but that will only happen when the Chinese have built their Blue Water navy and, equally importantly, are prepared to deploy it.

The US 5th Fleet is not about to sail away from its port in Bahrain – that is a piece of concrete it would give up reluctantly. However, if the energy supplies of Saudi Arabia, Kuwait, the UAE and Qatar are no longer required to keep American lights on, and cars on the road, the American public and Congress will ask, what is it there for? If the response is 'to check Iran' it may not be enough to quash the debate.

Elsewhere in the Middle East, US policy in the short term is to prevent Iran from becoming too strong whilst at the same time reaching for what is known as the 'grand bargain' – an agreement settling the many issues which divide the two countries, and ending three and a half decades of enmity. The Trump Presidency inherited this policy, and agrees with it, but seeks to achieve it via a more aggressive route.

The USA under Trump has gone in hard against Iran, albeit stopping short of military action. Sanctions continued to hurt the regime in 2018 as the USA pulled out of the joint comprehensive plan of action – better known as the 'Iran nuclear deal' – in which Tehran had agreed to halt activity related to its nuclear programme. In April 2019 the USA followed this up by designating the elite revolutionary guard corps as a 'foreign terrorist organisation'. This was the first time it had labelled an-other country's military as such, and it allowed the Trump administration to go after the guards' massive business interests via further sanctions.

These policies may cause flare ups and, with each side loath to back down, could lead to confrontation. However, neither side wants war, the Europeans are in no mood at all to completely unpick the jointly agreed nuclear deal, and the US administration is aware that when it comes to events in the 'Wider Middle East' Tehran gets a vote on what happens.

So, while the Trump White House has taken a more hostile attitude, and is backing the Arab Sunni states in their stand off with Iran, as with so much else, the pre-election anti-Iran rhetoric has been tempered by the realities of office.

With the Arab nations engaged in what may be a decades-long struggle with armed Islamists, Washington looks as if it has given up on the optimistic idea of encouraging Jeffersonian democracies to emerge, and will concentrate on attempting to manage the situation whilst at the same time desperately trying not to get sand on the boots of US soldiers.

The close relationship with Israel may cool, albeit slowly, as the demographics of the USA change. The children of the Hispanic and Asian immigrants now arriving in the United States will be more interested in Latin America and the Far East than in a tiny country on the edge of a region no longer vital to American interests. It's possible the Trump–Netanyahu love-in may be the high point of this relationship.

The policy in Latin America will be to ensure that the Panama Canal remains open, to enquire about the rates to pass through the proposed Nicaraguan canal to the Pacific, and to keep an eye on the rise of Brazil in case it gets any ideas about its influence in the Caribbean Sea. Economically, the USA will also compete with China throughout Latin America for influence – but only in Cuba would Washington pull out all the stops to ensure it dominates the post-Castro/Communist era. The proximity of Cuba to Florida and the historic (albeit mixed) relationship between Cuba and the USA, combined with Chinese pragmatism, should be enough to pave the way for the USA to be the dominant power in the new Cuba. President Obama's historic visit to the island in the spring of 2016 went a long way towards ensuring that. He is the first sitting US President to visit Havana since Calvin Coolidge in 1928. The former Cuban leader, the late Fidel Castro huffed and puffed about the event, and the state controlled media dutifully reported his negative remarks, but there was a sense that this was only to keep the old man happy; the collective decision had been made, the new era had begun.

In Africa, the Americans are but one nation seeking the continent's natural wealth, but the nation finding most of it is China. As in the Middle East, the USA will watch the Islamist struggle in North Africa with interest but try not to get involved much closer than 30,000 feet above the ground.

America's experiment with nation-building overseas appears to be over.

In Iraq, Afghanistan and elsewhere, the USA underestimated the mentality and strength of small powers and of tribes. The Americans' own history of physical security and unity may have led them to overestimate the power of their democratic rationalist argument, which believes that compromise, hard work and even voting would triumph over atavistic, deep-seated historical fears of 'the other', be they Sunni, Shia, Kurd, Arab, Muslim or Christian. They assumed people would want to come together whereas in fact many dare not try and would prefer to live apart because of their experiences. It is a sad reflection upon humanity, but it appears throughout many periods of history, and in many places, to be an unfortunate truth. The American actions took the lid off a simmering pot which had temporarily hidden that truth.

This does not make American policymakers 'naive', as some of the snootier European diplomats like to believe; but they do have a 'can do' and a 'can fix' attitude which inevitably will not always work.

The election of Mr Trump demonstrated that democracies are not immune to the cult of personality and the attraction of a strong man with easy answers to hard questions. He is the result of an increasing disdain among sections of the Western electorates for 'politics as usual'. His mantra of 'America first' has been put into action, especially in economic policy, but in some respects he has not broken from the truism that 'America has presidents and it has interests; the presidents come and go – the interests remain'. After all, previous presidents also felt it was in the USA's interests to curtail North Korea's nuclear expansion, to persuade NATO countries to spend more on defence and to prevent the rise of one overly dominant power on the European continent.

Trump has followed all these policies but gone about them in a different way, using language that many people see as undiplomatic. The moral stature of the USA as the leader of the free world, and indeed the presidency, may have been damaged but that is more down to the ugly belligerence of Trump rather than the massive and sudden complete reversal of decades of policy.

Trump plays with fire and risks the world burning, especially with his loose talk about not necessarily guaranteeing NATO's policy that 'an attack on one member state is an attack on all of them', but how much fundamentally has changed? Yes, he's pulled out of arms treaties with Russia regarding Europe, but he's engaged in arms reduction talks on the nuclear issue. The 'pivot to China' had begun already, as had the loosening of ties with Europe. In the Middle East the USA has only ever focused when it thought its interests might be harmed – hence Obama's casual treatment of the Syria crisis. Even the tearing up of the Iran nuclear deal is not a revolutionary change in

American foreign policy but a return to their previous harder line. Declining to join the Paris climate agreement has not been a global game changer – many individual US states are committed to meeting its targets. California is one and its economy is bigger than every country in the world other than Germany, China, Japan and the USA itself.

Put simply, at the personal level, the arrival of Mr Trump is new and may be part of the cheapening of political dialogue in a new age of populist leaders, but at the strategic level, the USA is behaving now as the USA has behaved before.

For thirty years it has been fashionable to predict the imminent or ongoing decline of the USA. This is as wrong now as it was in the past. The planet's most successful country is about to become self-sufficient in energy, it remains the pre-eminent economic power and it spends more on research and development for its military than the overall military budget of all the other NATO countries combined. Its population is not ageing as in Europe and Japan, and a 2013 Gallup study showed that 25 per cent of all people hoping to emigrate put the USA as their first choice of destination. In the same year Shanghai University listed what its experts judged the top twenty universities of the world: seventeen were in the USA.

The Prussian statesman Otto von Bismarck, in a double-edged remark, said more than a century ago that 'God takes special care of drunks, children and the United States of America.' It appears still to be true.

CHAPTER 4

WESTERN EUROPE

'Here the past was everywhere, an entire continent sown with memories.'

Miranda Richmond Mouillot, *A Fifty-Year Silence: Love, War and a Ruined House in France*

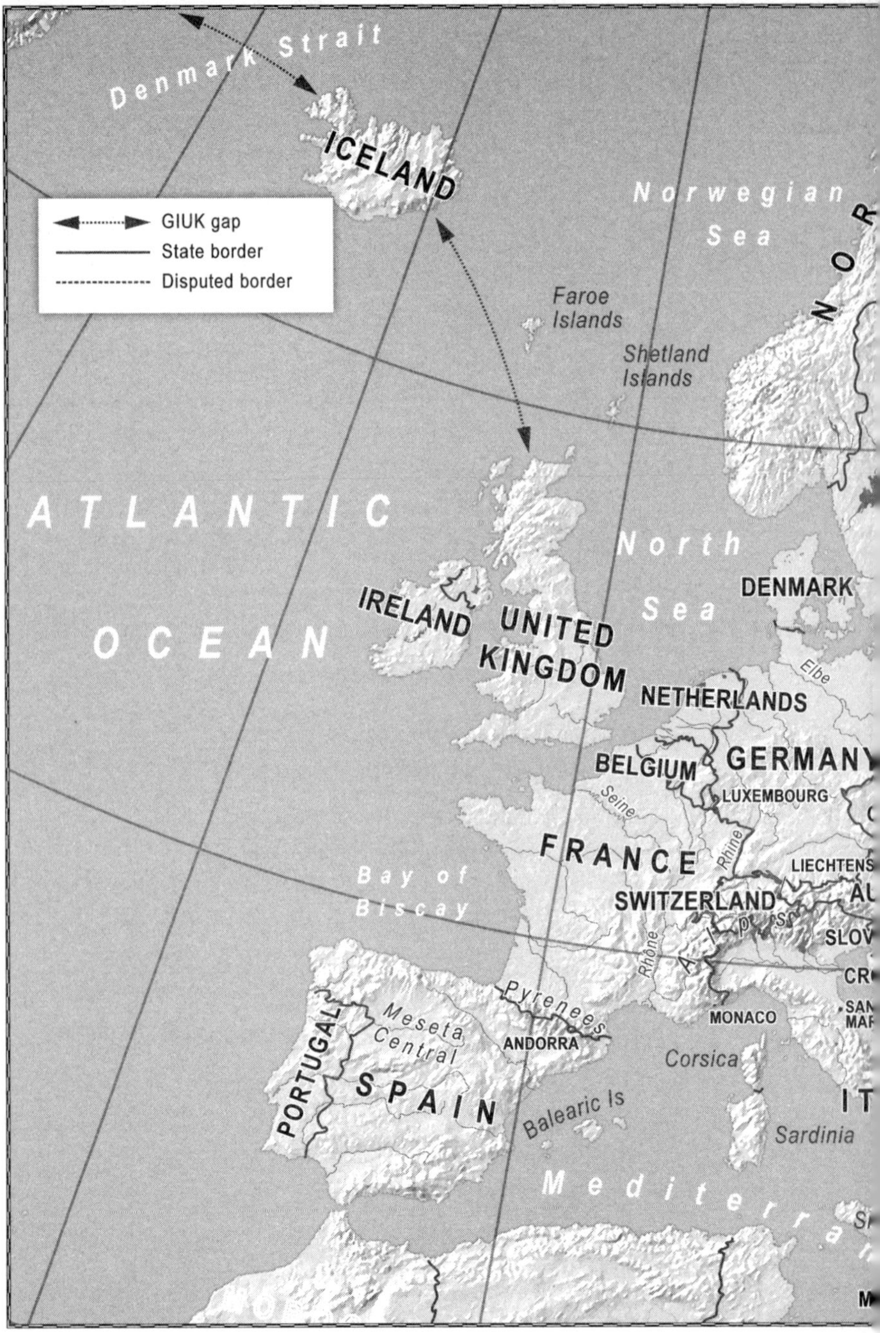

Denmark Strait
ICELAND
GIUK gap
State border
Disputed border
Norwegian Sea
Faroe Islands
Shetland Islands
ATLANTIC OCEAN
North Sea
DENMARK
IRELAND
UNITED KINGDOM
NETHERLANDS
Elbe
BELGIUM
GERMANY
LUXEMBOURG
Seine
Rhine
FRANCE
LIECHTENS
Bay of Biscay
SWITZERLAND
Alps
Rhône
MONACO
Pyrenees
Meseta Central
ANDORRA
PORTUGAL
SPAIN
Corsica
Balearic Is
Sardinia
Mediterra

500miles
500km
SWEDEN
FINLAND
RUSSIA
North European Plain
Baltic Sea
ESTONIA
LATVIA
LITHUANIA
Kaliningrad
(RUS. FED.)
BELARUS
POLAND
UKRAINE
SLOVAKIA
Carpathian Mtns
MOLDOVA
HUNGARY
ROMANIA
Sava
BOS. &
HERZ.
SERBIA
Danube
BULGARIA
Black Sea
GEORGIA
ARMENIA
MONTENEGRO
MACEDONIA
ALBANIA
TURKEY
Aegean
Sea
GREECE
SYRIA
CYPRUS
LEBANON
Crete

THE MODERN WORLD, FOR BETTER OR WORSE, SPRINGS from Europe. This western outpost of the great Eurasian land mass gave birth to the Enlightenment, which led to the Industrial Revolution, which has resulted in what we now see around us every day. For that we can give thanks to, or blame, Europe's location.

The climate, fed by the Gulf Stream, blessed the region with the right amount of rainfall to cultivate crops on a large scale, and the right type of soil for them to flourish in. This allowed for population growth in an area in which, for most, work was possible all year round, even in the heights of summer. Winter actually adds a bonus, with temperatures warm enough to work in but cold enough to kill off many of the germs which to this day plague huge parts of the rest of the world.

Good harvests mean surplus food that can be traded; this in turn builds up trading centres which become towns. It also allows people to think of more than just growing food and turn their attention to ideas and technology.

Western Europe has no real deserts, the frozen wastes are confined to a few areas in the far north, and earthquakes, volcanoes and massive flooding are rare. The rivers are long, flat, navigable and made for trade. As they empty into a variety of seas and oceans they flow into coastlines which are, west, north and south, abundant in natural harbours.

If you are reading this trapped in a snowstorm in the Alps, or waiting for flood waters to subside back into the Danube, then Europe's geographical blessings may not seem too apparent; but, relative to many places, blessings they are. These are the factors which led to the Europeans creating the first industrialised nation states, which in turn led them to be the first to conduct industrial-scale war.

If we take Europe as a whole we see the mountains, rivers and valleys that explain why there are so many nation states. Unlike the USA, in which one dominant language and culture pressed rapidly and violently ever westward, creating a giant country, Europe grew organically over millennia and remains divided between its geographical and linguistic regions.

The various tribes of the Iberian Peninsula, for example, prevented from expanding north into France by the presence of the Pyrenees, gradually came together over thousands of years to form Spain and Portugal – and even Spain is not an entirely united country, with Catalonia increasingly vocal about wanting its independence. France has also been formed by natural barriers, framed as it is by the Pyrenees, the Alps, the Rhine and the Atlantic Ocean.

Europe's major rivers do not meet (unless you count the Sava, which drains into the Danube in Belgrade). This partly explains why there are so many countries in what is a relatively small space. Because they do not connect, most of the rivers act, at some point, as boundaries, and each is a sphere of economic influence in its own right; this gave rise to at least one major urban development on the banks of each river, some of which in turn became capital cities.

Europe's second-longest river, the Danube (1,780 miles), is a case in point. It rises in Germany's Black Forest and flows south on its way to the Black Sea. In all, the Danube basin affects eighteen countries and forms natural borders along the way, including those of Slovakia and Hungary, Croatia and Serbia, Serbia and Romania, and Romania and Bulgaria. Over 2,000 years ago it was one of the borders of the Roman Empire, which in turn helped it to become one of the great trading routes of medieval times and gave rise to the present

The Danube Basin illustrates the geographical advantages of the terrain in Europe; interconnected rivers on a flat plain provided natural borders and an easily navigable transport network that encouraged a booming trade system.

capital cities of Vienna, Bratislava, Budapest and Belgrade. It also formed the natural border of two subsequent empires, the Austro-Hungarian and the Ottoman. As each shrank, the nations emerged again, eventually becoming nation states. However, the geography of the Danube region, especially at its southern end, helps explain why there are so many small nations there in comparison to the bigger countries in and around the North European Plain.

The countries of northern Europe have been richer than those of the south for several centuries. The north industrialised earlier than the south and so has been more economically successful. As many of the northern countries comprise the heartland of Western Europe, their trade links were easier to maintain, and one wealthy neighbour could trade with another – whereas the Spanish, for example, either had to cross the Pyrenees to trade, or look to the limited markets of Portugal and North Africa.

There are also unprovable theories that the domination of Catholicism in the south has held it back, whereas the Protestant work ethic propelled the northern countries to greater heights. Each time I visit the Bavarian city of Munich I reflect on this theory, and while driving past the gleaming temples of the headquarters of BMW, Allianz and Siemens have cause to doubt it. In Germany 34 per cent of the population is Catholic, and Bavaria itself is predominantly Catholic, yet their religious predilections do not appear to have influenced either their progress or their insistence that Greeks should work harder and pay more taxes.

The contrast between northern and southern Europe is also at least partly attributable to the fact that the south has fewer coastal plains suitable for agriculture, and has suffered more from drought and natural disasters than the north, albeit on a lesser scale than in other parts of the world. As we saw in Chapter One, the North European Plain is a corridor that stretches from France to the Ural Mountains in Russia, bordered to the north by the North and Baltic seas. The land allows for successful farming on a massive scale, and the waterways enable the crops and other goods to be moved easily.

Of all the countries on the plain, France was best situated to take advantage of it. France is the only European country to be both a northern and southern power. It contains the largest expanse of fertile land in Western Europe, and many of its rivers connect with each other; one flows west all the way to the Atlantic (the Loire), another south to the Mediterranean (the Rhône). These factors, together with its relative flatness, lent themselves to unification of regions, and – especially from the time of Napoleon – centralisation of power.

But to the south and west many countries remain in the second tier of European power, partially because of their location. The south of Italy, for example, is still well behind the north in terms of development, and although it has been a unified state (including Venice and Rome) since 1871, the strains of the rift between north and south are greater now than they have been since before the Second World War. The heavy industry, tourism and financial centres of the north have long meant a higher standard of living there, leading to the formation of political parties agitating for cutting state subsidies to the south, or even breaking away from it.

Spain is also struggling, and has always struggled because of its geography. Its narrow coastal plains have poor soil, and access to markets is hindered internally by its short rivers and the Meseta Central, a highland plateau surrounded by mountain ranges, some of which cut through it. Trade with Western Europe is further hampered by the Pyrenees, and any markets to its south on the other side of the Mediterranean are in developing countries with limited income. It was left behind after the Second World War, as under the Franco dictatorship it was politically frozen out of much of modern Europe. Franco died in 1975 and the newly democratic Spain joined the EU in 1986. By the 1990s it had begun to catch up with the rest of Western Europe, but its inherent geographical and financial weaknesses continue to hold it back and have intensified the problems of overspending and loose central fiscal control. It has been among the countries hit worst by the 2008 economic crisis.

Greece suffers similarly. Much of the Greek coastline comprises steep cliffs and there are few coastal plains for agriculture. Inland are more steep cliffs, rivers which will not allow transportation, and few wide, fertile valleys. What agricultural land there is is of high quality; the problem is that there is too little of it to allow Greece to become a major agricultural exporter, or to develop more than a handful of major urban areas containing highly educated, highly skilled and technologically advanced populations. Its situation is further exacerbated by its location, with Athens positioned at the tip of a peninsula, almost cut off from land trade with Europe. It is reliant on the Aegean Sea for access to maritime trade in the region – but across that sea lies Turkey, a large potential enemy. Greece fought several wars against Turkey in the late nineteenth and early twentieth centuries, and in modern times still spends a vast amount of euros, which it doesn't have, on defence.

The mainland is protected by mountains, but there are about 1,400 Greek islands (6,000 if you include various rocks sticking out of the Aegean) of which about 200 are inhabited. It takes a decent navy just to patrol this territory, never mind one strong enough to deter any attempt to take them over. The result is a huge cost in military spending that Greece cannot afford. During the Cold War the Americans, and to a lesser extent the British, were content to underwrite some of the military requirements in order to keep the Soviet Union out of the Aegean and the Mediterranean. When the Cold War ended, so did the cheques. But Greece kept spending.

This historical split continues to have an impact to this day in the wake of the financial crash that hit Europe in 2008 and the ideological rift in the eurozone. In 2012, when the European financial bailouts began and demands for Greek austerity measures were made to keep the country afloat and in the eurozone, the geographical divide soon became obvious. The donors and demanders were the northern countries, the recipients and supplicants mostly southern. It didn't take long for people in Germany to point out that they were working until sixty-five but paying taxes which were going to Greece so that people could retire at fifty-five. They then asked – why? And the answer, 'in sickness and in health', was unsatisfactory.

The Germans led the bailout-imposed austerity measures, the Greeks led the backlash. For example, the German Finance Minister Wolfgang Schäuble commented that he was 'not yet sure that all political parties in Greece are aware of their responsibility for the difficult situation their country is in'. To which the Greek president, Karolos Papoulias, who had fought the Nazis, replied, 'I cannot accept Mr Schäuble insulting my country . . . Who is Mr Schäuble to insult Greece? Who are the Dutch? Who are the Finnish?' He also made a pointed reference to the Second World War: 'We were always proud to defend not only our freedom, our country, but Europe's freedom too.' The stereotypes of profligate, slack southerners and careful, industrious northerners soon resurfaced, with the Greek media responding with constant and crude reminders of Germany's past, including superimposing a Hitler moustache on a front-page photograph of Chancellor Merkel.

The Greek taxpayer – of whom there are not enough to sustain the country's economy – has a very different view, asking: 'Why should the Germans dictate to us, when the euro benefits them more than anyone else?' In Greece and elsewhere austerity measures imposed from the north are seen as an assault on sovereignty.

Cracks are appearing in the edifice of the 'family of Europe' and not only because of the British voting for Brexit. That was a symptom of a problem, not the cause. On the periphery of Western Europe the financial crisis has left Greece looking like a semi-detached member; to the east it has again seen conflict. If the aberration of the past seventy years of peace is to continue through this century, that peace will need love, care and attention.

The post-Second-World-War generations have grown up with peace as the norm, but what is different about the current generation is that Europeans find it difficult to imagine the opposite. Wars now seem to be what happens elsewhere or in the past – at worst they happen on the 'periphery' of Europe. The trauma of two world wars, followed by seven decades of peace and then the collapse of the Soviet Union, persuaded many people that Western Europe was a 'post-conflict' region.

There are reasons to believe that this may still hold true in the future, but potential sources of conflict bubble under the surface, and the tension between the Europeans and the Russians may result in a confrontation. For example, history and geographical shape-shifting haunts Polish foreign policy even if the country is currently at peace, successful and one of the bigger EU states, with a population of 38 million. It is also physically one of the larger members and its economy has doubled since it emerged from behind the Iron Curtain, but still it looks to the past as it tries to secure its future.

The corridor of the North European Plain is at its narrowest between Poland's Baltic coast in the north and the beginning of the Carpathian Mountains in the south. This is where, from a Russian military perspective, the best defensive line could be placed or, from an attacker's viewpoint, the point at which its forces would be squeezed together before breaking out towards Russia.

The Poles have seen it both ways as armies have swept east and west across it, frequently changing borders. If you take *The Times Atlas of European History* and flick through the pages quickly as if it were a flip-book, you see Poland emerge *c.*1000, then continually change shape, disappear and reappear before assuming its present form in the late twentieth century.

The location of Germany and Russia, coupled with the Poles' experience of these two countries, does not make either a natural ally for Warsaw. Like France, Poland wants to keep Germany locked inside the EU and NATO, while not-so-ancient fears of Russia have come to the fore with the crisis in Ukraine. Over the centuries Poland has seen the Russian tide ebb and flow from and to them. After the low tide at the end of the Soviet (Russian) empire, there was only one direction it could subsequently flow.

Relations with Britain, as a counterweight to Germany within the EU, came easily despite the betrayal of 1939: Britain and France had signed a treaty guaranteeing to come to Poland's aid if Germany invaded. When the attack came the response to the Blitzkrieg was a 'Sitzkrieg' – both Allies sat behind the Maginot Line in France as Poland was swallowed up. Despite this, relations with the UK are strong, even if the main ally the newly liberated Poland sought out in 1989 was the USA.

The Americans embraced the Poles and vice versa: both had the Russians in mind. In 1999 Poland joined NATO, extending the Alliance's reach 400 miles closer to Moscow. By then several other former Warsaw Pact countries were also members of the Alliance and in 1999 Moscow watched helplessly as NATO went to war with its ally, Serbia. In the 1990s Russia was in no position to push back, but after the chaos of the Yeltsin years Putin stepped in on the front foot and came out swinging.

The best-known quote attributed to Henry Kissinger originated in the 1970s, when he is reported to have asked: 'If I want to phone Europe – who do I call?' The Poles have an updated question: 'If the Russians threaten, do we call Brussels or Washington?' They know the answer.

The Balkan countries are also once again free of empire. Their mountainous terrain led to the emergence of so many small states in the region, and is one of the things that has kept them from integrating – despite the best efforts of the experiment of the Union of Southern Slavs, otherwise known as Yugoslavia.

With the wars of the 1990s behind them, most of the former Yugoslav countries are looking westward, but in Serbia the pull of the east, with its Orthodox religion and Slavic peoples, remains strong. Russia, which has yet to forgive the Western nations for the bombing of Serbia in 1999 and the separation of Kosovo, is still attempting to coax Serbia into its orbit via the gravitational pull of language, ethnicity, religion and energy deals.

Bismarck famously said that a major war would be sparked by 'some damned fool thing in the Balkans'; and so it came to pass. The region is now an economic and diplomatic battleground with the EU, NATO, the Turks and the Russians all vying for influence. Albania, Bulgaria, Croatia and Romania have made their choice and are inside NATO – and, apart from Albania, are also in the EU, as is Slovenia.

The tensions extend into the north and Scandinavia.

Denmark is already a NATO member and the recent resurgence of Russia has caused a debate in Sweden over whether it is time to abandon the neutrality of two centuries and join the Alliance. In 2013 Russian jets staged a mock bombing run on Sweden in the middle of the night. The Swedish defence system appears to have been asleep, failing to scramble any jets, and it was the Danish air force that took to the skies to shepherd the Russians away. Despite that, the majority of Swedes remain against NATO membership, but the debate is ongoing, informed by Moscow's statement that it would be forced to 'respond' if either Sweden or Finland were to join the Alliance.

The EU and NATO countries need to present a united front to these challenges, but this will be impossible unless the key relationship in the EU remains intact – that between France and Germany.

As we've seen, France was best placed to take advantage of Europe's climate, trade routes and natural borders. It is partially protected, except in one area – the north-east, at the point where the flatland of the North European Plain becomes what is now Germany. Before Germany existed as a single country this was not a problem. France was a considerable distance from Russia, far from the Mongol hordes, and had the Channel between it and England, meaning that an attempt at a full-scale invasion and total occupation could probably be repulsed. In fact France was the pre-eminent power on the Continent: it could even project its power as far as the gates of Moscow.

But then Germany united.

It had been doing so for some time. There had been the 'idea' of Germany for centuries: the Eastern Frankish lands which became the Holy Roman Empire in the tenth century were sometimes called 'the Germanies', comprising as they did up to 500 Germanic mini-kingdoms. After the Holy Roman Empire was dissolved in 1806 the German Confederation of thirty-nine statelets came together in 1815 at the Congress of Vienna. This in turn led to the North German Confederation, and then the unification of Germany in 1871 after the Franco-Prussian War in which victorious German troops occupied Paris. Now France had a neighbour on its border that was geographically larger than itself, with a similar size of population but one with a better growth rate, and that was more industrialised.

The unification was announced at the Palace of Versailles near Paris after the German victory. The weak spot in the French defence, the North European Plain, had been breached. It would be again, twice, in the following seventy years, after which France would use diplomacy instead of warfare to try to neutralise the threat from the east.

Germany had always had bigger geographical problems than France. The flatlands of the North European Plain gave it two reasons to be fearful: to the west the Germans saw their long-unified and powerful neighbour France, and to the east the giant Russian Bear. Their ultimate fear was of a simultaneous attack by both powers across the flat land of the corridor. We can never know if it would have happened, but the fear of it had catastrophic consequences.

France feared Germany, Germany feared France, and when France joined both Russia and Britain in the Triple Entente of 1907, Germany feared all three. There was now also the added dimension that the British navy could, at a time of its choosing, blockade German access to the North Sea and the Atlantic. Its solution, twice, was to attack France first.

The dilemma of Germany's geographical position and

belligerence became known as 'the German Question'. The answer, after the horrors of the Second World War, indeed after centuries of war, was the acceptance of the presence in the European lands of a single overwhelming power, the USA, which set up NATO and allowed for the eventual creation of the European Union. Exhausted by war, and with safety 'guaranteed' by the American military, the Europeans embarked on an astonishing experiment. They were asked to trust each other.

What is now the EU was set up so that France and Germany could hug each other so tightly in a loving embrace that neither would be able to get an arm free with which to punch the other. It has worked brilliantly and created a huge geographical space now encompassing the biggest economy in the world.

It has worked particularly well for Germany, which rose from the ashes of 1945 and used to its advantage the geography it once feared. It became Europe's great manufacturer. Instead of sending armies across the flatlands it sent goods with the prestigious tag 'Made in Germany', and these goods flowed down the Rhine and the Elbe, along the autobahns and out into Europe and the world, north, south, west and, increasingly since 1990, east.

However, what began in 1951 as the six-nation European Steel and Coal Community became the multi-nation EU with an ideological core of 'ever closer union'. After the first major financial crisis to hit the Union, that ideology is on an uncertain footing and the ties that bind are fraying. There are signs within the EU of, as the geopolitical writer Robert Kaplan puts it, 'the revenge of geography'.

Ever closer union led, for nineteen of the member states, to a single currency – the euro. All twenty-eight members, except for Denmark and the UK, committed to joining it if and when they meet the criteria. What is clear now, and was to some clear at the time, is that at its launch in 1999 many countries which did join were simply not ready.

In 1999 many of the countries went into the newly defined relationship with eyes wide shut. They were all supposed to have levels of debt, unemployment and inflation within certain limits. The problem was that some, notably Greece, were cooking the books. Most of the experts knew, but because the euro is not just a currency – it is also an ideology – the members turned a blind eye.

The eurozone countries agreed to be economically wedded, as the Greeks point out, 'in sickness and in health', but when the economic crisis of 2008 hit, the wealthier countries had to bail out the poorer ones, and a bitter domestic row broke out. The partners are still throwing dishes at each other to this day.

The euro crisis and wider economic problems have revealed the cracks in the House of Europe (notably along the old fault line of the north–south divide). The dream of ever closer union appears to be frozen, or possibly even in reverse. In the spring of 2017 the EU Commission circulated a paper laying out several options on the direction in which the EU should be going. The choice of more power for Brussels was roundly rejected in most European capitals.

President Macron of France tried again in March 2019, with an open letter to EU citizens calling for a 'European renaissance'. It was published in at least one newspaper in each of the twenty-eight member states. He called for a 'stronger, more united continent' and a 'reset' of the open-border Schengen Zone and the free movement of people. He even went so far as to suggest that workers from across the EU should receive the same pay for the same job at the same company regardless of its location in Europe. That proposition would be welcomed by, say, a Romanian worker in Bucharest employed by a German company with offices around the continent, but the German company might have a different view.

There was also talk of hastening a move towards an EU defence force. This didn't go down well with several member states concerned about undermining NATO. Mr Macron's passionate call was debated for several days and then it faded from view.

The 2016 vote in the UK to leave the EU was a deep psychological blow to the European dream. If the EU splinters then the German question may return. Seen through the prism of seven decades of peace, this may seem alarmist, and Germany is among the most peaceful and democratic members of the European family; but seen through the prism of seven centuries of European warfare, it cannot be ruled out.

Germany is determined to remain a good European. Germans know instinctively that if the Union fragments the old fears of Germany will reappear, especially as it is now by far the most populous and wealthy European nation, with 82 million inhabitants and the world's fourth-biggest economy. A failed Union would also harm Germany economically: the world's third-largest exporter of goods does not want to see its closest market fragment into protectionism.

The German nation state, despite being less than 150 years old, is now Europe's indispensable power. In economic affairs it is unrivalled, it speaks quietly but carries a large euro-shaped stick, and the Continent listens. However, on global foreign policy it simply speaks quietly, sometimes not at all, and has an aversion to sticks.

The shadow of the Second World War still hangs over Germany. The Americans, and eventually the West Europeans, were willing to accept German rearmament due to the Soviet threat, but Germany rearmed almost reluctantly and has been loath to use its military strength. It played a walk-on part in Kosovo and Afghanistan, but chose to sit out the Libyan conflict.

Its most serious diplomatic foray into a non-economic crisis has been in Ukraine, which tells us a lot about where Germany is now looking. The Germans were involved in the machinations that overthrew Ukraine's President Yanukovych in 2014 and they were sharply critical of Russia's subsequent annexation of Crimea. However, mindful of the gas pipelines, Berlin was noticeably more restrained in its criticism and support for sanctions than, for example, the UK, which is far less reliant on Russian energy. Through the EU and NATO Germany is anchored in Western Europe, but in stormy weather anchors can slip, and Berlin is geographically situated to shift the focus of its attention east if required and forge much closer ties with Moscow.

Watching all of these Continental machinations from the sidelines of the Atlantic is the UK, sometimes present on the territory of the Continent, sometimes in 'splendid isolation', always fully engaged in ensuring that no power greater than it will rise in Europe. This is as true now in the diplomatic chambers of the EU as it was on the battlefields of Agincourt, Waterloo or Balaclava.

In modern times, the UK seeks to insert itself into the great post-war Franco-German alliances. Failing that, it seeks alliances among other, smaller, member states to build enough support to challenge policies with which it disagrees. For several centuries, the British sought to ensure that there was not an overwhelmingly dominant power on the continent. This policy continued during EU membership, and will in the future, whether the UK is a member or not.

Geographically, the Brits are in a good place. Good farmland, decent rivers, excellent access to the seas and their fish stocks, close enough to the European Continent to trade and yet protected by dint of being an island race – there have been times when the UK gave thanks for its geography as wars and revolutions swept over its neighbours.

The British losses in, and experience of, the world wars are not to be underestimated, but they are dwarfed by what happened in Continental Europe in the twentieth century and indeed before that. The British are at one remove from living with the historical collective memory of frequent invasions and border changes.

There is a theory that the relative security of the UK over the past few hundred years is why it has experienced more freedom and less despotism than the countries across the Channel. The theory goes that there were fewer requirements for 'strong men' or dictators, which, starting with Magna Carta (1215) and then the Provisions of Oxford (1258), led to forms of democracy years ahead of other countries.

It is a good talking point, albeit one not provable. What is undeniable is that the water around the island, the trees upon it which allowed a great navy to be built, and the economic conditions which sparked the Industrial Revolution all led to Great Britain controlling a global empire. Britain may be the biggest island in Europe, but it is not a large country. The expansion of its power across the globe in the eighteenth, nineteenth and twentieth centuries is remarkable, even if its position has since declined.

Its location still grants it certain strategic advantages, one of which is the GIUK (Greenland, Iceland and the UK) gap. This is a choke point in the world's sea lanes – it is hardly as important as the Strait of Hormuz or the Strait of Malacca, but it has traditionally given the UK an advantage in the North Atlantic. The alternative route for north European navies (including Belgium, the Netherlands and France) to access the Atlantic is through the English Channel, but this is narrow – only 20 miles across at the Strait of Dover – and very well defended. Any Russian naval ship coming from the Arctic also has to pass through the GIUK on its way to the Atlantic.

This strategic advantage has diminished in tandem with the reduced role and power of the Royal Navy, but in time of war it would again benefit the UK. The GIUK is one of many reasons why London flew into a panic in 2014 when, briefly, the vote on Scottish independence looked as if might result in a Yes. The loss of power in the North Sea and North Atlantic would have been a strategic blow and a massive dent to the prestige of whatever was left of the UK.

What the British have now is a collective memory of greatness. That memory is what persuades many people on the island that if something in the world needs to be done, then Britain should be among the countries which do it. The British remain within Europe, and yet outside it; it is an issue still to be settled.

Forty years after joining the EU, the British decided to hold a referendum on whether to remain a part of it. The majority voted Leave, but the result could well threaten the unity of the UK as it revealed divides across the union. In particular, the majority in Scotland voted to Remain, and so the Leave victory has once again raised the question of Scotland's independence; on the other hand, the drive for Scottish independence may be impeded by the supposed difficulties of rejoining the EU. Brussels has already made it clear to Catalonia, in response to the crisis that started in 2017, that if it were to leave Spain, it might take more than a decade to become an EU member. If the same applied to Scotland, it would then be out of the UK and out of the EU – and for a small nation with limited resources that would be an uncomfortable position.

Catalonia is symptomatic of something that was subsumed during the heyday of the EU – the feelings of smaller nations, and even regions, within the nation states. With these areas having been ignored for decades, the nationalism on display in the Catalonian crisis took many Europeans by surprise. Catalonia does not want to leave the EU, nor does Scotland, but significant numbers of the electorates are prepared to risk that in order to leave a united Spain and a United Kingdom. The 2014 Scottish referendum on independence resulted in a 55.3 per cent vote against it, but the issue has not gone away – neither there nor in Catalonia.

The two main issues that caused the British to edge towards the exit door are related: sovereignty and immigration. Anti-EU opinion, backed by some EU waverers, has been fuelled by the amount and type of laws enacted by the EU, which the UK, as part of the membership deal, had to abide by. For example, headlines were made about foreign criminals convicted of serious crimes in the UK who cannot be deported because of rulings from the European Court of Justice.

At the same time, the wave of economic immigrants and refugees arriving in Europe from the Middle East and Africa has also driven anti-EU feeling as many of those migrants want to reach Britain, and it is believed they have been encouraged to so do by the EU countries through which they pass.

Prejudice against immigrants always rises during times of economic recession, such as recently suffered in Europe, and the effects have been seen right across the continent and resulted in the rise of right-wing political parties, all of which militate against pan-nationalism and thus weaken the fabric of the EU.

A stark example came in early 2016 when, for the first time in half a century, Sweden began checking the documents of travellers from Denmark. This was a direct response to the numbers of refugees and migrants flowing into northern Europe from the wider Middle East and to the IS attacks on Paris in November 2015. The idea of the EU's 'Schengen Zone', a border-free area comprising twenty-six countries, has taken some heavy blows, with different countries at different times reintroducing border controls on the grounds of security. Fearing a bottleneck, Denmark then began checking people crossing from Germany. This all has an economic cost, makes travel more difficult, and is both a physical and conceptual attack on 'ever closer union'. Some analysts have begun to speak of a 'Fortress Europe' due to bids to reduce immigration levels, but this misses the fact that there is also a drift towards a 'Fortress Nation State'.

Europe's traditional white population is greying. Population projections predict an inverted pyramid, with older people at the top and fewer younger people to look after them or pay taxes. However, such forecasts have not made a dent in the strength of anti-immigrant feeling among what was previously the indigenous population, which struggles to deal with the rapid changes to the world in which it grew up.

This demographic change is in turn having an effect on the foreign policy of nation states, particularly towards the Middle

East. On issues such as the Iraq War or the Israeli/Palestinian conflict, for example, many European governments must, at the very least, take into account the feelings of their Muslim citizens when formulating policy.

The characters and domestic social norms of the European countries are also impacted. Debates about women's rights and the veiling of women, blasphemy laws, freedom of speech and many other issues have all been influenced by the presence of large numbers of Muslims in Europe's urban areas. Voltaire's maxim that he would defend to the death the right of a person to say something, even if he found it offensive, was once taken as a given. Now, despite many people having been killed *because* what they said was insulting, the debate has shifted. It is not uncommon to hear the idea that perhaps insulting religion should be beyond the pale, possibly even made illegal.

Whereas previously liberals would have been entirely behind Voltaire, there are now shades of relativism. The massacre of journalists at the French satirical magazine *Charlie Hebdo* in 2015 was followed by widespread condemnation and revulsion; however, sections of liberal condemnation were tinged with a 'but perhaps the satirists went too far'. This is something new for Europe in the modern age and is part of its culture wars, all of which loop back into attitudes towards the European political structures.

NATO is fraying at the edges at the same time as is the European Union. Both can be patched up, but if not, then over time they may become either defunct or irrelevant. At this point we would return to a Europe of sovereign nation states, with each state seeking alliances in a balance of power system. The Germans would again be fearing encirclement by the Russians and French, the French would again be fearing their bigger neighbour, and we would all be back at the beginning of the twentieth century.

For the French this is a nightmare. They successfully helped tie Germany down inside the EU, only to find that after German reunification they became the junior partner in a twin-engine motor they had hoped to be driving. This poses Paris a problem it does not appear to be able to solve. Unless it quietly accepts that Berlin calls the European shots, it risks further weakening the Union. But if it accepts German leadership, then its own power is diminished.

France is capable of an independent foreign policy – indeed, with its 'Force de frappe' nuclear deterrent, its overseas territories and its aircraft carrier-backed armed forces, it does just that – but it operates safe in the knowledge that its eastern flank is secure and it can afford to raise its eyes to the horizon.

Both France and Germany are currently working to keep the Union together: they see each other now as natural partners. But only Germany has a Plan B – Russia.

The end of the Cold War saw most of the Continental powers reducing their military budgets and cutting back their armed forces. It has taken the shock of the Russian–Georgian war of 2008 and the annexation of Crimea by Russia in 2014 to focus attention on the possibility of the age-old problem of war in Europe.

Now the Russians regularly fly missions aimed at testing European air defence systems and are busy consolidating themselves in South Ossetia, Abkhazia, Crimea, Transnistria and eastern Ukraine. They maintain their links with the ethnic Russians in the Baltics, and they still have their exclave of Kaliningrad on the Baltic Sea.

The Europeans have begun doing some serious

recalculation on their military spending, but there isn't much money around, and they face difficult decisions. While they debate those decisions the maps are being dusted down, and the diplomats and military strategists see that, while the threats of Charlemagne, Napoleon, Hitler and the Soviets may have vanished, the North European Plain, the Carpathians, the Baltic and the North Sea are still there.

In his book *Of Paradise and Power* the historian Robert Kagan argues that Western Europeans live in paradise but shouldn't seek to operate by the rules of paradise once they move out into the world of power. Perhaps, as the euro crisis diminishes and we look around at paradise, it seems inconceivable that we could go backwards; but history tells us how much things can change in just a few decades, and geography tells us that if humans do not constantly strive to overcome its 'rules', its 'rules' will overcome us.

This is what Helmut Kohl meant when he warned, upon leaving the Chancellorship of Germany in 1998, that he was the last German leader to have lived through the Second World War and thus to have experienced the horrors it wrought. In 2012 he wrote an article for Germany's best-selling daily newspaper, *Bild*, and was clearly still haunted by the possibility that because of the financial crisis the current generation of leaders would not nurture the post-war experiment in European trust: 'For those who didn't live through this themselves and who especially now in the crisis are asking what benefits Europe's unity brings, the answer despite the unprecedented European period of peace lasting more than 65 years and despite the problems and difficulties we must still overcome is: peace.'

CHAPTER 5

AFRICA

'It always seems impossible until it is done.'

Nelson Mandela

SPAIN
Algiers
Mediterranean Sea
ITALY
GREECE
TURKEY
Madeira Island
(PORTUGAL)
Rabat
Tunis
TUNISIA
Tripoli
SYRIA
LEBANON
ISRAEL
IRAQ
IRAN
MOROCCO
Canary Islands
(SPAIN)
Suez
Canal
JORDAN
KUWAIT
Cairo
Persian Gulf
ALGERIA
LIBYA
Laayoune
Western
Sahara
BAHRAIN
QATAR
U.A.E.
Nile
EGYPT
SAUDI
ARABIA
Sahara
Red Sea
Nouakchott
MAURITANIA
MALI
NIGER
CHAD
SUDAN
Sahel
Niger
ERITREA
Asmara
YEMEN
Dakar
SENEGAL
GAMBIA
Banjul
BURKINA
FASO
Niamey
Khartoum
Socotra
(YEMEN)
Bamako
Ouagadougou
N'djamena
DJIBOUTI
Djibouti
Bissau
GUINEA-
BISSAU
GUINEA
Conakry
Freetown
SIERRA LEONE
Monrovia
LIBERIA
CÔTE
D'IVOIRE
Yamoussoukro
GHANA
TOGO
BENIN
Porto
Novo
Lome
Accra
NIGERIA
Abuja
ETHIOPIA
Addis
Ababa
SOUTH
SUDAN
CENTRAL
AFRICAN REPUBLIC
Bangui
Juba
SOMALIA
CAMEROON
Yaoundé
Malabo
Gulf of Guinea
Congo
EQ. GUINEA
SAO TOME AND
PRINCIPE
Principé
São Tomé
Libreville
UGANDA
Kampala
KENYA
Nairobi
Mogadishu
Equator
Equator
GABON
DEMOCRATIC

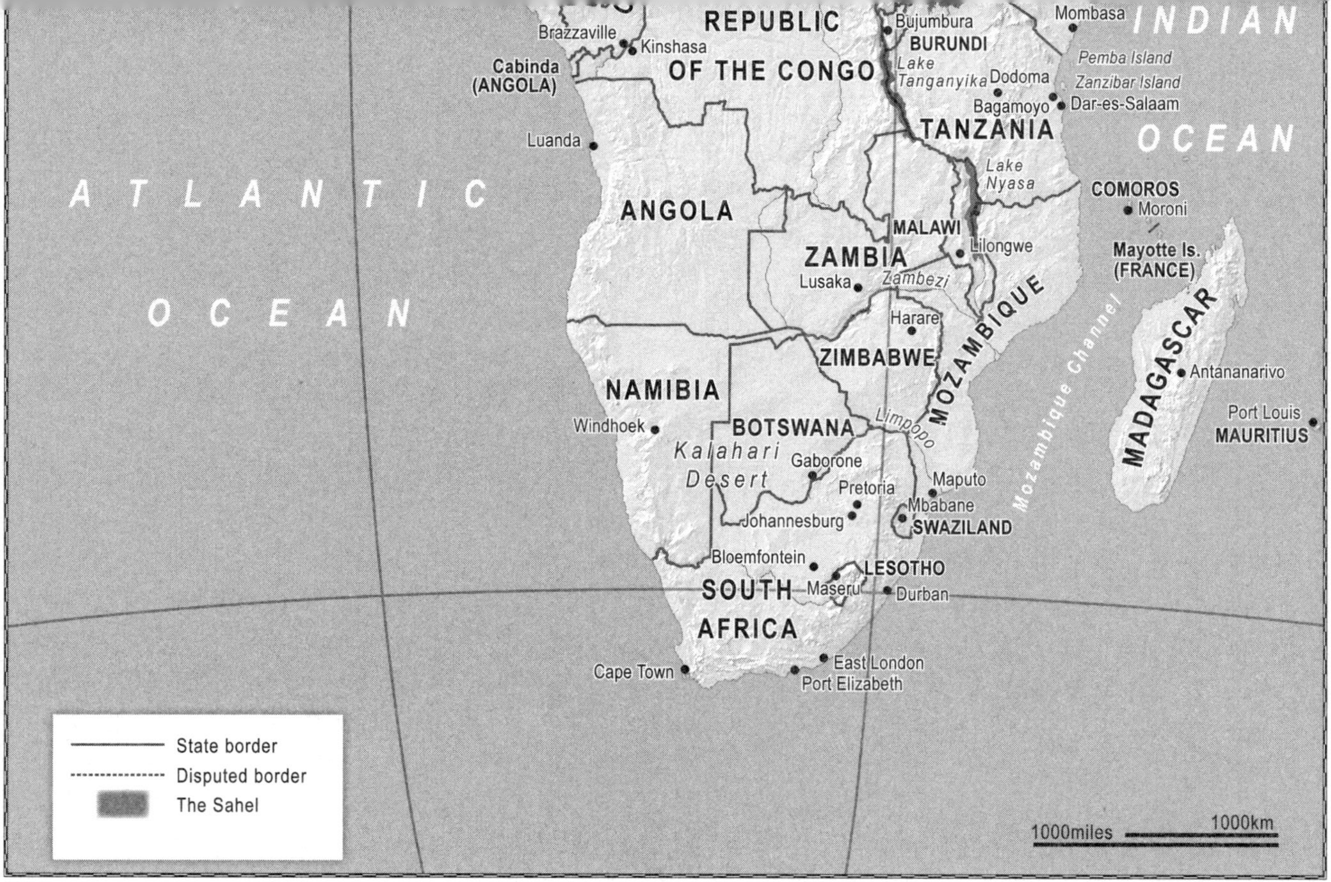
REPUBLIC OF THE CONGO
Brazzaville
Kinshasa
Cabinda (ANGOLA)
Luanda
ATLANTIC OCEAN
ANGOLA
NAMIBIA
Windhoek
BOTSWANA
Kalahari Desert
Gaborone
Pretoria
Johannesburg
Bloemfontein
SOUTH AFRICA
Maseru
Cape Town
East London
Port Elizabeth
Durban
LESOTHO
SWAZILAND
Mbabane
Maputo
Limpopo
ZIMBABWE
Harare
ZAMBIA
Lusaka
Zambezi
MALAWI
Lilongwe
Lake Nyasa
MOZAMBIQUE
Mozambique Channel
TANZANIA
Bujumbura
BURUNDI
Lake Tanganyika
Dodoma
Bagamoyo
Dar-es-Salaam
Mombasa
Pemba Island
Zanzibar Island
INDIAN OCEAN
COMOROS
Moroni
Mayotte Is. (FRANCE)
MADAGASCAR
Antananarivo
Port Louis
MAURITIUS
State border
Disputed border
The Sahel
1000miles
1000km

AFRICA'S COASTLINE? GREAT BEACHES, REALLY, REALLY lovely beaches, but terrible natural harbours. Rivers? Amazing rivers, but most of them are rubbish for actually transporting anything, given that every few miles you go over a waterfall. These are just two in a long list of problems which help explain why Africa isn't technologically or politically as successful as Western Europe or North America.

There are lots of places that are unsuccessful, but few have been as unsuccessful as Africa, and that despite having a head start as the place where *Homo sapiens* originated about 200,000 years ago. As that most lucid of writers, Jared Diamond, put it in a brilliant *National Geographic* article in 2005, 'It's the opposite of what one would expect from the runner first off the block.' However, the first runners became separated from everyone else by the Sahara Desert and the Indian and Atlantic oceans. Almost the entire continent below the Sahara developed in isolation from the Eurasian land mass, where ideas and technology were exchanged from east to west, and west to east, but not north to south.

Africa, being a huge continent, has always consisted of different regions, climates and cultures, but what they all had in common was their isolation from each other and the outside world, especially in the interior regions where, most notably, the Congo rainforests were a massive barrier to trade routes. That is less the case now, but the legacy remains.

The world's idea of African geography is flawed. Few people realise just how big it is. This is because most of us use the standard Mercator world map. This, as do other maps, depicts a sphere on a flat surface and thus distorts shapes. Africa is far, far longer than usually portrayed, which explains what an achievement it was to round the Cape of Good Hope, and is a reminder of the importance of the Suez Canal to world trade. Making it around the Cape was a momentous achievement, but once it became unnecessary to do so, the sea journey from Western Europe to India was reduced by 6,000 miles.

If you look at a world map and mentally glue Alaska onto California, then turn the USA on its head, it appears as if it would roughly fit into Africa with a few gaps here and there. In fact Africa is three times bigger than the USA. Look again at the standard Mercator map and you see that Greenland appears to be the same size as Africa, and yet Africa is actually fourteen times the size of Greenland! You could fit the USA, Greenland, India, China, Spain, France, Germany and the UK into Africa and still have room for most of Eastern Europe. We know Africa is a massive land mass, but the maps rarely tell us how massive.

The geography of this immense continent can be explained in several ways, but the most basic is to think of Africa in terms of the top third and bottom two-thirds.

The top third begins on the Mediterranean coastlines of the North African Arabic-speaking countries. The coastal plains quickly become the Sahara, the world's largest dry desert, which is almost as big as the USA. Directly below the Sahara is the Sahel region, a semi-arid, rock-strewn, sandy strip of land measuring more than 3,000 miles at its widest points and stretching from Gambia on the Atlantic coast through Niger, Chad and right across to Eritrea on the Red Sea. The word Sahel comes from the Arabic *sahil*, which means coast, and is how the people living in the region think of it – as the shoreline of the vast sand sea of the Sahara. It is another sort of shore, one where the influence of Islam diminishes. From the Sahel to the Mediterranean the vast majority of people are Muslims. South of it there is far more diversity in religion.

Indeed, south of the Sahel, in the bottom two-thirds of Africa, there is more diversity in most things. The land becomes more temperate and green vegetation appears, which becomes jungle as we approach Congo and the Central African Republic. Towards the east coast are the great lakes in Uganda and Tanzania, while across to the west more deserts appear in Angola and Namibia. By the time we reach the tip of South Africa the climate is again 'Mediterranean', even though we have travelled almost 5,000 miles from the northernmost point in Tunisia on the Mediterranean coast.

Given that Africa is where humans originated, we are all African. However, the rules of the race changed *c.* 8000 BCE when some of us, who'd wandered off to places such as the Middle East and around the Mediterranean region, lost the wanderlust, settled down, began farming and eventually congregated in villages and towns.

But back south there were few plants willing to be domesticated, and even fewer animals. Much of the land consists of jungle, swamp, desert or steep-sided plateau, none of which lend themselves to the growing of wheat or rice, or sustaining herds of sheep. Africa's rhinos, gazelles and giraffes stubbornly refused to be beasts of burden – or as Diamond puts it in a memorable passage, 'History might have turned out differently if African armies, fed by barnyard-giraffe meat and backed by waves of cavalry mounted on huge rhinos, had swept into Europe to overrun its mutton-fed soldiers mounted on puny horses.' But Africa's head start in our mutual story did allow it more time to develop something else which to this day holds it back: a virulent set of diseases, such as malaria and yellow fever, brought on by the heat and now complicated by crowded living conditions and poor healthcare infrastructure. This is true of other regions – the subcontinent and South America, for example – but sub-Saharan Africa has been especially hard hit, for example by the HIV virus, and has a particular problem because of the prevalence of the mosquito and the Tsetse fly.

Most of the continent's rivers also pose a problem, as they begin in high land and descend in abrupt drops which thwart navigation. For example, the mighty Zambezi may be Africa's fourth-longest river, running for 1,600 miles, and may be a stunning tourist attraction with its white-water rapids and the Victoria Falls, but as a trade route it is of little use. It flows through six countries, dropping from 4,900 feet to sea level when it reaches the Indian Ocean in Mozambique. Parts of it are navigable by shallow boats, but these parts do not interconnect, thus limiting the transportation of cargo.

Unlike in Europe, which has the Danube and the Rhine, this drawback has hindered contact and trade between regions – which in turn affected economic development, and hindered the formation of large trading regions. The continent's great rivers, the Niger, the Congo, the Zambezi, the Nile and others, don't connect and this disconnection has a human factor. Whereas huge areas of Russia, China and the USA speak a unifying language which helps trade, in Africa thousands of languages exist and no one culture emerged to dominate areas of similar size. Europe, on the other hand, was small enough to have a 'lingua franca' through which to communicate, and a landscape that encouraged interaction.

Even had technologically productive nation states arisen, much of the continent would still have struggled to connect to the rest of the world because the bulk of the land mass is framed by the Indian and Atlantic oceans and the Sahara Desert. The exchange of ideas and technology barely touched sub-Saharan Africa for thousands of years. Despite this, several African empires and city states did arise after about the sixth century CE: for example the Mali Empire (thirteenth–sixteenth century), and the city state of Great Zimbabwe (eleventh–fifteenth century), the latter in land between the Zambezi and Limpopo rivers. However, these and others were isolated to relatively small regional blocs, and although the myriad cultures which did emerge across the continent may have been politically sophisticated, the physical landscape remained a barrier to technological development: by the time the outside world arrived in force, most had yet to develop writing, paper, gunpowder or the wheel.

Traders from the Middle East and the Mediterranean had been doing business in the Sahara, after the introduction of camels, from about 2,000 years ago, notably trading the vast resources of salt there; but it wasn't until the Arab conquests of the seventh century CE that the scene was set for a push southward. By the ninth century they had crossed the Sahara, and by the eleventh were firmly established as far south as modern-day Nigeria. The Arabs were also coming down the east coast and establishing themselves in places such as Zanzibar and Dar es Salaam in what is now Tanzania.

When the Europeans finally made it down the west coast in the fifteenth century they found few natural harbours for their ships. Unlike Europe or North America, where the jagged coastlines give rise to deep natural harbours, much of the African coastline is smooth. And once they did make land they struggled to penetrate any further inland than about 100 miles due to the difficulty of navigating the rivers, as well as the challenges of the climate and disease.

Both the Arabs and then the Europeans brought with them new technology which they mostly kept to themselves, and took away whatever they found of value, which was mainly natural resources and people.

Slavery existed long before the outside world returned to where it had originated. Traders in the Sahel region used thousands of slaves to transport vast quantities of the region's then most valuable commodity, salt, but the Arabs began the practice of subcontracting African slave-taking to willing tribal leaders who would deliver them to the coast. By the time of the peak of the Ottoman Empire in the fifteenth and sixteenth centuries hundreds of thousands of Africans (mostly from the Sudan region) had been taken to Istanbul, Cairo, Damascus and across the Arabian world. The Europeans followed suit, outdoing the Arabs and Turks in their appetite for, and mistreatment of, the people brought to the slave ships anchored off the west coast.

Back in the great capital cities of London, Paris, Brussels and Lisbon, the Europeans then took maps of the contours of Africa's geography and drew lines on them – or, to take a more aggressive approach, lies. In between these lines they wrote words such as Middle Congo or Upper Volta and called them countries. These lines were more about how far which power's explorers, military forces and businessmen had advanced on the map than what the people living between the lines felt themselves to be, or how they wanted to organise themselves. Many Africans are now partially the prisoners of the political geography the Europeans made, and of the natural barriers to progression with which nature endowed them. From this they are making a modern home and, in some cases, vibrant, connected economies.

There are now fifty-six countries in Africa. Since the 'winds of change' of the independence movement blew through the mid twentieth century, some of the words between the lines have been altered – for example, Rhodesia is now Zimbabwe – but the borders are, surprisingly, mostly intact. However, many encompass the same divisions they did when first drawn, and those formal divisions are some of the many legacies colonialism bequeathed the continent.

The ethnic conflicts within Sudan, Somalia, Kenya, Angola, the Democratic Republic of the Congo, Nigeria, Mali and elsewhere are evidence that the European idea of geography did not fit the reality of Africa's demographics. There may have always been conflict: the Zulus and Xhosas had their differences long before they had ever set eyes on a European. But colonialism forced those differences to be resolved within an artificial structure – the European concept of a nation state. The modern civil wars are now partially because the colonialists told different nations that they were one nation in one state, and then after the colonialists were chased out a dominant people emerged within the state who wanted to rule it all, thus ensuring violence.

Take, for example, Libya, an artificial construct only a few decades old which at the first test fell apart into its previous incarnation as three distinct geographical regions. In the west it was, in Greek times, Tripolitania (from the Greek *tri polis,* three cities, which eventually merged and became Tripoli). The area to the east, centred on the city of Benghazi but stretching down to the Chad border, was known in both Greek and Roman times as Cyrenaica. Below these two, in what is now the far south-west of the country, is the region of Fezzan.

Tripolitania was always orientated north and north-west, trading with its southern European neighbours. Cyrenaica always looked east to Egypt and the Arab lands. Even the sea current off the coast of the Benghazi region takes boats naturally eastwards. Fezzan was traditionally a land of nomads who had little in common with the two coastal communities.

This is how the Greeks, Romans and Turks all ruled the area – it is how the people had thought of themselves for centuries. The mere decades-old European idea of Libya will struggle to survive and already one of the many Islamist groups in the east has declared an 'emirate of Cyrenaica'. While this may not come to pass, it is an example of how the concept of the region originated merely in lines drawn on maps by foreigners.

However, one of the biggest failures of European line-drawing lies in the centre of the continent, the giant black hole known as the Democratic Republic of the Congo – the DRC. Here is the land in which Joseph Conrad set his novel *Heart of Darkness*, and it remains a place shrouded in the darkness of war. It is a prime example of how the imposition of artificial borders can lead to a weak and divided state, ravaged by internal conflict, and whose mineral wealth condemns it to being exploited by outsiders.

The DRC is an illustration of why the catch-all term 'developing world' is far too broad-brush a way to describe countries which are not part of the modern industrialised world. The DRC is not developing, nor does it show any signs of so doing. The DRC should never have been put together; it has fallen apart and is the most under-reported war zone in the world, despite the fact that six million people have died there during wars which have been fought since the late 1990s.

The DRC is neither democratic, nor a republic. It is the second-largest country in Africa with a population of about 81 million, although due to the situation there it is difficult to find accurate figures. It is bigger than Germany, France and Spain combined and contains the Congo Rainforest, second only to the Amazon as the largest in the world.

The people are divided into more than 200 ethnic groups, of which the biggest are the Bantu. There are several hundred languages, but the widespread use of French bridges that gap to a degree. The French comes from the DRC's years as a Belgian colony (1908–60) and before that, when King Leopold of the Belgians used it as his personal property from which to steal its natural resources to line his pockets. Belgian colonial rule made the British and French versions look positively benign and was ruthlessly brutal from start to finish, with few attempts to build any sort of infrastructure to help the inhabitants. When the Belgians went in 1960 they left behind little chance of the country holding together.

The civil wars began immediately and were later intensified by a blood-soaked walk-on role in the global Cold War. The government in the capital, Kinshasa, backed the rebel side in Angola's war, thus bringing itself to the attention of the USA, which was also supporting the rebel movement against the Soviet-backed Angolan government. Each side poured in hundreds of millions of dollars' worth of arms.

When the Cold War ended both great powers had less interest in what by then was called Zaire and the country staggered on, kept afloat by its natural resources. The Rift Valley curves into the DRC in its south and east and it has exposed huge quantities of cobalt, copper, diamonds, gold, silver, zinc, coal, manganese and other minerals, especially in Katanga Province.

In King Leopold's days the world wanted the region's rubber for the expanding motor car industry; now China buys more than 50 per cent of the DRC's exports, but still the population lives in poverty. In 2014 the United Nations Human Development Index placed the DRC 186th out of 187 countries it measured. The bottom eighteen countries in that list are all in Africa.

Because it is so resource-rich and so large, everyone wants a bite out of the DRC, which, as it lacks a substantive central authority, cannot really bite back.

The region is also bordered by nine countries. They have all played a role in the DRC's agony, which is one reason why the Congo wars are also known as 'Africa's world war'. To the south is Angola, to the north the Republic of the Congo and the Central African Republic, to the east Uganda, Rwanda, Burundi, Tanzania and Zambia. The roots of the wars go back decades, but the worst of times was triggered by the disaster that hit Rwanda in 1994 and swept westward in its aftermath.

After the genocide in Rwanda the Tutsi survivors and moderate Hutus formed a Tutsi-led government. The killing machines of the Hutu militia, the Interahamwe, fled into eastern DRC but conducted border raids. They also joined with sections of the DRC army to kill the DRC's Tutsis, who live near the border region. In came the Rwandan and Ugandan armies, backed by Burundi and Eritrea. Allied with opposition militias, they attacked the Interahamwe and overthrew the DRC government. They also went on to control much of the country's natural wealth, with Rwanda in particular shipping back tons of coltan, which is used in the making of mobile phones and computer chips. However, what had been the government forces did not give up and – with the involvement of Angola, Namibia and Zimbabwe – continued the fight. The country became a vast battleground, with more than twenty factions involved in the fighting.

The wars have killed, at a low estimate, tens of thousands of people, and have resulted in the deaths of another six million due to disease and malnutrition. The UN estimates that almost 50 per cent of the victims have been children aged under five.

In recent years the fighting has died down, but the DRC is home to the world's most deadly conflict since the Second World War and still requires the UN's largest peacekeeping mission to prevent full-scale war from breaking out again. Now the job is not to put Humpty Dumpty together again, because the DRC was never whole. It is simply to keep the pieces apart until a way can be found to join them sensibly and peacefully. The European colonialist created an egg without a chicken, a logical absurdity repeated across the continent and one that continues to haunt it.

Burundi is another example, with ethnically rooted political tensions simmering throughout 2015 and worsening in 2016. Formerly part of German East Africa when it included what is now Tanzania, it was divided between Belgium and the UK after the First World War and administered by Belgium from 1945 until independence in 1962. The Belgians used the Tutsi people to govern over the Hutus and, despite being just 15 per cent of the population, the Tutsi continue to dominate politics, economics and the military. More than 300,000 people died in the civil war between 1993 and 2005. Levels of violence began to rise again in 2015/16 after President Pierre

Nkurunziza reinterpreted the constitution to allow him to run for a third term. This was not quite what President Obama had in mind when, during his Africa tour in July 2015, he criticised African leaders, saying, 'The continent will not advance if its leaders refuse to step down when their terms end . . . Sometimes you will hear leaders say, "I'm the only person who can hold this nation together." If that's true then that leader has truly failed to build their nation.' That sentence encompassed both the colonial legacy of Africa and how its modern leaders have often been part of the problem rather than the solution to that legacy.

Africa has been equally cursed and blessed by its resources – blessed in so far as it has natural riches in abundance, but cursed because outsiders have long plundered them. In more recent times the nation states have been able to claim a share of these riches, and foreign countries now invest rather than steal, but still the people are rarely the beneficiaries.

In addition to its natural mineral wealth, Africa is also blessed with many great rivers – although most of its rivers do not encourage trade, they are good for hydroelectricity. However, this too is a source of potential conflict.

The Nile, the longest river in the world (4,100 miles), affects ten countries considered to be in the proximity of its basin – Burundi, the DRC, Eritrea, Ethiopia, Kenya, Rwanda, Sudan, Tanzania, Uganda and Egypt. As long ago as the fifth century BCE the historian Herodotus said: 'Egypt is the Nile, and the Nile is Egypt.' It is still true, and so a threat to the supply to Egypt's 700-mile-long, fully navigable section of the Nile is for Cairo a concern – one over which it would be prepared to go to war. Without the Nile, there would be no one there. It may be a huge country, but the vast majority of its

97 million population lives within a few miles of the Nile. Measured by the area in which people dwell, Egypt is one of the most densely populated countries in the world.

Egypt was, arguably, a nation state when most Europeans were living in mud huts, but it was only ever a regional power. It is protected by deserts on three sides and might have become a great power in the Mediterranean region but for one problem. There are hardly any trees in Egypt, and for most of history, if you didn't have trees you couldn't build a great navy with which to project your power. There has always been an Egyptian navy – it used to import cedar from Lebanon to build ships at huge expense – but it has never been a Blue Water navy.

Modern Egypt now has the most powerful armed forces of all the Arab states, thanks to American military aid; but it remains contained by deserts, the sea and its peace treaty with Israel. It will remain in the news as it struggles to cope with feeding 97 million people a day while battling an Islamist insurgency, especially in the Sinai, and guarding the Suez Canal, through which passes 8 per cent of the world's entire trade every day. Some 2.5 per cent of the world's oil passes this way daily; closing the canal would add about fifteen days' transit time to Europe and ten to the USA, with concurrent costs.

Despite having fought five wars with Israel, the country Egypt is most likely to come into conflict with next is Ethiopia, and the issue is the Nile. Two of the continent's oldest countries, with the largest armies, have at times edged towards conflict over the region's major source of water.

The Blue Nile, which begins in Ethiopia, and the White Nile meet in the Sudanese capital, Khartoum, before flowing through the Nubian Desert and into Egypt. By this point the majority of the water is from the Blue Nile.

Ethiopia is sometimes called 'Africa's water tower' due to its high elevation and has more than twenty dams fed by the rainfall in its highlands. In 2011 Addis Ababa announced a joint project with China to build a massive hydroelectric project on the Blue Nile near the Sudanese border called the Grand Renaissance Dam. In 2017 the dam was almost complete, but it will take several years to fill the reservoir with water. The dam will be used to create electricity, and the flow to Egypt should continue; but in theory the reservoir could also hold a year's worth of water, and completion of the project would give Ethiopia the potential to hold the water for its own use, thus drastically reducing the flow into Egypt.

As things stand Egypt has a more powerful military, but that is slowly changing, and Ethiopia, a country of 105 million people, is a growing power. Cairo knows this, and also that once the dam is built, destroying it would create a flooding catastrophe in both Ethiopia and Sudan. However, at the moment it does not have a *casus belli* to strike before completion, and despite the fact that several years ago a Cabinet minister was caught on microphone recommending bombing, the next few years are more likely to see intense negotiations, with Egypt wanting cast-iron guarantees that the flow will never be stopped. Water wars are considered to be among the potential coming conflicts this century and this remains one to watch. Around 85 per cent of the Nile waters emerge from the Ethiopian highlands, and by the summer of 2019 the two sides had yet to agree on the speed of the water flow or how quickly Ethiopia will fill the dam.

After being distracted during the Arab uprisings, during which first President Mubaran and then President Morsi were overthrown, Cairo is now focusing again on the issue. Given that the UN predicts the country will begin to suffer water shortages by 2025 regardless of what Ethiopia does, that is not surprising.

Another hotly contested liquid is oil.

Nigeria is sub-Saharan Africa's largest producer of oil, and all of this high-quality oil is in the south. Nigerians in the north complain that the profits from that oil are not shared equitably across the country's regions. This in turn exacerbates the ethnic and religious tensions between the peoples from the Nigerian delta and those in the north-east.

By size, population and natural resources, Nigeria is West Africa's most powerful country. It is the continent's most populous nation, with 191 million people, which with its size and natural resources makes it the leading regional power. It is formed from the territories of several ancient kingdoms which the British brought together as an administrative area. In 1898 they drew up a 'British Protectorate on the River Niger' which in turn became Nigeria.

It may now be an independent regional powerhouse, but its people and resources have been mismanaged for decades. In colonial times the British preferred to stay in the south-western area along the coast. Their 'civilising' mission rarely extended to the highlands of the centre, nor up to the Muslim populations in the north, and this half of the country remains less developed than the south. Much of the money made from oil is spent paying off the movers and shakers in Nigeria's complex tribal system. The onshore oil industry in the delta is also being threatened by the Movement for the Emancipation of the Niger Delta, a fancy name for a group which does operate in a region devastated by the oil industry, but which uses it as a cover for terrorism and extortion. The kidnapping of foreign oil workers is making it a less and less attractive place to do business. The offshore oilfields are mostly free of this activity and that is where the investment is heading.

The Islamist group Boko Haram, which wants to establish a caliphate in the Muslim areas, has used the sense of injustice engendered by underdevelopment to gain ground in the north. Boko Haram fighters are usually ethnic Kanuris from the north-east. They rarely operate outside of their home territory, not even venturing west to the Hausa region, and certainly not way down south to the coastal areas. This means that when the Nigerian military come looking for them Boko Haram are operating on home ground. Much of the local population will not co-operate with the military, either for fear of reprisal or due to a shared resentment of the south. Despite several major operations against it by the army, the group looks far from defeated. In 2017 it was still strong enough to go on the offensive, killing dozens of civilians in a series of raids. Since it first appeared in 2009 more than 20,000 people have been killed and thousands more abducted.

The territory taken by Boko Haram does not yet endanger the existence of the state of Nigeria. The group does not even pose a threat to the capital Abuja, despite it being situated halfway up the country; but they do pose a daily threat to people in the north and they damage Nigeria's reputation abroad as a place to do business.

Most of the villages they have captured are on the Mandara mountain range, which backs onto Cameroon. This means the national army is operating a long way from its bases, and cannot surround a Boko Haram force. Cameroon's government does not welcome Boko Haram, but the countryside gives the fighters space to retreat to if required. The situation will not burn itself out for several years, during which time Boko Haram will try to form alliances with the jihadists up north in the Sahel region.

The Americans and French have tracked the problem for several years and now operate surveillance drones in response to the growing threat of violence projecting out of the Sahel/ Sahara region and connecting with northern Nigeria. The Americans use several bases, including the one in Djibouti which is part of the US Africa Command, set up in 2007, and the French have access to concrete in various countries in what they call 'Francophone Africa'.

The dangers of the threat spreading across several countries has been a wake-up call. Nigeria, Cameroon and Chad are all now involved militarily and co-ordinating with the Americans and French.

Further south, down the Atlantic coast, is sub-Saharan Africa's second-largest oil producer – Angola. The former Portuguese colony is one of the African nation states with natural geographical borders. It is framed by the Atlantic Ocean to the west, by jungle to the north and desert to the south, while the eastern regions are sparsely populated rugged land which acts as a buffer zone with the DRC and Zambia.

The majority of the 29 million-strong population live in the western half, which is well watered and can sustain agriculture; and off the coast in the west lie most of Angola's oilfields. The rigs out in the Atlantic are mostly owned by American companies, but over half of the output ends up in China. This makes Angola (dependent on the ebb and flow of sales) second only to Saudi Arabia as the biggest supplier of crude oil to the Middle Kingdom.

Angola is another country familiar with conflict. Its war

for independence ended in 1975 when the Portuguese gave up, but it instantly morphed into a civil war between tribes disguised as a civil war over ideology. Russia and Cuba supported the 'socialists', the USA and apartheid South Africa backed the 'rebels'. Most of the socialists of the MPLA (Popular Movement for the Liberation of Angola) were from the Mbundu tribe, while the opposition rebel fighters were mostly from two other main tribes, the Bakongo and the Ovimbundu. Their political disguise was as the FNLA (National Liberation Front of Angola) and UNITA (National Union for the Total Independence of Angola). Many of the civil wars of the 1960s and 1970s followed this template: if Russia backed a particular side, that side would suddenly remember that it had socialist principles while its opponents would become anti-Communist.

The Mbundu had the geographical but not the numerical advantage. They held the capital, Luanda, had access to the oilfields and the main river, the Kwanza, and were backed by countries which could supply them with Russian arms and Cuban soldiers. They prevailed in 2002 and their top echelons immediately undermined their own somewhat questionable socialist credentials by joining the long list of colonial and African leaders who enriched themselves at the expense of the people.

This sorry history of domestic and foreign exploitation continues in the twenty-first century.

As we've seen, the Chinese are everywhere, they mean business and they are now every bit as involved across the continent as the Europeans and Americans. About a third of China's oil imports come from Africa, which – along with the precious metals to be found in many African countries – means they have arrived, and will stay. European and American oil companies and big multinationals are still far more heavily involved in Africa, but China is quickly catching up. For example, in Liberia it is seeking iron ore, in the DRC and Zambia it's mining copper and, also in the DRC, cobalt. It has already helped to develop the Kenyan port of Mombasa and is now embarking on more huge projects just as Kenya's oil assets are beginning to become commercially viable.

China's state-owned China Road and Bridge Corporation is building a $14 billion rail project to connect Mombasa to the capital city of Nairobi. Analysts say the time taken for goods to travel between the two cities will be reduced from thirty-six hours to eight hours, with a corresponding cut of 60 per cent in transport costs. There are even plans to link Nairobi up to South Sudan, and across to Uganda and Rwanda. Kenya intends, with Chinese help, to be the economic powerhouse of the eastern seaboard.

Over the southern border Tanzania is trying a rival bid to become East Africa's leader and has concluded billions of dollars' worth of deals with the Chinese on infrastructure projects. It has also signed a joint agreement with China and an Omani construction company to overhaul and extend the port of Bagamoyo, as the main port in Dar es Salaam is severely congested. It is planned that Bagamoyo will be able to handle 20 million cargo containers a year, which will make it the biggest port in Africa. Tanzania also has good transport links in the 'Southern Agricultural Growth Corridor of Tanzania' and is connecting down into the fifteen-nation Southern African Development Community. This in turn links into the North–South Corridor, which connects the port of Durban to the copper regions of the DRC and Zambia with spurs linking the port of Dar es Salaam to Durban and Malawi.

Despite this, Tanzania looks as if it will be the second-tier power along the east coast. Kenya's economy is the powerhouse in the five-nation East African Community, accounting for about 40 per cent of the region's GDP. It may have less arable land than Tanzania, but it uses what it has much more efficiently. Its industrial system is also more efficient, as is its system of getting goods to market – both domestic and international. If it can maintain political stability it looks destined to remain the dominant regional power in the near to medium term.

China's presence also stretches into Niger, with the Chinese National Petroleum Corporation investing in the small oilfield in the Ténéré fields in the centre of the country. And Chinese investment in Angola over the past decade exceeds $8 billion and is growing every year. The Chinese Railway Engineering Corporation (CREC) has already spent almost $2 billion modernising the Benguela railway line which links the DRC to the Angolan port of Lobito on the Atlantic coast 800 miles away. This way come the cobalt, copper and manganese with which Katanga Province in the DRC is cursed and blessed.

In Luanda CREC is constructing a new international airport, and around the capital huge apartment blocks built to the Chinese model have sprung up to house some of the estimated 150,000–200,000 Chinese workers now in the country. Thousands of these workers are also trained in military skills and could provide a ready-made militia if China so required.

What Beijing wants in Angola is what it wants everywhere: the materials with which to make its products, and political stability to ensure the flow of those materials and products. So when former president José Eduardo dos Santos, who had been in charge for thirty-six years, decided to pay Mariah Carey $1 million to sing at his birthday party in 2013, that was his affair – as was any other way he chose to spend his vast wealth in his poverty-stricken country. And if the Mbundu, to which dos Santos belongs, continue to dominate, that is theirs. China does not have a view on human rights or corruption in Africa – only on economics.

Chinese involvement is an attractive proposition for many African governments. Beijing and the big Chinese companies don't ask difficult questions about human rights, they don't demand economic reform or even suggest that certain African leaders stop stealing their countries' wealth as the IMF or World Bank might. For example, China is Sudan's biggest trading partner, which goes some way to explaining why China consistently protects Sudan at the UN Security Council and continued to back its President Omar al-Bashir even when there was an arrest warrant out for him issued by the International Criminal Court. Western criticism of this gets short shrift in Beijing, however; it is regarded as simply another power play aimed at stopping China doing business, and hypocrisy given the West's history in Africa.

All the Chinese want is the oil, the minerals, the precious metals and the markets. This is an equitable government-to-government relationship, but we will see increasing tension between local populations and the Chinese workforces often brought in to assist the big projects. This in turn may draw Beijing more into the local politics, and require it to have some sort of minor military presence in various countries.

South Africa is China's largest trading partner in Africa. The two countries have a long political and economic history and are well placed to work together. Hundreds of Chinese companies, both state owned and private, now operate in Durban, Johannesburg, Pretoria, Cape Town and Port Elizabeth.

South Africa's economy is ranked second-biggest on the continent behind Nigeria. It is certainly the powerhouse in the south in terms of its economy (three times the size of Angola's), military and population (56 million). South Africa is more developed than many African nations, thanks to its location at the very southern tip of the continent with access to two oceans, its natural wealth of gold, silver and coal and a climate and land that allow for large-scale food production.

Because it is located so far south, and the coastal plain quickly rises into high land, South Africa is one of the very few African countries that do not suffer from the curse of malaria, as mosquitoes find it difficult to breed there. This allowed the European colonialists to push into its interior much further and faster than in the malaria-riddled tropics, settle, and begin small-scale industrial activity which grew into what is now southern Africa's biggest economy.

For most of Southern Africa, doing business with the outside world means doing business with Pretoria, Bloemfontein and Cape Town.

South Africa has used its natural wealth and location to tie its neighbours into its transport system, meaning there is a two-way rail and road conveyer belt stretching from the ports in East London, Cape Town, Port Elizabeth and Durban stretching north through Zimbabwe, Botswana, Zambia, Malawi and Tanzania, reaching even into Katanga Province of the DRC and eastward into Mozambique. The new Chinese-built railway from Katanga to the Angolan coast has been laid to challenge this dominance and might take some traffic from the DRC, but South Africa looks destined to maintain its advantages.

During the apartheid years the ANC (African National Congress) backed Angola's MPLA in its fight against Portuguese colonisation. However, the passion of a shared struggle is turning into a cooler relationship now that each party controls its respective country and competes at a regional level. Angola has a long way to go to catch up with South Africa. This will not be a military confrontation: South Africa's dominance is near-total. It has large, well-equipped armed forces comprising about 100,000 personnel, dozens of fighter jets and attack helicopters, as well as several modern submarines and frigates.

In the days of the British Empire, controlling South Africa meant controlling the Cape of Good Hope and thus the sea lanes between the Atlantic and Indian oceans. Modern navies can venture much further out from the southern African coastline if they wish to pass by, but the Cape is still a commanding piece of real estate on the world map and South Africa is a commanding presence in the whole of the bottom third of the continent.

There is a new scramble for Africa in this century, but this time it is two-pronged. There are the well-publicised outside interests, and meddling, in the competition for resources, but there is also the 'scramble within', and South Africa intends to scramble fastest and furthest.

It dominates the fifteen-nation Southern African Development Community (SADC) and has managed to gain a permanent place at the International Conference on the Great Lakes Region, of which it is not even a member. The SADC is rivalled by the East African Community (EAC) comprising Burundi, Kenya, Rwanda, Uganda and Tanzania. The latter is also a member of the SADC and the other EAC members take a dim view of its flirtation with South Africa. For its part South Africa appears to view Tanzania as its vehicle for gaining greater influence in the Great Lakes region and beyond.

The South African National Defence Force has a brigade in the DRC officially under the command of the UN, but it was sent there by its political masters to ensure that South Africa is not left out from the spoils of war in that mineral-rich country. This has brought it into competition with Uganda, Burundi and Rwanda, which have their own ideas about who should be in charge in the DRC.

The Africa of the past was given no choice – its geography shaped it – and then the Europeans engineered most of today's borders. Now, with its booming populations and developing mega-cities, it has no choice but to embrace the modern globalised world to which it is so connected. In this, despite all the problems we have seen, it is making huge strides.

The same rivers that hampered trade are now harnessed for hydroelectric power. From the earth that struggled to sustain large-scale food production come minerals and oil, making some countries rich even if little of the wealth reaches the people. Nevertheless, in most, but not all, countries poverty has fallen as healthcare and education levels have risen. Many countries are English-speaking, which in an English-language-dominated global economy is an advantage, and the continent has seen economic growth over most of the past decade.

On the downside, economic growth in many countries is dependent on global prices for minerals and energy. Countries whose national budgets are predicated on receiving $100 dollars per barrel of oil, for example, have little to fall back on when prices drop to $80 or $60. Manufacturing output levels are close to where they were in the 1970s. Corruption remains rampant across the continent, and as well as the few 'hot' conflicts (Somalia, Nigeria, Sudan, for example) there are several more that are merely frozen.

Nevertheless, every year more roads and railways are being built connecting this incredibly diverse space. The vast distances of the oceans and deserts separating Africa from everywhere have been overcome by air travel, and industrial muscle has created harbours in places nature had not intended them to be.

In every decade since the 1960s optimists have written about how Africa is on the brink of prevailing over the hand history and nature have dealt it. Perhaps this time it is true. It needs to be. Sub-Saharan Africa currently holds 1.1 billion people, by some estimates – by 2050 that may have more than doubled to 2.4 billion.

CHAPTER 6

THE MIDDLE EAST

'We've broken Sykes–Picot!'

Islamic State fighter, 2014

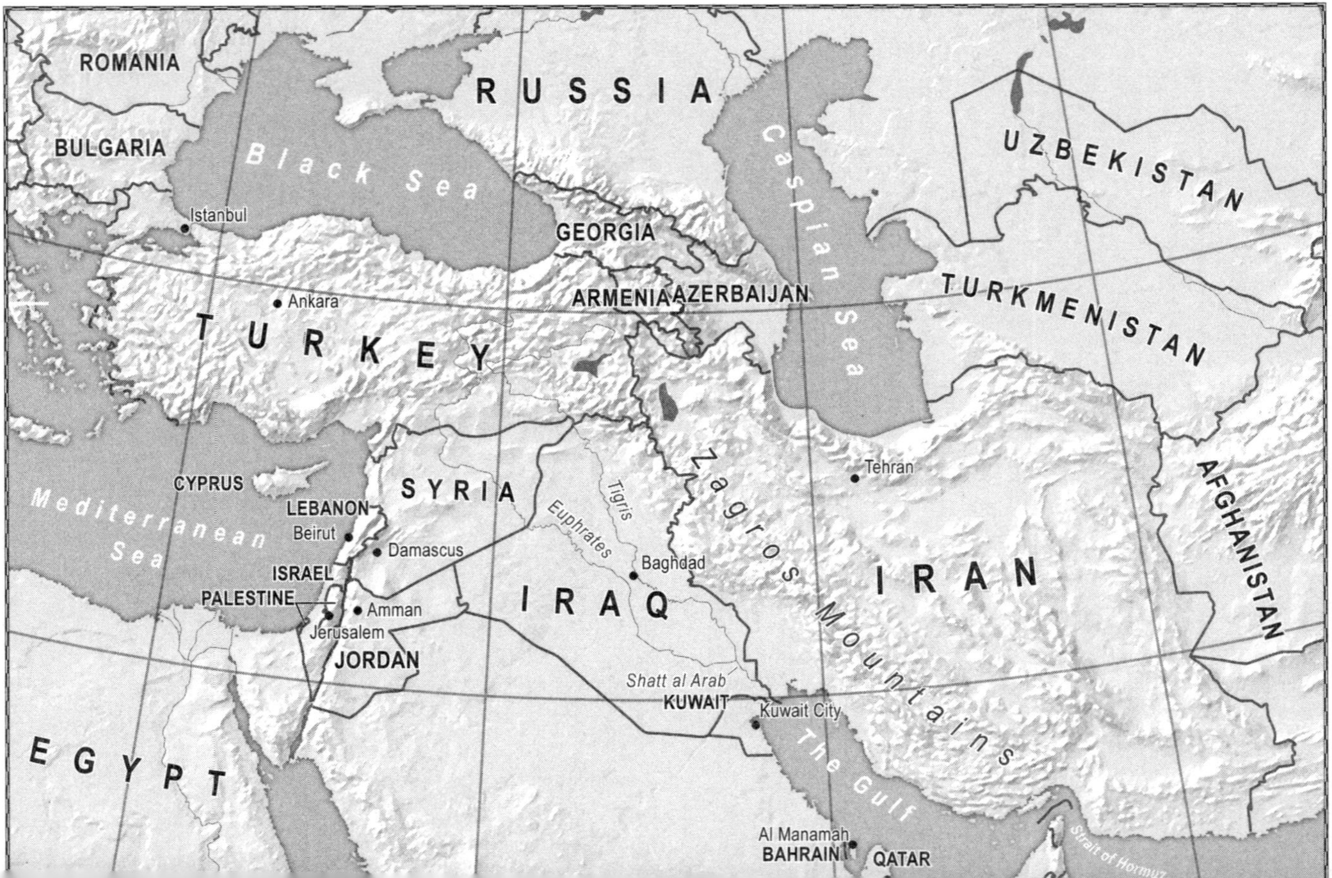
ROMANIA
BULGARIA
RUSSIA
Black Sea
Istanbul
GEORGIA
UZBEKISTAN
Caspian Sea
ARMENIA
AZERBAIJAN
TURKMENISTAN
Ankara
TURKEY
CYPRUS
Mediterranean Sea
LEBANON
Beirut
SYRIA
Damascus
ISRAEL
PALESTINE
Amman
Jerusalem
JORDAN
Euphrates
Tigris
Baghdad
IRAQ
Zagros Mountains
Tehran
IRAN
AFGHANISTAN
Shatt al Arab
KUWAIT
Kuwait City
The Gulf
Al Manamah
BAHRAIN
QATAR
Strait of Hormuz
EGYPT

SAUDI ARABIA
UNITED ARAB EMIRATES
Muscat
Mecca
Red Sea
Rub al'Khali
OMAN
SUDAN
Nile
ERITREA
YEMEN
Sana'a
Socotra (YEMEN)
Gulf of Aden
DJIBOUTI
SOMALIA
ETHIOPIA
Arabian Sea
State border
Disputed border
500miles
500km

THE MIDDLE OF WHAT? EAST OF WHERE? THE REGION'S very name is based on a European view of the world, and it is a European view of the region that shaped it. The Europeans used ink to draw lines on maps: they were lines that did not exist in reality and created some of the most artificial borders the world has seen. An attempt is now being made to redraw them in blood.

One of the most important pieces of video to emerge from the Middle East in 2014 was overshadowed that year by footage of explosions and beheadings. It is a piece of slick propaganda by Islamic State and shows a bulldozer wiping, or rather pushing, the Iraqi–Syrian border out of existence. The border is simply a high berm of sand. Move the sand and the border no longer *physically* exists. This 'line' still exists in theory. The next few years will determine whether those words of the Islamic State fighter are prophetic, or mere bravado: 'We are destroying the borders and breaking the barriers. Thanks be to Allah.'

After the First World War, there were fewer borders in the wider Middle East than currently exist, and those that did exist were usually determined by geography alone. The spaces within them were loosely subdivided and governed according to geography, ethnicity and religion, but there was no attempt to create nation states.

The Greater Middle East extends across 1,000 miles, west to east, from the Mediterranean Sea to the mountains of Iran. From north to south, if we start at the Black Sea and end on the shores of the Arabian Sea off Oman, it is 2,000 miles long. The region includes vast deserts, oases, snow-covered mountains, long rivers, great cities and coastal plains. And it has a great deal of natural wealth in the form that every industrialised and industrialising country around the world needs – oil and gas.

It also contains the fertile region known as Mesopotamia, the 'land between the rivers' (the Euphrates and Tigris). However, the most dominant feature is the vast Arabian Desert and scrubland in its centre which touches parts of Israel, Jordan, Syria, Iraq, Kuwait, Oman, Yemen and most of Saudi Arabia including the Rub' al Khali or 'Empty Quarter'. This is the largest continuous sand desert in the world, incorporating an area the size of France. It is due to this feature not only that the majority of the inhabitants of the region live on its periphery, but also that until European colonisation most of the people within it did not think in terms of nation states and legally fixed borders.

The notion that a man from a certain area could not travel across a region to see a relative from the same tribe unless he had a document, granted to him by a third man he didn't know in a faraway town, made little sense. The idea that the document was issued because a foreigner had said the area was now two regions and had made up names for them made no sense at all and was contrary to the way in which life had been lived for centuries.

The Ottoman Empire (1299–1922) was ruled from Istanbul. At its height it stretched from the gates of Vienna, across Anatolia and down through Arabia to the Indian Ocean. From west to east it took in what are now Algeria, Libya, Egypt, Israel/Palestine, Syria, Jordan, Iraq and parts of Iran. It had never bothered to make up names for most of these regions; in 1867 it simply divided them into administrative areas known as 'Vilayets', which were usually based on where certain tribes lived, be they the Kurds in present-day Northern

Iraq, or the tribal federations in what is now part of Syria and part of Iraq.

When the Ottoman Empire began to collapse, the British and French had a different idea. In 1916 the British diplomat Colonel Sir Mark Sykes took a chinagraph pencil and drew a crude line across a map of the Middle East. It ran from Haifa on the Mediterranean in what is now Israel to Kirkuk (now in Iraq) in the north-east. It became the basis of his secret agreement with his French counterpart François Georges-Picot to divide the region into two spheres of influence should the Triple Entente defeat the Ottoman Empire in the First World War. North of the line was to be under French control, south of it under British hegemony.

The term 'Sykes–Picot' has become shorthand for the various decisions made in the first third of the twentieth century which betrayed promises given to tribal leaders and which partially explain the unrest and extremism of today. This explanation can be overstated, though: there was violence and extremism before the Europeans arrived. Nevertheless, as we saw in Africa, arbitrarily creating 'nation states' out of people unused to living together in one region is not a recipe for justice, equality and stability.

Prior to Sykes–Picot (in its wider sense), there was no state of Syria, no Lebanon, nor were there Jordan, Iraq, Saudi Arabia, Kuwait, Israel or Palestine. Modern maps show the borders and the names of nation states, but they are young and they are fragile.

Islam is the dominant religion of the Middle East, but contains within it many different versions. The most important division within Islam is almost as old as the religion itself: the split between Sunni and Shia Muslims dates back to 632 CE when the prophet Muhammad died, leading to a dispute over his succession.

The Sunni Muslims form the majority among Arabs, and indeed among the world's Muslim population, comprising perhaps 85 per cent of the total, although within some of the Arab countries the percentages are less distinct. The name comes from 'Al Sunna' or 'people of tradition'. Upon the death of the Prophet, those who would become Sunni argued that his successor should be chosen using Arab tribal traditions. They regard themselves as Orthodox Muslims.

The word Shia derives from 'Shiat Ali', literally 'the party of Ali', and refers to the son-in-law of the Prophet Muhammad. Ali and his sons Hassan and Hussein were all assassinated and thus denied what the Shia feel was their birthright – to lead the Islamic community.

From this sprang several doctrinal disputes and cultural practices dividing the two main branches of Islam that have led to disputes and warfare, although there have also been long periods of peaceful coexistence.

There are also divisions within the division. For example, there are various branches of Sunni Islam that follow particular great scholars from the past, including the strict Hanbali tradition, named after the ninth-century Iraqi scholar Ahmad ibn Hanbal, favoured by many Sunnis from Qatar and Saudi Arabia; this in turn has influenced the ultra-puritanical Salafi thought, which predominates among jihadists.

Shia Islam has three main divisions, the best known of which is probably the Twelvers, who adhere to the teaching of the Twelve Imams, but even that contains divisions. The Ismaili school disputes the lineage of the seventh Imam, while the Zaidi school disputes that of the fifth Imam. There are also several offshoots from mainstream Shia Islam, with the Alawites (Alawis) and Druze being considered so far away from traditional Islamic thought that many other Muslims, especially among the Sunni, do not even recognise them as being part of the religion.

The legacy of European colonialism left the Arabs grouped into nation states and ruled by leaders who tended to favour whichever branch of Islam (and tribe) they themselves came from. These dictators then used the machinery of state to ensure their writ ruled over the entire area within the artificial lines drawn by the Europeans, regardless of whether this was historically appropriate and fair to the different tribes and religions that had been thrown together.

Iraq is a prime example of the ensuing conflicts and chaos. The more religious among the Shia never accepted that a Sunni-led government should have control over their holy cities such as Najaf and Karbala, where their martyrs Ali and Hussein are said to be buried. These communal feelings go back centuries; a few decades of being called 'Iraqis' was never going to dilute such emotions.

As rulers of the Ottoman Empire the Turks saw a rugged, mountainous area dominated by Kurds, then, as the mountains fell away into the flatlands leading towards Baghdad, and west to what is now Syria, they saw a place where the majority of people were Sunni Arabs. Finally, after the two great rivers the Tigris and the Euphrates merged and ran down to the Shatt al-Arab waterway, the marshlands and the city of Basra, they saw more Arabs, most of whom were Shia. They ruled this space accordingly, dividing it into three administrative regions: Mosul, Baghdad and Basra.

In antiquity, the regions very roughly corresponding to the

above were known as Assyria, Babylonia and Sumer. When the Persians controlled the space they divided it in a similar way, as did Alexander the Great, and later the Umayyad Empire. The British looked at the same area and divided the three into one, a logical impossibility Christians can resolve through the Holy Trinity, but which in Iraq has resulted in an unholy mess.

Many analysts say that only a strong man could unite these three areas into one country, and Iraq had one strong man after another. But in reality the people were never unified, they were only frozen with fear. In the one place which the dictators could not see, people's minds, few bought into the propaganda of the state, wallpapering as it did over the systematic persecution of the Kurds, the domination by Saddam's Sunni Muslim clan from his home town of Tikrit, nor the mass slaughter of the Shia after their failed uprising in 1991.

The Kurds were the first to leave. The smallest minorities in a dictatorship will sometimes pretend to believe the propaganda that their rights are protected because they lack the strength to do anything about the reality. For example, Iraq's Christian minority, and its handful of Jews, felt they might be safer keeping quiet in a secular dictatorship, such as Saddam's, than risk change and what they feared might, and indeed has, followed. However, the Kurds were geographically defined and, crucially, numerous enough to be able to react when the reality of dictatorship became too much.

Iraq's five million Kurds are concentrated in the north and north-eastern provinces of Irbil, Sulaymaniyah and Dahuk and their surrounding areas. It is a giant crescent of mostly hills and mountains, which meant the Kurds retained their distinct identity despite repeated cultural and military attacks against them, such as the al-Anfal campaign of 1988, which included aerial gas attacks against villages. During the eight-stage campaign, Saddam's forces took no prisoners and killed all males aged between fifteen and fifty that they came across. Up to 100,000 Kurds were murdered and 90 per cent of their villages wiped off the map.

When in 1990 Saddam Hussein over-reached into Kuwait, the Kurds went on to seize their chance to make history and turn Kurdistan into the reality they had been promised after the First World War in the Treaty of Sèvres (1920), but never granted. At the tail end of the Gulf War conflict the Kurds rose up, the Allied forces declared a 'safe zone' into which Iraqi forces were not allowed, and a de facto Kurdistan began to take shape. The 2003 invasion of Iraq by the USA cemented what appears to be a fact – Baghdad will not again rule the Kurds.

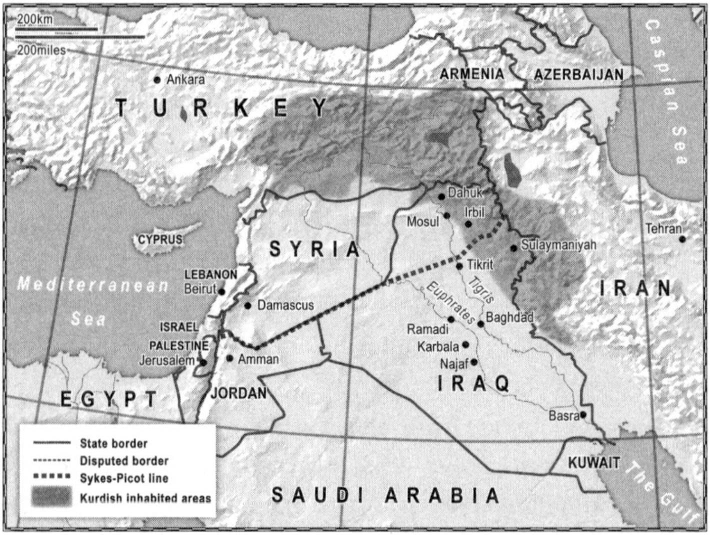

Although not a recognised state, there is an identifiable 'Kurdistan' region. Crossing borders as it does, this is an area of potential trouble should the Kurdish regions attempt to establish an independent country.

Iraqi Kurdistan is not a recognised sovereign state but it has many of the trappings of one. However, a move towards full independence via a referendum in 2017 backfired badly. Baghdad sent in the Iraqi military, backed by Shia militia. They confronted the Kurdish Peshmerga fighters and took control of the city of Kirkuk after just a few days of fighting. The Kurds had taken it from Islamic State and had hoped that the city, which lies adjacent to a huge oil field, might one day be their sovereign capital. But with their common enemy routed, the rivalry between the Kurdish regional government and the Iraqi capital soon resurfaced. Now the Iraqi flag once again flies over Kirkuk and the oil revenues once again flow to Baghdad.

Without a fully independent Kurdistan carved out of Iraq, the chances of a 'greater Kurdistan', stretching from the Iraqi mountains to the Mediterranean, have receded. Syria, Turkey and Iran have followed Iraq's lead and seen to that.

There is another problem: unity among the Kurds. Iraqi Kurdistan has long been divided between two rival families and all the different Kurdish regions have their divisions. Syria's Kurds are still trying to create a statelet they call Rojava but President Assad's military victories since 2017 have put that in doubt. Nevertheless, Syria's Kurds still see Rojava as part of a future greater Kurdistan, but having been used as 'boots on the ground' by the Western powers to beat Islamic State in Syria, they are once more being abandoned. Yet again they will repeat their old adage: 'The Kurds have no friends but the mountains'. In the event of its creation questions would arise as to who would have how much power, and where. If Kurdistan does become an internationally recognised state then the shape of Iraq will change. That assumes there will be an Iraq. There may not be.

The Hashemite Kingdom, as Jordan is also known, is another place that was carved out of the desert by the British, who in 1918 had one large piece of territory to administer and several problems to solve.

Various Arabian tribes had helped the British against the Ottomans during the First World War, but there were two in particular which London promised to reward at the war's end. Unfortunately both were promised the same thing – control of the Arabian Peninsula. Given that the Saud and Hashemite tribes frequently fought each other, this was a little awkward. So London dusted down the maps, drew some lines and said the head of the Saud family could rule over one region, and the head of the Hashemites could rule the other, although each would 'need' a British diplomat to keep an eye on things. The Saudi leader eventually landed on a name for his territory, calling it after himself, hence we know the area as Saudi Arabia – the rough equivalent would be calling the UK 'Windsorland'.

The British, sticklers for administration, named the other area 'Transjordan', which was shorthand for 'the other side of the Jordan River'. A dusty little town called Amman became the capital of Transjordan, and when the British went home in 1948 the country's name changed to Jordan. But the Hashemites were not from the Amman area: they were originally part of the powerful Qureshi tribe from the Mecca region, and the original inhabitants were mostly Bedouin. The majority of the population is now Palestinian: when the Israelis occupied the West Bank in 1967 many Palestinians fled to Jordan, which was the only Arab state to grant them citizenship. We now have a situation where the majority of Jordan's 9.7 million citizens are Palestinian, many of whom do not regard themselves as loyal subjects of the current

Hashemite ruler, King Abdullah. Added to this problem are the one million Iraqi and Syrian refugees the country has also taken in who are putting a huge strain on its extremely limited resources.

Such changes to a country's demographics can cause serious problems, and nowhere more so than in Lebanon.

Until the twentieth century, the Arabs in the region saw the area between the Lebanese mountains and the sea as simply a province of the region of Syria. The French, into whose grasp it fell after the First World War, saw things differently.

The French had long allied themselves with the region's Arab Christians and by way of thanks made up a country for them in a place in which they appeared in the 1920s to be the dominant population. As there was no other obvious name for this country the French named it after the nearby mountains, and thus Lebanon was born. This geographical fancy held until the late 1950s. By then the birth rate among Lebanon's Shia and Sunni Muslims was growing faster than that of the Christians, while the Muslim population had been swollen by Palestinians fleeing the 1948 Arab–Israeli War in neighbouring Israel/Palestine. There has only been one official census in Lebanon (in 1932), because demographics is such a sensitive issue and the political system is partially based on population sizes.

There have long been bouts of fighting between the various confessional groups in the area, and what some historians call the first Lebanese civil war broke out in 1958 between the Maronite Christians and the Muslims, who by this time probably slightly outnumbered the Christians. They are now in a clear majority but there are still no official figures, and academic studies citing numbers are fiercely contested.

Some parts of the capital, Beirut, are exclusively Shia Muslim, as is most of the south of the country. This is where the Shia Hezbollah group (backed by Shia-dominated Iran) is dominant. Another Shia stronghold is the Beqaa Valley, which Hezbollah has used as a staging post for its forays into Syria to support government forces there. Other towns are overwhelmingly Sunni Muslim. For example Tripoli, in the north, is thought to be 80 per cent Sunni, but it also has a sizeable Alawite minority, and given the Sunni–Alawite tensions next door in Syria this has led to sporadic bouts of fighting.

Lebanon appears to be a unified state only from the perspective of seeing it on a map. It takes just a few minutes after arriving at Beirut Airport to discover it is far from that. The drive from the airport to the centre takes you past the exclusively Shia southern suburbs, which are partially policed by the Hezbollah militia, probably the most efficient fighting force in the country. The Lebanese army exists on paper, but in the event of another civil war such as that of 1975–90, it would fall apart, as soldiers in most units would simply go back to their home towns and join the local militias.

That is, in part, what happened to the Syrian armed forces once the civil war there really took hold towards the end of 2011.

Syria is another multi-faith, multi-confessional, multi-tribal state which fell apart at the first time of asking. Typical of the region, the country is majority Sunni Muslim – about 70 per cent – but has substantial minorities of other faiths. Until 2011 many communities lived side by side in the towns, cities and countryside, but there were still distinct areas in which a particular group dominated. As in Iraq, locals would always tell you, 'We are one people, there are no divisions between us.' However, as in Iraq, your name, place of birth or place of habitation usually meant your background could be easily identified, and, as in Iraq, it didn't take much to pull the one people apart into many.

When the French ruled the region they followed the British example of divide and rule. At that time the Alawites were known as Nusayris. Many Sunnis do not count them as Muslims, and such was the hostility towards them they rebranded themselves as Alawites (as in 'followers of Ali') to reinforce their Islamic credentials. They were a backward hill people, at the bottom of the social strata in Syrian society. The French took them and put them into the police force and military, from where over the years they established themselves as a major power in the land.

Fundamentally, everyone was aware of the tension of having leaders from a small minority of the population ruling the majority. The Assad clan, from which President Bashar al-Assad comes, is Alawite, a group that comprises approximately 12 per cent of the population. The family has ruled the country since Bashar's father, Hafez, took power in a coup d'état in 1970. In 1982 Hafez crushed a Muslim Brotherhood Sunni uprising in Hama, killing perhaps 30,000 people over several days. The Brotherhood never forgave or forgot, and when the nationwide uprising began in 2011 there were scores to be settled. In some respects the ensuing civil war was simply Hama, Part Two.

The final shape and make-up of Syria remain in question, but since the Russians intervened in late 2015 the possibility of the regime being defeated is over. It holds most of the country, including its core and all of the major urban areas. The rebel groups are in essence beaten and IS is scattered. The

Kurdish forces have carved out territory they control, but this in turn has brought in the Turkish army which is determined to prevent a Kurdish state emerging from the wreckage. Even the prospect of regional autonomy was complicated by the arrival of large numbers of Turkish troops and armour in 2018. President Erdoğan was not prepared to risk a 'mini Kurdistan' on his Syrian border as that in turn would risk invigorating Turkish Kurds with ideas of their own autonomous region, which might one day join with its Syrian counterpart.

In the near future most of Syria looks as if it is destined to be ruled by the Assad regime, as long as Iran and Russia continue to back it. However, as of the summer of 2019 the Kurds and Turkey still hold territory, and various jihad groups form pockets of resistance. The deep divisions in Syrian society revealed by the war have not healed, and without a redistribution of power and wealth by the Assad regime, there will always be elements waiting for another chance to overthrow it.

However, while President Putin is willing to use military power to back the regime, it should survive. Putin saw that Obama's lack of focus on Syria gave Russia an opportunity. It could reinsert itself into the Middle East, make Russia part of the solution to the Syrian problem, and try to link cooperation on resolving the crisis with the easing of sanctions against Moscow, which had been put in place following its annexation of Crimea.

The first two were the easy bit; he's still working on the third. Russia already had a lease on part of the small port of Tartus, on Syria's Mediterranean coast, a foothold in the Middle East it didn't want to lose in the event of a regime change. Moscow had been frozen out by President Sadat's Egypt in the early 1970s and then out of Iraq following the overthrow of Saddam Hussein in 2003. So Putin ensured that President Assad could not lose power by sending in his troops and warplanes. The Russian sector of the Tartus port was extended and a 100-year lease granted for a large air base for Russian forces in the Latakia region. President Assad was in President Putin's pocket.

Syria has become, like Lebanon, a place used by outside powers to further their own aims. Russia, Iran and Lebanese Hezbollah support the Syrian government forces. The Arab countries support the opposition, but different states support different opposition groups: the Saudis and Qataris, for example, are both vying for influence, but each backs a different proxy to achieve it.

It will require skill, courage and an element so often lacking – compromise – to hold many of these regions together as a single, governable space. Especially as Sunni jihadist fighters are trying to pull them apart in order to widen their 'caliphate'.

Groups such as Al Qaeda and, more recently, Islamic State have garnered what support they have partially because of the humiliation caused by colonialism and then the failure of pan-Arab nationalism – and to an extent the Arab nation state. Arab leaders have failed to deliver prosperity or freedom, and the siren call of Islamism, which promises to solve all problems, has proved attractive to many in a region marked by a toxic mix of piety, unemployment and repression. The Islamists hark back to a golden age when Islam ruled an empire and was at the cutting edge of technology, art, medicine and government. They have helped bring to the surface the ancient suspicions of 'the other' throughout the Middle East.

Islamic State grew out of the 'Al Qaeda in Iraq' franchise group in the late 2000s, which nominally was directed by the remnants of the Al Qaeda leadership. By the time the Syrian Civil War was in full flow the group had split from Al Qaeda and renamed itself. At first it was known by the outside world as ISIL ('Islamic State In the Levant') but as the Arabic word for the Levant is Al Sham, gradually it became ISIS. In the summer of 2014 the group began calling itself Islamic State, having proclaimed such an entity in large parts of Iraq and Syria.

It quickly became the 'go to' jihadist group, drawing thousands of foreign Muslims to the cause, partially due to its pious romanticism and partially for its brutality. Its main attraction, though, was its success in creating a caliphate; where Al Qaeda murdered people and captured headlines, IS murdered people and captured territory.

IS also seized upon an area that is increasingly important in the internet age – psychological space. It built on the pioneering work of Al Qaeda in social media and took it to new heights of sophistication and brutality. By 2015 IS was ahead of any government in levels of public messaging using jihadists brought up on the sometimes brutalising effects of the internet and its obsession with violence and sex. They are Generation Jackass Jihadis and they are ahead of the deadly game.

By the summer of 2015, many Arabs across the Middle East, including most of the regional media, were calling IS by another name, one which encapsulated how repulsive many ordinary people felt the organisation to be – Daesh.

It is an acronym of sorts formed from the group's previous name in Arabic, *Dawlat al Islamiya Iraq Wa al Shams*, but the reason people tend to use the name is because IS members hate the term. It sounds similar to the verb *daes* (one who is underhand and sows dissent); it rhymes with negative words such as *fahish* (a sinner); and best of all for those who despise the organisation's particular brand of Islam, is that it rhymes with and sounds a bit like *jahesh*, meaning 'stupid ass'. In Arabic culture, this is quite a serious insult, one which simultaneously demeans the subject and reduces its power to instil fear.

In 2015, the war raged back and forth across parts of Iraq with IS losing the town of Tikrit, but taking Ramadi. Suddenly the US Air force found itself in the odd position of flying reconnaissance missions, and limited air strikes, which assisted Iranian Republican Guard commanders. IS wanted Tikrit, partially to guard against the Iraqi government trying to retake Mosul to the north, but Ramadi was far more important to them. It is in Anbar province, which is an overwhelmingly Sunni region of Iraq and links through to the Syrian border. Holding the territory strengthened their claim to be a 'state'.

In August 2014 the American-led coalition had begun air strikes against IS in both Iraq and Syria. The air cover allowed various anti-IS forces to successfully go on the offensive. By 2019 there had been thousands of airstrikes with many of the US planes flying from the USS *George H.W. Bush* and USS *Carl Vinson* aircraft carriers in the Gulf, and others from Kuwait and a base in the UAE. The planes included the F-22 Raptor Stealth jet fighter which attacked Islamic State's oil facilities. The US pilots, who flew the majority of the missions, suffered from not having enough American Special Forces forward air controllers calling in the coordinates for the strikes. As targets were frequently in the urban areas, the 'rules of engagement' meant many planes returned to their bases without firing their weapons. However, there was also a significant loss of life among civilians on the ground.

IS began losing territory in the summer of 2015, with urban areas such as the Syrian town of Kobane being overrun by Kurdish forces. The following year the major Iraqi city of Ramadi was retaken by the army and supporting militia.

The outside world became more and more involved in Syria as the years passed. The Russians struck both Free Syrian Army and IS targets in Syria, following the alleged IS attack on one of its passenger airliners in Egypt. The French responded to the terror attacks on Paris in November 2015 with massive airstrikes on IS, and then asked the UK for assistance. The British Parliament voted to extend its air strikes in Iraq to include Syria.

The result has seen IS's 'Caliphate' destroyed. The loss of Mosul, recaptured by the Iraqi army in 2017, was a huge set back for IS, both militarily and psychologically: it was from the Great Mosque in the city that the 'Caliphate' had been declared three years previously. By 2019, the 'Caliphate' no longer existed. Thousands of its fighters had been killed or captured, many others tried to return home, and those who stayed retreated into remote parts of the Euphrates valley in an attempt to regroup and begin hit-and-run attacks. It's not necessarily the end of IS, though. By 2017 hundreds of fighters had headed to Libya to set up another base, and many of the non-Arab foreign fighters attempted to return to their home countries in Europe and the Central Asian states, all of which look destined to be plagued by violent Islamism for years to come.

However, the militaries of several outside countries are still operating in Syria. The Russians, British, French, Iranians, Turks and others remain militarily committed there, even if the Americans have reduced their footprint on the ground and some of their air power.

Thousands of drone missions have been flown, some from

within the continental United States. Drones are a clear, modern example of technology overcoming some of the restrictions of geography – but at the same time they serve to underline geography's importance. The US houses its growing fleet of drones in at least ten bases around the world. This allows a person sitting in an air-conditioned office in Nevada with a joystick to hit targets or transfer control to an operative near the target. But it also means the US needs to keep good relations with whichever country is housing the regional drone headquarters. For example, the signal sent from Nevada may need to travel through an underwater cable to Germany and then be sent up to a satellite belonging to a third country that sells bandwidth to the Pentagon. This is a reminder of the conceptual map of US power, which is needed in order to fully understand geopolitics today.

Drone strikes have been used to devastating effect against individual targets. From 2014 to 2019 they made a huge contribution to reclaiming several thousand square miles of territory in Iraq from IS, even if it was still in control of large swathes of the Sunni-dominated regions of the country.

Sunni Islamist fighters from across the globe, drawn like moths to the light of a billion pixels, took advantage of the three-way split between Kurds, Sunni and Shia in Iraq. They offer the Sunni Arabs a heady mix of the promise of restoring them to their 'rightful' place as the dominant force in the region, and the re-establishment of the caliphate in which their version of all true believers (Sunni Muslims) live under one ruler.

However, it is the very fanaticism of their beliefs and practices that explains why they cannot achieve their utopian fantasies.

Firstly, only some of the Sunni Iraqi tribes will support the jihadist aims, and even then only to achieve their own ends – which do not include a return to the sixth century. Once they get what they want they will then turn on the jihadists, especially the foreign ones. Secondly, the jihadists have demonstrated that there is no mercy for anyone who opposes them and that being a non-Sunni is akin to a death sentence. So, all non-Sunni Muslims and all the minorities in Iraq, Christians, Chaldeans, Yazidis and others, are against them, as are dozens of Western and Muslim countries.

The non-jihadist Iraqi Sunnis are in a difficult position. In the event of either a fragmented or a legally federalised Iraq they are stuck in the middle, surrounded by sand in an area that is known as the Sunni Triangle, with its points roughly located just east of Baghdad, west of Ramadi and north of Tikrit. Sunnis living here often have more in common with their related tribes in Syria than they do with the Kurds in the north or the Shia of the south.

There is not enough economic diversity within the triangle to sustain a Sunni entity. History bequeathed oil to 'Iraq', but the de facto division of the country means the oil is mostly in the Kurdish and Shia areas; and if there is no strong, unified Iraq, then the oil money flows back to where the oil is found. The Kurdish lands cannot be brought under their control, the cities south of Baghdad such as Najaf and Karbala are overwhelmingly Shia, and the ports of Basra and Umm Qasr are far away from the Sunni territory. This dilemma leaves the Sunnis fighting for an equal share in a country they once ruled, sometimes toying with the idea of separation, but knowing that their future would probably be self-rule over not very much.

In the event of a split the Shia are geographically best placed to take advantage. The region they dominate has oilfields, 35 miles of coastline, the Shatt al-Arab waterway, ports, access to the outside world and a religious, economic and military ally next door in the form of Iran.

The jihadist fantasy is global domination by Salafi Islam. In their more lucid, yet still wild, moments they plan, and fight, for a more limited aim – a caliphate throughout the Middle East. One of the jihadists' battle cries is 'From Mosul to Jerusalem!', meaning that they hope to control the area from Mosul in Iraq right across to Beirut in Lebanon, Amman in Jordan and Jerusalem in Israel. However, the real size of Islamic State's geographical caliphate is limited by its capabilities.

This is not to underestimate the problem or the scale of what may be the Arab version of Europe's Thirty Years' War (1618–48). It is not just a Middle Eastern problem. Many of the international jihadists who survived are now trying to return home to Europe, North America, Indonesia, the Caucasus and Bangladesh, where they are unlikely to settle for a quiet life. The intelligence services in London believe that around 2015 there were more British Muslims fighting in the wider Middle East region for jihadist groups than were serving in the British Army. They had identified about 500 but believed there might be another 200–300. The radicalisation programme undertaken by the Islamists began several decades before the de-radicalisation initiatives now under way in European countries.

Most countries in the region face their own version of this generational struggle to a greater or lesser degree. Saudi Arabia, for example, has taken on Al Qaeda cells over the past decade but, having mostly taken them apart, it now faces renewed challenges from the next generation of jihadists. It has another problem in the south, on the border with Yemen, which itself is blighted with violence, separatist movements and a strong jihadist element.

There is also a simmering Islamist movement in Jordan, especially in the town of Zarqa, in the north-east towards the Syrian and Iraqi borders, which is home to some of the several thousand supporters of groups such as Al Qaeda and Islamic State. The authorities are fearful of a jihadist group in Iraq or Syria reaching the now fragile borders in strength and crossing into Jordan. The British-trained Jordanian Army is thought to be one of the most robust in the Middle East, but it might struggle to cope if local Islamists and foreign fighters took to the streets in guerrilla warfare. If the Palestinian Jordanians declined to defend the country it is not unrealistic to believe that it would descend into the sort of chaos we now see in Syria. This is the last thing the Hashemite rulers want – and it's the last thing the Israelis want as well.

The battle for the future of the Arab Middle East has to an extent taken the spotlight off the Israeli–Arab struggle. The fixation with Israel/Palestine does sometimes return, but the magnitude of what is going on elsewhere has finally enabled at least some observers to understand that the problems of the region are not down to the existence of Israel. That was a lie peddled by the Arab dictators as they sought to deflect attention from their own brutality, and it was bought by many people across the area and the dictators' useful idiots in the West. Nevertheless the Israeli/Palestinian joint tragedy continues, and such is the obsession with this tiny piece of land that it may again come to be considered by some to be the most pressing conflict in the world.

The Ottomans had regarded the area west of the River Jordan to the Mediterranean Coast as a part of the region of Syria. They called it Filistina. After the First World War, under the British Mandate this became Palestine.

The Jews had lived in what used to be called Israel for millennia, but the ravages of history had dispersed them across the globe. Israel remained for them the 'promised land' and Jerusalem in particular was sacred ground. However, by 1948 Arab Muslims and Christians had been a clear majority in the land for more than a thousand years.

In the twentieth century, with the introduction of the Mandate for Palestine, the Jewish movement to join their minority co-religionists grew and, propelled by the pogroms in Eastern Europe, more and more Jews began to settle there. The British looked favourably on the creation of a 'Jewish homeland' in Palestine and allowed Jews to move there and buy land from the Arabs. After the Second World War and the Holocaust, Jews tried to get to Palestine in even greater numbers. Tensions between Jews and non-Jews reached boiling point, and an exhausted Britain handed over the problem to the United Nations in 1948, which voted to partition the region into two countries. The Jews agreed, the Arabs said 'No'. The outcome was war, which created the first wave of Palestinian refugees fleeing the area and Jewish refugees coming in from across the Middle East.

Jordan occupied the West Bank region, including East Jerusalem. Egypt occupied Gaza, considering it to be an extension of its territory. Neither was minded to give the people living there citizenship or statehood as Palestinians, nor was there any significant movement by the inhabitants calling for the creation of a Palestinian state. Syria, meanwhile, considered

The Golan Heights, the West Bank and Gaza remain contested territory following the Six-Day War in 1967.

the whole area to be part of greater Syria and the people living there as Syrians.

To this day Egypt, Syria and Jordan are suspicious of Palestinian independence, and if Israel vanished and was replaced by Palestine, all three might make claims to parts of the territory. In this century, however, there is a fierce sense of nationhood among the Palestinians, and any Arab dictatorship seeking to take a chunk out of a Palestinian state of whatever shape or size would be met with massive opposition. The Palestinians are very aware that most of the Arab countries, to which some of them fled in the twentieth century, refuse to give them citizenship; these countries insist that the status of their children and grandchildren remains 'refugee', and work to ensure that they do not integrate into the country.

During the Six-Day War of 1967 the Israelis won control of all of Jerusalem, the West Bank and Gaza. In 2005 they left Gaza, but hundreds of thousands of settlers remain in the West Bank.

Israel regards Jerusalem as its eternal, indivisible capital. The Jewish religion says the rock upon which Abraham prepared to sacrifice Isaac is there, and that it stands directly above the Holy of Holies, King Solomon's Temple. For the Palestinians Jerusalem has a religious resonance which runs deep throughout the Muslim world: the city is regarded as the third most holy place in Islam because the Prophet Muhammad is said to have ascended to heaven from that same rock, which is on the site of what is now the 'Furthest Mosque' (Al Aqsa). Militarily the city is of only moderate strategic geographical importance – it has no real industry to speak of, no river and no airport – but it is of overwhelming significance in cultural and religious terms: the ideological need for the place is of more importance than its location. Control of, and access to, Jerusalem is not an issue upon which a compromise solution can be easily achieved.

In December 2017 President Trump said the USA would now recognise Jerusalem as Israel's capital. Congress had supported such a policy back in 1995 and voted for funds to move the US embassy. However, Presidents Clinton, Bush and Obama all signed waivers every six months postponing the move and Trump had been following suit before abruptly changing his mind. The embassy was officially relocated in

March 2018. The White House suggested it was still being impartial in the Palestine/Israel dispute and that this was simply a recognition of the obvious. It also said the move did not rule out East Jerusalem becoming the capital of a Palestinian state one day. It wasn't seen that way by the Palestinians; to many it was confirmation of decades of suspicions that the USA favoured Israel, especially when, in early 2019, Trump also recognised Israel's annexation of the Golan Heights. But it was notable that although the Arab world condemned both actions, it quickly moved on.

In comparison to the West Bank, Gaza was easier for the Israelis to give up (although it was still difficult). Whether the people living there have gained much by the Israeli departure, however, is open to debate.

Gaza is by far the worse off of the two current Palestinian 'entities'. It is only 25 miles long and 7.5 miles wide. Crammed into this space are 1.8 million people. It is in effect a 'city state', albeit a horribly impoverished one. Due to the conflict with Israel its citizens are penned in on three sides by a security barrier created by Israel and Egypt, and by the sea to their west. They can only build to within a certain distance of the border with Israel because the Israelis are trying to limit the ability of rocket fire from Gaza to reach deep into Israel. The last decade has seen an asymmetric arms race gain pace, with militants in Gaza seeking rockets that can fire further, and Israel developing its anti-missile defence system.

Because of its urban density Gaza makes good fighting ground for its defenders but it is a nightmare for its civilians, who have little or no shelter from war and no link to the West Bank, although the distance between the two is only 25 miles at its narrowest point. Until a peace deal is agreed there is nowhere for the Gazans to go, and little for them to do at home.

The West Bank is almost seven times the size of Gaza but is landlocked. Much of it comprises a mountain ridge which runs north to south. From a military perspective, this gives whoever commands the high ground control of the coastal plain on the western side of the ridge, and of the Jordan Rift Valley to its east. Leaving to one side the ideology of Jewish settlers, who claim the biblical right to live in what they call Judea and Samaria, from a military perspective the Israeli view is that a non-Israeli force cannot be allowed to control these heights, as heavy weapons could be fired onto the coastal plain where 70 per cent of Israel's population lives. The plain also includes its most important road systems, many of its successful high-tech companies, the international airport and most of its heavy industry.

This is one reason for the demand for 'security' by the Israeli side and its insistence that, even if there is an independent Palestinian state, that state cannot have an army with heavy weapons on the ridge, and that Israel must also maintain control of the border with Jordan. Because Israel is so small it has no real 'strategic depth', nowhere to fall back to if its defences are breached, and so militarily it concentrates on trying to ensure no one can get near it. Furthermore, the distance from the West Bank border to Tel Aviv is about 10 miles at its narrowest; from the West Bank ridge, any half decent military could cut Israel in two. Likewise, in the case of the West Bank Israel prevents any group from becoming powerful enough to threaten its existence.

Under current conditions Israel faces threats to its security and to the lives of its citizens by terrorist attacks and rocket fire from its immediate neighbours, but not a threat to its very existence. Egypt, to the south-west, is not a threat. There is a peace treaty that currently suits both sides, and the partially demilitarised Sinai Peninsula acts as a buffer between them. East of this, across the Red Sea at Aqaba in Jordan, the desert also protects Israel, as does its peace treaty with Amman. To the north there is a potential menace from Lebanon, one which is growing. The Iranian presence in neighbouring Syria has given Tehran a 'land bridge' across the Middle East, stretching from its capital to Beirut. It has used this bridge to increase its arms shipments to the huge Hezbollah Shia militia. Analysts suggest Hez-bollah now has an arsenal of up to 150,000 missiles, some of them guided, others long range. If and when Hezbollah in Lebanon uses its larger and longer-range rockets to reach deep into Israel on a significant scale, the response will be massive.

Another serious potential threat comes from Lebanon's bigger neighbour Syria. Historically, Damascus wants and needs direct access to the coast. It has always regarded Lebanon as part of Syria (as indeed it was) and remains bitter about its troops having been forced to leave in 2005. If that route to the sea is blocked, the alternative is to cross the Golan Heights and descend to the hilly region around the Sea of Galilee en route to the Mediterranean. But the Heights were seized by Israel during the Six-Day War in 1967, and it would take an enormous onslaught by a Syrian army to break through to the coastal plain leading to the major Israeli population centres. This cannot be discounted at some future point, but in the medium term it remains extremely unlikely.

That leaves the question of Iran – a more serious consideration as it raises the issue of nuclear weapons.

Iran is a non-Arabic, majority Farsi-speaking giant. It is bigger than France, Germany and the UK combined, but while the populations of those countries amount to 215 million people, Iran has only 81 million. With limited habitable space, most live in the mountains; the great deserts and salt plains of the interior of Iran are no place for human habitation. Just driving through them can subdue the human spirit, and living in them is a struggle few undertake.

There are two huge mountain ranges in Iran: the Zagros and the Elburz. The Zagros runs from the north, 900 miles down along Iran's borders with Turkey and Iraq, ending almost at the Strait of Hormuz in the Gulf. In the southern half of the range there is a plain to the west where the Shatt al-Arab divides Iran and Iraq. This is also where the major Iranian oilfields are, the others being in the north and centre. Together they are thought to comprise the world's fourth-largest reserves. Despite this Iran remains relatively poor due to mismanagement, corruption, mountainous topography that hinders transport connections and economic sanctions which have, in part, prevented certain sections of industry from modernising.

The Elburz range also begins in the north, but along the border with Armenia. It runs the whole length of the Caspian Sea's south shore and on to the border with Turkmenistan before descending as it reaches Afghanistan. This is the mountain range you can see from the capital, Tehran, towering above the city to its north. It provides spectacular views, and also a better-kept secret than the Iranian nuclear project: the skiing conditions are excellent for several months each year.

Iran is defended by this geography, with mountains on three sides, swampland and water on the fourth. The Mongols were the last force to make any progress through the territory in 1219–21 and since then attackers have ground themselves into dust trying to make headway across the mountains. By the time of the Second Gulf War in 2003 even the USA, the greatest fighting force the world has seen, thought better than to take a right turn once it had entered Iraq from the south, knowing that even with its superior firepower Iran was not a country to invade. In fact, the US military had a catchphrase at the time: 'We do deserts, not mountains.'

In 1980, when the Iran–Iraq War broke out, the Iraqis used six divisions to cross the Shatt al-Arab in an attempt to annex the Iranian province of Khuzestan. They never even made it off the swamp-ridden plains, let alone entered the foothills of the Zagros. The war dragged on for eight years, taking at least a million lives.

The mountainous terrain of Iran means that it is difficult to create an interconnected economy, and that it has many minority groups each with keenly defined characteristics. Khuzestan, for example, is ethnically majority Arab, and elsewhere there are Kurds, Azeri, Turkmen and Georgians, among others. At most 60 per cent of the country speaks Farsi, the language of the dominant Persian majority. As a result of this diversity, Iran has traditionally centralised power and used force and a fearsome intelligence network to maintain internal stability. Tehran knows that no one is about to invade Iran, but also that hostile powers can use its minorities to try and stir dissent and thus endanger its Islamic revolution.

Iran also has a nuclear industry which many countries, particularly Israel, believe is being used to prepare for the construction of nuclear weapons, increasing tensions in the region. The Israelis feel threatened by the prospect of Iranian nuclear weapons. It is not just Iran's potential to rival their own arsenal and wipe out Israel with just one bomb: if Iran were to get the bomb, then the Arab countries would probably panic and attempt to get theirs as well. The Saudis, for example, fear that the ayatollahs want to dominate the region, bring all the Shia Arabs under their guidance, and even have designs on controlling the holy cities of Mecca and Medina. A nuclear-armed Iran would be the regional superpower par excellence, and to counter this danger the Saudis would probably try to buy nuclear weapons from Pakistan (with whom they have close ties). Egypt and Turkey might follow suit.

This means that the threat of an Israeli air strike on Iran's nuclear facilities is a constant presence, but there are many restraining factors. One is that in a straight line it is 1,000 miles from Israel to Iran. The Israeli air force would need to cross two sovereign borders, those of Jordan and Iraq; the latter would certainly tell Iran that the attack was coming. Another is that any other route requires refuelling capabilities which may be beyond Israel, and which (if flying the northern route) also overfly sovereign territory. A final reason is that Iran holds what might be a trump card – the ability to close the Strait of Hormuz in the Gulf through which passes each day, depending on sales, about 20 per cent of the world's oil needs. At its narrowest point the Strait, which is regarded as the most strategic in the world, is only 21 miles across. The industrialised world fears the effect of Hormuz being closed possibly for months on end, with ensuing spiralling prices. This is one reason why so many countries pressure Israel not to act.

In the 2000s the Iranians feared encirclement by the Americans. The US navy was in the Gulf, and American troops were in Iraq and Afghanistan. With the military drawdowns in both countries Iranian fears have now faded, and Iran is left in the dominant position with a direct line to its allies in Shia-dominated Iraq. The south of Iraq is also a bridge for Iran to its Alawite allies in Damascus, and then to its Shia allies in the form of Hezbollah in Lebanon on the Mediterranean coast.

In the sixth to the fourth centuries BCE the Persian Empire stretched all the way from Egypt to India. Modern-day Iran has no such imperial designs, but it does seek to expand its influence, and the obvious direction is across the flatlands to its west – the Arab world and its Shia minorities. It has made ground in Iraq since the US invasion delivered a Shia-majority government. This has alarmed Sunni-dominated Saudi Arabia and helped fuel the Middle East's version of the Cold War with the Saudi–Iranian relationship at its core. Saudi Arabia may be bigger than Iran, it may be many times richer than Iran due to its well-developed oil and gas industries, but its population is much smaller (33 million Saudis as opposed to 81 million Iranians) and militarily it is not confident about its ability to take on its Persian neighbour if this cold war ever turns hot and their forces confront each other directly. Each side has ambitions to be the dominant power in the region, and each regards itself as the champion of its respective version of Islam. When Iraq was under the heel of Saddam, a powerful buffer separated Saudi Arabia and Iran; with that buffer gone, the two countries now glare at each other across the Gulf. The American-led deal on Iran's nuclear facilities, which was concluded in the summer of 2015, has in no way reassured the Gulf States that the threat to them from Iran has diminished, and the increasingly bitter war of words between Saudi Arabia and Iran continues, along with a war sometimes fought by proxy elsewhere most notably in Yemen.

That war, which began in 2011, has dragged on for years. In 2019 the UN Human Rights Commission estimated that nearly 7,000 civilians had been killed, mostly following air strikes by the Saudi-led coalition forces, although many observers believe the actual figure is much higher. Hundreds of thousands of people have also been displaced. The situation was described by the UN as 'the world's worst humanitarian disaster'. Media coverage has been patchy – it became so dangerous to cover the conflict that by 2018 few media organisations were prepared to let teams take the risk of going to Yemen.

With Iran accused of backing the Houthi rebels, and Saudi Arabia supporting the Yemen government, the battle for influence in the Middle East continues between the two countries, hence Saudi Arabia's dislike of the Iran nuclear deal. Western media reporting concentrated on the Israeli reaction to the deal, but the Arab media across the entire region was wholly against it, with some newspapers comparing it to the Munich Agreement of 1938. One leading Saudi columnist called for the kingdom to begin building a bomb to be ready for when Iran does the same.

This was the background to the shocking events of early 2016, when Saudi Arabia (a majority Sunni country) executed forty-seven prisoners in a single day, among them the country's most senior Shia sheikh, Nimr al Nimr. This was a calculated move by the ruling Sunni royal family to show the world, including America, that nuclear deal or no nuclear deal, the Saudis were going to face down Iran. Demonstrations broke out across the Shia Muslim world, the Saudi embassy in Tehran was duly ransacked and set on fire, diplomatic relations were broken between the two countries, and the scene was set for the continuation of the bitter Sunni/Shia civil war. This has played out in a number of ways and even pitted Sunni states against each other diplomatically. In 2017 Saudi Arabia, the UAE, Bahrain and Egypt broke relations with Qatar, accusing it of supporting terrorism. An economic blockade ensued, leading Qatar to accept aid flown in from Iran, which was quick to see an opportunity to help further divide the Gulf States.

West of Iran is a country that is both European and Asian. Turkey lies on the borders of the Arab lands but is not Arabic, and although most of its land mass is part of the wider Middle East region, it tries to distance itself from the conflicts taking place there.

The Turks have never been truly recognised as part of Europe by their neighbours to the north and north-west. If Turkey *is* European, then Europe's borders are on the far side of the vast Anatolian Plain, meaning they stop at Syria, Iraq and Iran. This is a concept few people accept. If it is *not* part of Europe, then where is it? Its greatest city, Istanbul, was European City of Culture 2010, it competes in the Eurovision Song Contest and the UEFA European Championship, it applied for membership of what is now the European Union in the 1970s; and yet less than 5 per cent of its territory is in Europe. Most geographers regard the small area of Turkey which is west of the Bosporus as being in Europe, and the rest of the country, south and south-east of the Bosporus, as being in the Middle East (in its widest sense).

That is one reason why Turkey has never been accepted into the EU. Other factors are its record on human rights, especially when it comes to the Kurds, and its economy. Its population is 79 million and European countries fear that, given the disparity in living standards, EU membership would result in a mass influx of labour. What may also be a factor, albeit unspoken within the EU, is that Turkey is a majority Muslim country (98 per cent). The EU is neither a secular nor a Christian organisation, but there has been a difficult debate about 'values'. For each argument for Turkey's EU membership there is an argument against, and in the past decade the prospects for Turkey joining have diminished. This has led the country to reflect on what other choices there may be.

In the 1920s, for one man at least, there was no choice. His name was Mustafa Kemal and he was the only Turkish general to emerge from the First World War with an enhanced reputation. After the victorious powers carved up Turkey he rose to become president on a platform of resisting the terms imposed by the Allies, but at the same time modernising Turkey and making it part of Europe. Western legal codes and the Gregorian calendar were introduced and Islamic public institutions banned. The wearing of the fez was forbidden, the Latin alphabet replaced Arabic script, and he even granted the vote to women (two years ahead of Spain and fifteen years ahead of France). In 1934, when Turks embraced legally binding surnames, Kemal was given the name 'Atatürk' – 'Father of the Turks'. He died in 1938 but subsequent Turkish leaders continued working to bring Turkey into the West European fold, and those that didn't found themselves on the wrong end of coups d'état by a military determined to complete Atatürk's legacy.

By the late 1980s, however, the continued rejection by Europe and the stubborn refusal of many ordinary Turks to become less religious resulted in a generation of politicians who began to think the unthinkable – that perhaps Turkey needed a Plan B. President Turgut Özal, a religious man, came to office in 1989 and began the change. He encouraged Turks again to see Turkey as the great land bridge between Europe, Asia and the Middle East, and a country which could again be a great power in all three regions. The current President, Recep Tayyib Erdoğan, has similar ambitions, perhaps even greater ones, but has faced similar hurdles in achieving them. These are in part geographical.

Politically, the Arab countries remain suspicious that Erdoğan wants to recreate the Ottoman Empire economically and they resist close ties. The Iranians see Turkey as their most powerful military and economic competitor in their own backyard. Relations, never warm, have cooled due to them being on opposite sides in support for factions involved in the Syrian civil war. Turkey's strong support for the Muslim Brotherhood government in Egypt was a policy that backfired when the Egyptian military staged its second coup and took power. Relations between Cairo and Ankara are now icy.

Worse still are relations between Ankara and Moscow. The Turks and Russians have been at odds for 500 years but over the past century have mostly learned to rub along without too much friction. The Syrian civil war has changed that, with Russia backing President Assad and Turkey working hard to help overthrow the Assad regime and replace it with a Sunni Muslim-led government. Things came to a head in late 2015 after the Russians intervened in Syria militarily. Turkey shot down a Russian SU 24 jet fighter, which it claimed had strayed into its airspace. A bitter war of words followed, there was even the vague threat of it turning into a shooting match, but both sides settled for vitriol and economic sanctions. This fierce row was not just about Syria and the Russian jet – it was about Turkey and Russia vying for influence in the Black Sea, the Caspian Sea, and among the Turkic peoples in countries such as Turkmenistan. They both know that as Turkey continues to grow, it will seek to rival Russia in the 'Stans' and neither is minded to back down on issues of sovereignty and 'honour'.

The Turkish elite have learnt that scoring Islamist points by picking fights with Israel results in Israel co-operating with Cyprus and Greece to create a trilateral energy alliance to exploit the gas fields off their respective coasts. The Egyptian government's dim view of Turkey is contributing to Cairo's interest in being a major customer for this new energy source. Meanwhile Turkey, which could have benefited from Israeli energy, remains largely reliant on its old foe Russia for its energy needs whilst simultaneously working with Russia to develop new pipelines to deliver energy to EU countries.

The Americans, alarmed at the new cold war between Turkey and Israel, two of its allies, are working to bring them together again. The USA wants a better relationship between them so as to strengthen NATO's position in the eastern Mediterranean. In NATO terms, Turkey is a key country because it controls the entrance to and exit from the Black Sea through the narrow gap of the Bosporus Strait. If it closes the Strait, which is less than a mile across at its narrowest point, the Russian Black Sea Fleet cannot break out into the Mediterranean and then the Atlantic. Even getting through the Bosporus only takes you into the Sea of Marmara; you still have to navigate through the Dardanelles Straits to get to the Aegean Sea en route to the Mediterranean.

Given its land mass Turkey is not often thought of as a sea power, but it borders three seas and its control of these waters has always made it a force to be reckoned with; it is also a trade and transportation bridge linking Europe with the Middle East, the Caucasus and on up to the Central Asian countries, with which it shares history and, in some regions, ethnic ties.

Turkey is determined to be at the crossroads of history even if the traffic can at times be hazardous. The webpage of the Turkish Foreign Ministry emphasises this in the section 'Synopsis of Foreign Policy': 'The Afro-Eurasian geography where Turkey is situated at the epicentre is an area where such opportunities and risks interact in the most intensive way.' It also says: 'Turkey is determined to become a full member of the European Union as part of its bicentennial effort to reach the highest level of contemporary civilisation.'

That looks unlikely in the short to medium term. Until a few years ago Turkey was held up as an example of how a Middle Eastern country, other than Israel, could embrace democracy. That example has taken some huge blows recently with the ongoing Kurdish problem, the difficulties facing some of the tiny Christian communities and the tacit support for Islamist groups in their fight against the Syrian government. The failed coup of 2016 opened the way for the Erdoğan government to crack down on all opposition. More than 50,000 people were subsequently arrested and about 150,000 fired from their jobs.

In 2018, Erdoğan won an election that granted him increased executive powers, in an attempt to cement his position as one of the leading 'strong men' in the world. He has sought to use this to create an increasingly nationalist Turkey, one which is looking to extend its influence in the Balkans, the Middle East and Central Asia. However, April 2019 brought a setback. His AKP party failed to win local elections despite controlling much of Turkey's media. Erdoğan, shocked at the prospect of losing control of Istanbul, demanded a recount of ballot papers, suggesting that 'organised crime' was involved in the election. The results were the same so he then said the whole vote should be rerun. A joke quickly spread around the city about four things people can't choose in life: place of birth, race, ethnicity and the mayor of Istanbul. The dark humour disguised both the unease and rage many people felt about the president's increasing authoritarianism.

President Erdoğan's remarks on Jews, race and gender equality, taken with the creeping Islamisation of Turkey, have also set alarm bells ringing. However, compared with the majority of Arab states Turkey is far more developed and recognisable as a democracy. Erdoğan may be undoing some of Atatürk's work, but the grandchildren of the Father of the Turks live more freely than anyone in the Arab Middle East.

Because the Arab states have not experienced a similar opening-up and have suffered from colonialism, they were not ready to turn the Arab uprisings (the wave of protests that started in 2010) into a real Arab Spring. Instead they soured into perpetual rioting and civil war.

The Arab Spring is a misnomer, invented by the media; it clouds our understanding of what is happening. Too many reporters rushed to interview the young liberals who were standing in city squares with placards written in English, and mistook them for the voice of the people and the direction of history. Some journalists had done the same during the 'Green Revolution', describing the young students of north Tehran as the 'Youth of Iran', thus ignoring the other young Iranians who were joining the reactionary Basij militia and Revolutionary Guard.

In 1989 in Eastern Europe there was one form of totalitarianism: Communism. In the majority of people's minds there was only one direction in which to go: towards democracy, which was thriving on the other side of the Iron Curtain. East and West shared a historical memory of periods of democracy and civil society. The Arab world of 2011 enjoyed none of those things and faced in many different directions. There were, and are, the directions of democracy, liberal democracy (which differs from the former), nationalism, the cult of the strong leader and the direction in which many people had been facing all along – Islam in its various guises, including Islamism.

In the Middle East power does indeed flow from the barrel of a gun. Some good citizens of Misrata in Libya may want to develop a liberal democratic party, some might even want to campaign for gay rights; but their choice will be limited if the local de facto power shoots liberal democrats and gays. Iraq is a case in point: a democracy in name only, far from liberal, and a place where people are routinely murdered for being homosexual.

The second phase of the Arab uprising is well into its stride. This is the complex internal struggle within societies where religious beliefs, social mores, tribal links and guns are currently far more powerful forces than 'Western' ideals of equality, freedom of expression and universal suffrage. The Arab countries are beset by prejudices, indeed hatreds of which the average Westerner knows so little that they tend not to believe them even if they are laid out in print before their eyes. We are aware of our own prejudices, which are legion, but often seem to turn a blind eye to those in the Middle East.

The routine expression of hatred for others is so common in the Arab world that it barely draws comment other than from the region's often Western-educated liberal minority who have limited access to the platform of mass media. Anti-Semitic cartoons which echo the Nazi *Der Stürmer* propaganda newspaper are common. Week in, week out, shock-jock imams are given space on prime-time TV shows.

Western apologists for this sort of behaviour are sometimes hamstrung by a fear of being described as one of Edward Said's 'Orientalists'. They betray their own liberal values by denying their universality. Others, in their naivety, say that these incitements to murder are not widespread and must be seen in the context of the Arabic language, which can be given to flights of rhetoric. This signals their lack of understanding of the 'Arab street', the role of the mainstream Arab media and a refusal to understand that when people who are full of hatred say something, they mean it.

When Hosni Mubarak was ousted as President of Egypt it was indeed people power that toppled him, but what the outside world failed to see was that the military had been waiting for years for an opportunity to be rid of him and his son Gamal, and that the theatre of the street provided the cover they needed. It was only when the Muslim Brotherhood called its supporters out that there was enough cover. There were only three institutions in Egypt: Mubarak's National Democratic Party, the military and the Brotherhood. The latter two destroyed the former, the Brotherhood then won an election, began turning Egypt into an Islamist state, and paid the price by itself being overthrown by the real power in the land – the military.

The Islamists remain the second power, albeit now underground. When the anti-Mubarak demonstrations were at their height the gatherings in Cairo attracted several hundred thousand people. After Mubarak's fall, when the radical Muslim Brotherhood preacher Yusuf al-Qaradawi returned from exile in Qatar, at least a million people came out to greet him, but few in the Western media called this the 'voice of the people'. The liberals never had a chance. Nor do they now. This is not because the people of the region are radical; it is because if you are hungry and frightened, and you are offered either bread and security or the concept of democracy, the choice is not difficult.

In impoverished societies with few accountable institutions, power rests with gangs disguised as 'militia' and 'political parties'. While they fight for power, sometimes cheered on by naive Western sympathisers, many innocent people die. It looks as if it will be that way in Libya, Syria, Yemen, Iraq and possibly other countries for years to come.

The Americans are keen to scale down their political and military investment in the region due to a reduction in their energy import requirements; if they do withdraw then China, and to a lesser extent India, may have to get involved in equal proportion to the US loss of interest. The Chinese are already major players in Saudi Arabia, Iraq and Iran. That scenario is on a global level and will be determined in the chancelleries of the capitals of the great powers. On the ground the game will be played with people's imaginations, wants, hopes and needs, and with their lives.

Sykes–Picot is breaking; putting it back together, even in a different shape, will be a long and bloody affair.

CHAPTER 7

INDIA AND PAKISTAN

'India is not a nation, nor a country. It is a subcontinent of nationalities.'

Muhammad Ali Jinnah

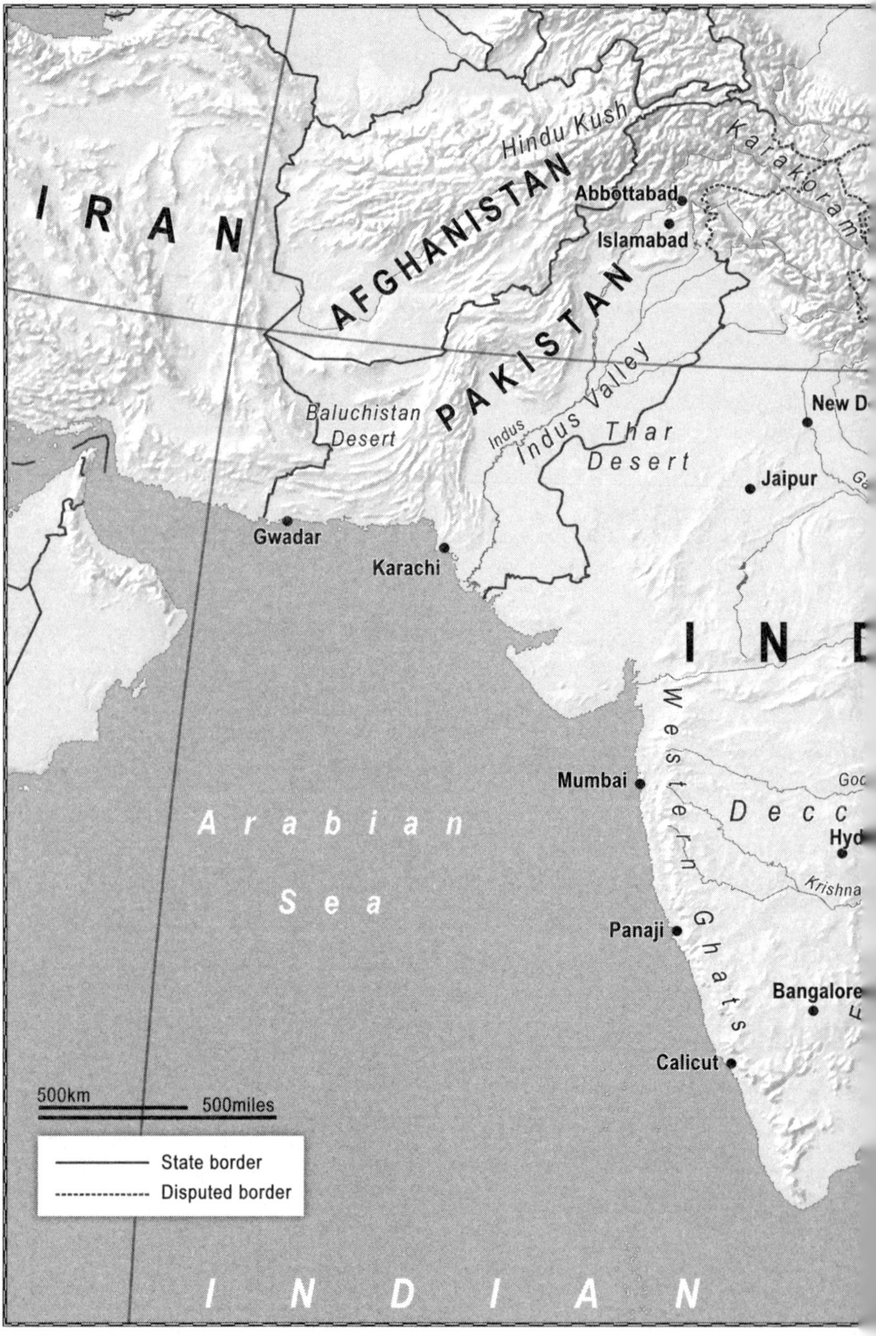
IRAN
AFGHANISTAN
PAKISTAN
Hindu Kush
Karakoram
Abbottabad
Islamabad
Indus Valley
Indus
Baluchistan Desert
Thar Desert
New Delhi
Jaipur
Gwadar
Karachi
Western Ghats
Mumbai
Krishna
Panaji
Bangalore
Calicut
Arabian Sea
INDIAN
500km
500miles
State border
Disputed border

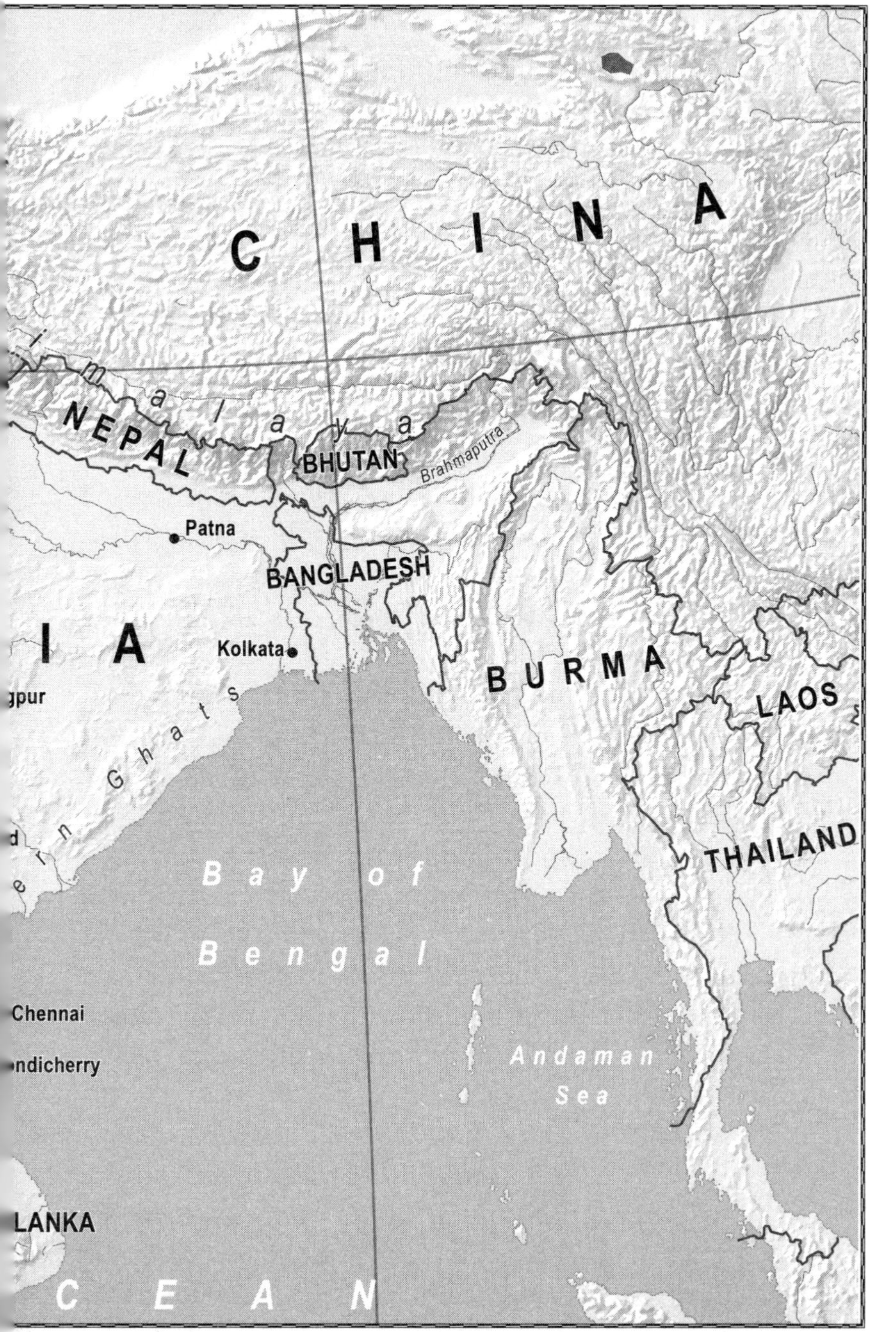

CHINA
NEPAL
BHUTAN
Brahmaputra
Patna
BANGLADESH
Kolkata
BURMA
LAOS
THAILAND
Bay of Bengal
Andaman Sea
Chennai
ndicherry
LANKA
gpur
CEAN

INDIA AND PAKISTAN CAN AGREE ON ONE THING: NEITHER wants the other one around. This is somewhat problematic given that they share a 1,900-mile long border. Each country fairly bristles with antagonism and nuclear weapons, so how they manage this unwanted relationship is a matter of life and death on a scale of tens of millions.

India has a population of 1.3 billion people, while Pakistan's is about 200 million. Impoverished, volatile and splintering, Pakistan appears to define itself by its opposition to India, while India, despite obsessing about Pakistan, defines itself in many ways, including that of being an emerging world power with a growing economy and an expanding middle class. From this vantage point it looks across at Pakistan and sees how it outperforms it on almost all economic and democratic indicators.

They have fought four major wars and many skirmishes. Emotions run hot. An oft-quoted remark by a Pakistani officer that Pakistan would make India bleed by a thousand cuts was addressed in late 2014 by military analyst Dr Amarjit Singh writing in the *Indian Defence Review*: 'Whatever others may believe, my opinion is simply that it is better for India to brave a costly nuclear attack by Pakistan, and get it over with even at the cost of tens of millions of deaths, than suffer ignominy and pain day in and day out through a thousand cuts and wasted energy in unrealized potential.' That may not reflect official government policy, but it is an indication of the depth of feeling at many levels in both societies. Modern Pakistan and India were born in fire; next time the fire could kill them.

The two are tied together within the geography of the Indian subcontinent, which creates a natural frame. The Bay of Bengal, the Indian Ocean and the Arabian Sea are respectively to the south-east, south, and south-west, the Hindu Kush to the north-west, and the Himalayas to the north. Moving clockwise, the plateau of the Baluchistan Desert climbs steadily before becoming the mountains of the North West Frontier, which rise even higher to become the Hindu Kush. A right turn east connects to the Karakoram Range, which then leads to the Himalayas. They sweep right along the border with China all the way to Myanmar. From there, as India curves around Bangladesh, the terrain descends south to the Bay of Bengal.

The interior of the frame contains what are modern-day India, Pakistan, Bangladesh, Nepal and Bhutan. The latter two are impoverished landlocked nations dominated by their giant neighbours, China and India. Bangladesh's problem is not that it lacks access to the sea, but that the sea has too much access to Bangladesh: flooding from the waters of the Bay of Bengal constantly afflicts the low-lying territory. Its other geographical problem is that it is almost entirely surrounded by India, because the 2,545-mile long frontier, agreed in 1974, wrapped India around Bangladesh, leaving it only a short border with Myanmar as an alternative land route to the outside world.

Bangladesh is volatile, and contains Islamist militants which trouble India; but none of these three smaller countries within the subcontinent can ever rise to threaten its undisputed master. Nor would Pakistan be considered a threat to India had it not mastered the technology of developing nuclear weapons in the decades following the partition of the region in 1947.

The area within our frame, despite being relatively flat, has always been too large and diverse to have strong central rule. Even the British colonial overlords, with their famed bureaucracy and connecting rail system, allowed regional autonomy and indeed used it to play local leaders off against each other. The linguistic and cultural diversity is partially due to the differences in climate – for example, the freezing north of the Himalayas in contrast to the jungles of the south – but it is also because of the subcontinent's rivers and religions.

Various civilisations have grown up along these rivers, such as the Ganges, the Brahmaputra and the Indus. To this day the population centres are dotted along their banks, and the regions, so different from each other – for example the Punjab, with its Sikh majority, and the Tamil speakers of Tamil Nadu – are based on these geographical divides.

Different powers have invaded the subcontinent over the centuries, but none have ever truly conquered it. Even now New Delhi does not truly control India and, as we shall see, to an even greater extent Islamabad does not control Pakistan. The Muslims had the greatest success in uniting the subcontinent under one leadership, but even Islam never overcame the linguistic, religious and cultural differences.

The first Muslim invasion was as early as the eighth century CE, when the Arabs of the Umayyad Caliphate made it as far as the Punjab in what is now Pakistan. From then until the eighteenth century various foreign invasions brought Islam to the subcontinent; however, east of the Indus River Valley a majority of the Hindu population resisted conversion, thus sowing the seeds for the eventual partition of India.

The British came, and went, and when they went the centre could not hold, and things fell apart. In truth, there was no real centre: the region has always been divided by the ancient disparities of the languages of the Punjab and Gujarat, the mountains and the deserts, and Islam and Hinduism. By 1947 the forces of post-colonial nationalism and religious separatism broke the subcontinent into two, and later three, major pieces: India, Pakistan and Bangladesh. The British, exhausted by two world wars, and aware that the days of empire were coming to a close, did not cover themselves in glory in the manner of their leaving.

On 3 June 1947 the announcement was made in the House of Commons: the British would withdraw – India was to be partitioned into the two independent dominions of India and Pakistan. Seventy-three days later, on 15 August, they were all but gone.

An extraordinary movement of people followed as millions of Muslims fled the new borders of India, heading west to Pakistan, with millions of Hindus and Sikhs coming the other way. Columns of people 30,000-strong were on the roads as whole communities moved. Trains packed full of refugees criss-crossed the subcontinent disgorging people into cities and making the return journey filled with those heading in the other direction.

It was carnage. Riots broke out across both countries as Muslims, Hindus, Sikhs and others turned on each other in panic and fear. The British government washed its hands and refused pleas from the new Indian and Pakistani leaders for the few troops still in the country to help maintain order. Estimates of the death toll vary, but at least a million people died and 15 million were displaced. The Muslim-majority areas in the west – the Indus Valley region west of the Thar Desert and the Ganges River basin – became West Pakistan while those to the east of Calcutta (now Kolkata) became East Pakistan.

What did Pakistan get out of this? Much less than India. It inherited India's most troublesome border, the North West Frontier with Afghanistan, and it was a state split into two non-contiguous regions with little to hold it together as 1,000 miles of Indian territory separated West Pakistan from East Pakistan. Alaska and the rest of the USA have managed the problem of non-contiguous distance without difficulty, but they are culturally, linguistically and economically linked and operating in a stable environment. The only connection between the two parts of Pakistan was Islam. They never really came together, so it was no surprise when they were torn apart; in 1971 East Pakistan rebelled against the dominance of West Pakistan, India intervened and, after much bloodshed, East Pakistan seceded, becoming Bangladesh.

However, back in 1947, twenty-five years after the end of the Ottoman Empire, Jinnah and the other leaders of the new Pakistan, amid much fanfare and promises of a bright future, claimed they had created a united Muslim homeland.

Pakistan is geographically, economically, demographically and militarily weaker than India. Its national identity is also not as strong. India, despite its size, cultural diversity, and secessionist movements, has built a solid secular democracy with a unified sense of Indian identity. Pakistan is an Islamic state with a history of dictatorship and populations whose loyalty is often more to their cultural region than to the state.

Secular democracy has served India well, but the 1947 division did give it a head start. Within the new borders of India was the vast majority of the subcontinent's industry, most of the taxable income base and the majority of the major cities. For example Calcutta, with its port and banking sector, went to India, thus depriving East Pakistan of this major income provider and connection to the outside world.

Pakistan received just 17 per cent of the financial reserves which had been controlled by the pre-partition government.

It was left with an agricultural base, no money to spend on development, a volatile western frontier and a state divided within itself in multiple ways.

The name Pakistan gives us clues about these divisions; *pak* means 'pure' and *stan* means 'land' in Urdu, so it is the land of the pure, but it is also an acronym. The P is for Punjab, A is for Afghania (the Pashtun area by the Afghan border), K for Kashmir, S for Sindh and T stands for 'tan', as in Baluchistan.

From these five distinct regions, each with their own language, one state was formed, but not a nation. Pakistan tries hard to create a sense of unity, but it remains rare for a

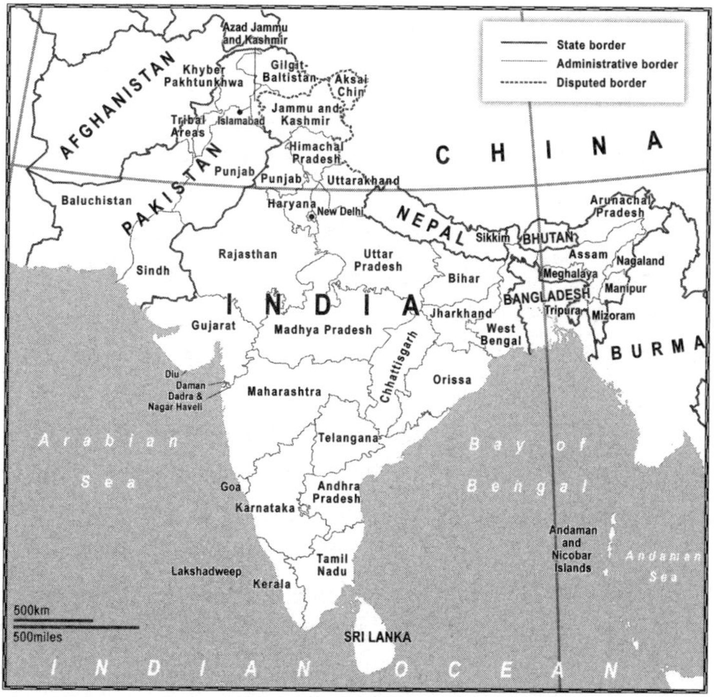

The regions that make up India and Pakistan – many have their own distinct identities and languages.

Punjabi to marry a Baluchi, or a Sindh to marry a Pashtun. The Punjabis comprise 60 per cent of the population, the Sindhs 14 per cent, Pashtuns 13.5 per cent and Baluchis 4.5 per cent. Religious tensions are ever present – not only in the antagonism sometimes shown to the country's Christian and Hindu minorities, but also between the majority Sunni and the minority Shia Muslims. In Pakistan there are several nations within one state.

The official language is Urdu, which is the mother tongue of the Muslims of India who fled in 1947, most of who settled in the Punjab. This does not endear the language to the rest of the country. The Sindh region has long chafed at what it feels to be Punjabi dominance and many Sindhs think they are treated as second-class citizens. The Pashtuns of the North West Frontier have never accepted the rule of outsiders: parts of the frontier region are named the Federally Administered Tribal Areas, but in reality they have never been administered from Islamabad. Kashmir remains divided between Pakistan and India, and although a majority of Kashmiris want independence, the one thing India and Pakistan can agree on is that they cannot have it. Baluchistan also has an independence movement which periodically rises up against the state.

Baluchistan is of crucial importance: while it may only contain a small minority of Pakistan's population, without it there is no Pakistan. It comprises almost 45 per cent of the country and holds much of its natural gas and mineral wealth. Another source of income beckons with the proposed overland routes to bring Iranian and Caspian Sea oil up through Pakistan to China. The jewel in this particular crown is the coastal city of Gwadar. Many analysts believe this strategic asset was the Soviet Union's long-term target when it invaded

Afghanistan in 1979: Gwadar would have fulfilled Moscow's long-held dream of a warm-water port. The Chinese have also been attracted by this jewel and invested billions of dollars in the region. A deep-water port was inaugurated in 2007 and the two countries are now working to link it to China. In the long run, China would like to use Pakistan as a land route for its energy needs. This would allow it to bypass the Strait of Malacca, which as we saw in the chapter on China is a choke point that could strangle Chinese economic growth.

In the spring of 2015, the two countries agreed a $46 billion deal to build a superhighway of roads, railways and pipelines running 1,800 miles from Gwadar to China's Xinjiang region. The China–Pakistan Economic Corridor, as it is called, will give China direct access to the Indian Ocean and beyond. In late 2015, China also signed a forty-year lease on 2,300 acres of land in the port area, to develop a massive 'special economic zone' and an international airport, all as part of the China–Pakistan Economic Corridor. Because both sides know that Baluchistan is likely to remain volatile, a security force of up to 25,000 men is being formed to protect the zone.

Massive Chinese investment in building a land route such as this would make Pakistan very happy, and this is one of the reasons Pakistan will always seek to crush any secessionist movements that arise in the province. However, until more of the wealth Baluchistan creates is returned home and used for its own development, the area is destined to remain restive and occasionally violent.

Islam, cricket, the intelligence services, the military and fear of India are what hold Pakistan together. None of these will be enough to prevent it from being pulled apart if the forces of separatism grow stronger. In effect Pakistan has been in a state of civil war for more than a decade, following periodic and ill-judged wars with its giant neighbour India.

The first was in 1947, shortly after partition, and was fought over Kashmir, which in 1948 ended up divided along the Line of Control (also known as Asia's Berlin Wall); however, both India and Pakistan continue to claim sovereignty.

Nearly twenty years later Pakistan miscalculated the strength of the Indian military because of India's poor performance in the 1962 India–China war. Tensions between India and China had risen due to the Chinese invasion of Tibet, which in turn had led India to give refuge to the Dalai Lama. During this brief conflict the Chinese military showed their superiority and pushed forward almost into the state of Assam near the Indian heartland. The Pakistan military watched with glee then, overestimating their own prowess, went to war with India in 1965 and lost.

In 1984 Pakistan and India fought skirmishes at an altitude of 22,000 feet on the Siachen Glacier, thought to be the highest battle in history. More fighting broke out in 1985, 1987 and 1995. Pakistan continued to train militants to infiltrate across the Line of Control and another battle broke out over Kashmir in 1999. By then both countries were armed with nuclear weapons, and for several weeks the unspoken threat of an escalation to nuclear war hovered over the conflict before American diplomacy kicked in and the two sides were talked down. They came close to war again in 2001, and gunfire still breaks out sporadically along the border.

Militarily, India and Pakistan are pitted against each other. Both sides say their posture is defensive, but neither believes the other and so they continue to mass troops on the border, locked together in a potential dance of death.

The relationship between India and Pakistan will never be friendly, but were it not for the thorn of Kashmir in both sides it could potentially be cordial. As it is, India is content to see Pakistan divided within itself and will work to maintain that situation, and Pakistan will seek to undermine India, with elements within the state even supporting terror attacks inside India, such as the Mumbai massacre of 2008.

The Kashmir issue is partially one of national pride, but it is also strategic. Full control of Kashmir would give India a window into Central Asia and a border with Afghanistan. It would also deny Pakistan a border with China and thus diminish the usefulness of a Chinese–Pakistani relationship. The Pakistani government likes to trumpet that its friendship with China is 'taller than the mountains and deeper than the oceans'. This is not true, but it is useful in sometimes making the Americans nervous about cutting Pakistan off from the massive financial aid it receives from Washington.

If Pakistan had full control of Kashmir it would strengthen Islamabad's foreign policy options and deny India opportunities. It would also help Pakistan's water security. The Indus River originates in Himalayan Tibet but passes through the Indian-controlled part of Kashmir before entering Pakistan and then running the length of the country and emptying into the Arabian Sea at Karachi.

The Indus and its tributaries provide water to two-thirds of the country: without it the cotton industry and many other mainstays of Pakistan's struggling economy would collapse. By a treaty that has been honoured through all of their wars, India and Pakistan agreed to share the waters; but both populations are growing at an alarming rate, and global warming could diminish the water flow. Annexing all of Kashmir would secure

Pakistan's water supply. Given the stakes, neither side will let go; and until they agree on Kashmir the key to unlocking the hostility between them cannot be found. Kashmir looks destined to remain a place where a sporadic proxy war between Pakistani-trained fighters and the Indian army is conducted – a conflict which threatens to spill over into full-scale war with the inherent danger of the use of nuclear weapons. Both countries will also continue to fight another proxy war – in Afghanistan – especially now that most NATO forces have left.

Pakistan lacks internal 'strategic depth' – somewhere to fall back to in the event of being overrun from the east – from India. The Pakistan/Indian border includes swampland in the south, the Thar Desert and the mountains of the north; all are extremely difficult territory for an army to cross. It can be done and both sides have battle plans of how to fight there. The Indian Army plan involves blockading the port of Karachi and its fuel storage depots by land and sea, but an easier invasion route is between the south and the north – it lies in the centre, in the more hospitable Punjab, and in the Punjab is Pakistan's capital – Islamabad.

The distance from the Indian border to Islamabad is less than 250 miles, most of it flat ground. In the event of a massive, overwhelming, conventional attack the Indian army could be in the capital within a few days. That they profess no desire to do so is not the point: from Pakistan's point of view they might, and the geographical possibility is enough for Pakistan to require a Plan A and a Plan B to counter the risk.

Plan A is to halt an Indian advance in the Punjab and possibly counter-attack across the border and cut the Indian Highway 1A, which is a vital supply route for the Indian military. The Indian Army is more than 1 million strong, twice the size of Pakistan's, but if it can't be supplied, it can't fight. Plan B is to fall back across the Afghan border if required, and that requires a sympathetic government in Kabul. Hence geography has dictated that Pakistan will involve itself in Afghanistan, as will India.

To thwart each other, each side seeks to mould the government of Afghanistan to its liking – or, to put it another way, each side wants Kabul to be an enemy of its enemy.

When the Soviets invaded Afghanistan in 1979 India gave diplomatic support to Moscow, but Pakistan was quick to help the Americans and Saudis to arm, train and pay for the Mujahedeen to fight the Red Army. Once the Soviets were beaten Pakistan's intelligence service, the ISI, helped to create, and then back, the Afghan Taliban, which duly took over the country.

Pakistan had a natural 'in' with the Afghan Taliban. Most are Pashtun, the same ethnicity as the majority of the Pakistanis of the North West Frontier (now known as Khyber Pakhtunkhwa). They have never thought of themselves as two peoples and consider the border between them as a Western invention, which in some ways it is.

The Afghan–Pakistani border is known as the Durand Line. Sir Mortimer Durand, the Foreign Secretary of the colonial government of India, drew it in 1893 and the then ruler of Afghanistan agreed to it. However, in 1949 the Afghan government 'annulled' the agreement, believing it to be an artificial relic of the colonial era. Since then Pakistan has tried to persuade Afghanistan to change its mind, Afghanistan refuses, and the Pashtuns each side of the mountains try to carry on as they have for centuries by ignoring the border and maintaining their ancient connections.

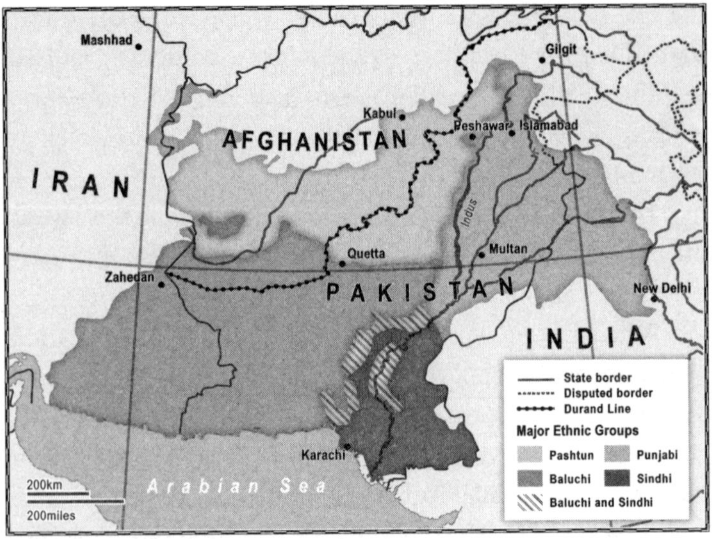

The main ethnic groups in the Afghan–Pakistani area did not fit into the border that was imposed in 1893 by the Durand Line; many of these groups continue to identify more with their tribes beyond the borders than with the rest of the nation.

Central to this area, sometimes called Pashtunistan, is the Pakistani city of Peshawar, a sort of urban Taliban military-industrial complex. Knock-off Kalashnikovs, bomb-making technology and fighters flow out from the city, and support from within sections of the state flows in.

It is also a staging post for ISI officers en route to Afghanistan with funds and instructions for the Talibanesque groups across the border. Pakistan has been involved militarily in Afghanistan for decades now, but it has overreached itself, and the tiger it was riding has bitten it.

In 2001 the Pakistani-created Taliban had been hosting the foreign fighters of Al Qaeda for several years. Then, on 9/11, Al Qaeda struck the USA on its home soil in an operation put together in Afghanistan. In response US military power ran the Taliban and Al Qaeda out of town. Afghan Northern Alliance anti-Taliban forces moved down to take over the country and a NATO stabilisation force followed.

Across the border on the day after 9/11, the Americans had begun breathing diplomatic fire on the Pakistanis, demanding their participation in the 'War on Terror' and an end to their support for terrorism. The then Secretary of State, Colin Powell, had phoned President Musharraf and demanded he come out of a meeting to take the call, in which he told him: 'You are either with us or against us.'

It has never been confirmed by the American side, but Musharraf has written that the call was followed up by Powell's deputy Richard Armitage ringing the head of the ISI and telling him 'that if we chose the terrorists, then we should be prepared to be bombed back to the Stone Age'. Pakistan co-operated, and that was that. Except – they hadn't fully co-operated, and that wasn't that.

Islamabad was forced to act, and did; but not everyone in the Pakistani system was on board. The government banned several militant groups and tried to rein in religious groups it deemed extremist. By 2004 it was involved militarily against groups in the North West Frontier and privately accepted the American policy of drone strikes on its territory whilst publically decrying them.

These were tough decisions. The Pakistan military and ISI had to turn on the very Taliban leaders they had trained and formed friendships with in the 1990s. The Taliban groups reacted with fury, seizing complete control of several regions in the tribal areas. Musharraf was the target of three failed assassination attempts, his would-be successor Benazir Bhutto was murdered, and amid the chaos of bombing campaigns and military offensives up to 50,000 Pakistani civilians have been killed.

The American/NATO operation in Afghanistan, and the Pakistani measures across the border, had helped scatter the Arab, Chechen and other foreign fighters of Al Qaeda to the corners of the earth, where their leadership was hunted down and killed; but the Taliban had nowhere to go – they were Afghans and Pakistanis – and, as they told these new technologically advanced foreign invaders from America and Europe, 'You may have the watches – but we have the time.' They would wait out the foreigners no matter what was thrown at them, and in this they would be helped by elements in Pakistan.

Within a couple of years it became clear: the Taliban had not been defeated, they had melted into where they came from, the Pashtun population, and were now emerging again at times and places of their choosing.

The Americans came up with a 'hammer and anvil' strategy. They would hammer the Afghan Taliban against the anvil of the Pakistani operation on the other side of the border. The 'anvil' in the tribal areas turned out instead to be a sponge that soaked up whatever was thrown at it, including any Afghan Taliban retreating from the American hammer.

In 2006 the British decided they would stabilise Helmand Province in the south, where the Afghan government's remit did not run far outside of the provincial capital, Lashkar Gah. This was Afghan Pashtun heartland territory. The British went in with good intentions, they knew their history, but it seems they just ignored it – the reason why remains a mystery. The then British Defence Secretary John Reid is wrongly quoted, and blamed, for having said that summer that he 'hoped not a shot will be fired in anger'. In fact he said, 'We're in the south to help and protect the Afghan people to reconstruct their economy and democracy. We would be perfectly happy to leave in three years' time without firing one shot.'

That may have been a fine aspiration, but was it ever feasible? That summer, after he gave a briefing at the Foreign Office in London, I had an exchange with the Defence Secretary, as follows:

> 'Don't worry, Tim. We're not going after the Taliban, we're there to protect people.'
> 'Don't worry, Secretary of State, the Taliban are going to come after you.'

It was an amicable exchange, conducted before more than 450 British soldiers had been killed, but to this day I don't know if the British government was softening up public opinion ahead of the deployment of troops whilst privately predicting it would be tough going, or whether it was being inexplicably naive about what lay ahead.

So the Taliban bled the British, bled the Americans, bled NATO, waited NATO out, and after thirteen years most of NATO went away. By 2019 there were only 14,000 US troops left in the country, along with about 8,500 European and other foreign troops, most of whom were no longer on the offensive. This was down from a peak of 130,000 in 2011. With President Trump keen to end US involvement in its 'longest war', negotiations began with the Taliban over a plan to withdraw all foreign forces within five years of an agreement that would leave the government in Kabul sharing power with the Taliban.

During the whole period leading up to this, members of the highest levels of Pakistan's establishment were playing a double game. America might have its strategy, but Pakistan knew what the Taliban knew: that one day the Americans would go away, and when they left, Pakistan's foreign policy would still require a Pakistan-friendly government in Afghanistan. Factions within the Pakistan military and government had continued to give help to the Taliban, gambling that after NATO's retreat the southern half of Afghanistan at the very least would revert to Taliban dominance, thus ensuring that Kabul would need to talk to Islamabad.

In 2011, Pakistan's perfidy had been laid bare when the Americans eventually found Al Qaeda's leader, Osama bin Laden, hiding in plain sight of the government in Abbottabad, a military garrison town. By that point, such was the Americans' lack of trust in their Pakistani 'allies' that they failed to tell Islamabad in advance about the Special Forces team which flew in to kill bin Laden. This was a breach of sovereignty that humiliated the military and government of Pakistan, as did the argument which went: 'If you didn't know he was there you were incompetent; if you did you were complicit.'

The Pakistani government had always denied playing the double game that resulted in the deaths of huge numbers of Afghans and Pakistanis, as well as relatively small numbers of Americans. After the Abbottabad mission Islamabad continued the denials, but now there were fewer people who believed them. If elements of the Pakistani establishment were prepared to give succour to America's most wanted man, even though he was by then of limited value to them, it was obvious they would support groups which furthered their ambitions to influence events in Afghanistan. The problem was that those groups now had their counterparts in Pakistan and they wanted to influence events there. The biter was bitten.

The Pakistani Taliban is a natural outgrowth of the Afghan version. Both are predominantly Pashtun and neither will accept domination from any non-Pashtun power, be it the British army of the nineteenth century or the Punjabi-dominated Pakistani army of the twenty-first century.

This was always understood and accepted by Islamabad. The Pakistani government pretended it ruled the entire country, and the Pashtun of the North West Frontier pretended they were loyal to the Pakistani state. This relationship worked until 11 September 2001.

The years since then have been exceptionally hard on Pakistan. The civilian death toll is enormous and foreign investment has dwindled away, making ordinary life even harder. The army, forced to go up against what was a de facto ally, has lost up to 5,000 men and the civil war has endangered the fragile unity of the state.

Things became so bad that the Pakistani military and government ended up having to give the US military intelligence and co-ordinates allowing them to conduct drone strikes against Pakistani Taliban targets in the North West Frontier. At the same time, when the strikes became apparent, Islamabad had to pretend to condemn them and describe them as a violation of Pakistani sovereignty due to the hundreds of civilian deaths attributed to mistakes by the US.

The drones were mostly flown out of a base in Afghanistan but some are thought to have been launched from a secret base inside Pakistan. Wherever they came from, there were a lot of them. Drone strikes in Afghanistan and Pakistan massively increased during the Obama Presidency from the numbers fired during George Bush's tenure.

By the spring of 2015 things had become even tougher. NATO had left Afghanistan and the Americans had announced an end to combat missions, leaving behind only a residual force. Officially this was to conduct Special Forces operations and training missions; unofficially it is to try to ensure that Kabul does not fall to the Taliban. Without NATO harrying the Taliban on the Afghan side of the border, Pakistan's job of beating the Pakistani Taliban became even harder. Washington continued to press Islamabad to go in hard. In a sense, the Pakistan military was also waiting out the Americans. It was losing personnel in a battle it knew it was unlikely to win. No foreign force has ever really defeated the tribes of the North West Frontier, and a Pakistani army containing Punjabis, Sindhis, Baluchis and Kashmiris (and some Pashtun) is considered a foreign force by many in the tribal areas.

As the US obsession with the 'war on terror' has diminished, the pressure on Islamabad to root out the Taliban in the North West Frontier has decreased. The Americans have limited interest in Afghanistan so long as the Taliban quietly promise not to host an international jihadist group again. The Pakistanis will maintain enough links with the Afghan Talibs to ensure that governments in Kabul will listen to Islamabad and not cosy up to India, and once the pressure is off they can do a deal with the Pakistani Taliban.

None of this would have been necessary if the Afghan Taliban, in part created by the Pakistani ISI, had not been stupid enough to host the Arabs of bin Laden's Al Qaeda and then after 9/11 had not fallen back upon the Pashtun culture of honouring guests, thus refusing to give them up when the

Americans came calling. In the event, after a decade and half of fighting, the situation remains so bad that the US government has had to reverse policy and keep thousands more troops than it had planned in Afghanistan. Despite wanting to get out of the country, they cannot completely abandon it. Not only would the Taliban take over even more of Afghanistan than they already control, but now IS is gaining a foothold there. In the event of the capital falling, the USA would no longer be able to pretend that the blood and treasure they have expended was a price worth paying. The potential of this massive propaganda defeat is what keeps them involved in their longest war, and why the Trump administration struggled to create a coherent policy upon taking office.

As for India, it can multi-task – indeed it has to, given that it has more to think about than only Pakistan, even if it is the number one foreign policy priority for New Delhi. Having a hostile nuclear-armed state next door is bound to focus the mind, but India also has to concentrate on managing 1.3 billion people whilst simultaneously emerging as a potential world power.

Its relationship with China would dominate its foreign policy, but for one thing – the Himalayas. Without the world's tallest mountain range between them, what is a lukewarm relationship would probably be frosty. A glance at the map indicates two huge countries cheek by jowl, but a closer look shows they are walled off from one another along what the CIA *World Factbook* lists as 1,652 miles of border.

There are issues which cause friction, chief among them Tibet, the highest region on earth. As previously discussed, China wanted Tibet, both to prevent India from having it, and – almost as bad in Beijing's view – to prevent an independent

Tibet allowing India to base military forces there, thus giving them the commanding heights.

India's response to the Chinese annexation of Tibet was to give a home to the Dalai Lama and the Tibetan independence movement in Dharamshala in the state of Himachal Pradesh. This is a long-term insurance policy, paid for by India but without the expectation that it will ever be cashed in. As things stand Tibetan independence looks impossible; but if the impossible were to occur, even in several decades' time, India would be in a position to remind a Tibetan government who their friends were during the years of exile.

The Chinese understand that this scenario is extremely unlikely, but remain irritated by Dharamshala. Their response is seen in Nepal, where Beijing ensures it has influence with the Maoist movement there.

India does not want to see a Maoist-dominated Nepal ultimately controlled by China, but knows that Beijing's money and trade is buying influence there. China may care little for Maoism these days, but it cares enough about Tibet to signal to India that it too can afford the payments on a long-term insurance policy. Any 'interference' in Tibet can be met with 'interference' in Nepal. The more India has to concentrate on the smaller states in its neighbourhood, the less it can concentrate on China.

In mid 2017 both were concentrating on the smaller state of Bhutan with which each has a border, leading to a minor confrontation over Bhutan's Doklam plateau. China claims part of the area and had begun constructing a highway there, but Indian troops soon showed up to block it. In the event of China controlling the tri-border area it would overlook Indian military positions, but more importantly would allow China to bring heavy armour closer to India, in particular the Siliguri Corridor, also known as Chicken's Neck: the thin stretch of land connecting India's north-eastern states to the rest of the country, which could be easily cut off.

There were further tensions in 2019: satellite imagery suggested that China was increasing its construction activity. A paved road had been lengthened and several 'semi-permanent' buildings were seen, among them what was thought to be hangars for helicopters. There is frequent dialogue between New Delhi and Beijing over the plateau, but the mutual suspicion between the two is likely to continue and the area remains a potential flashpoint.

Another related issue between the two giants is the north-eastern Indian state of Arunachal Pradesh, which China claims as 'South Tibet'. As China's confidence grows, so does the amount of territory there it says is Chinese. Until recently China only claimed the Tawang area in the extreme west of the state. However, in the early 2000s Beijing decided that all of Arunachal Pradesh was Chinese, which was news to the Indians who have exercised sovereignty over it since 1955. The Chinese claim is partly geographical and partly psychological. Arunachal Pradesh borders China, Bhutan and Myanmar, making it strategically useful, but the issue is also valuable to China as a reminder to Tibet that independence is a non-starter.

That is a message India also has to send periodically to several of its own regions. There are numerous separatist movements, some more active than others, some dormant, but none that look set to achieve their aims. For example, the Sikh movement to create a state for Sikhs out of part of both Indian and Pakistani Punjab has for the moment gone quiet, but could flare up again. The state of Assam has several competing movements, including the Bodo-speaking peoples, who want a state for themselves, and the Muslim United Liberation Tigers of Assam, who want a separate country created within Assam for Muslims.

There is even a movement to create an independent Christian state in Nagaland, where 75 per cent of the population are Baptist; however, the prospect of the Nagaland National Council achieving its aims is as remote as the land it seeks to control, and that looks to be true of all of the separatist movements.

Despite these, and other, groups seeking independence, a Sikh population of 21 million people and a Muslim minority of perhaps 172 million, India retains a strong sense of itself and unity within diversity. This will help as it emerges further onto the world stage.

The world has so marvelled at China's stunning rise to power that its neighbour is often overlooked, but India may yet rival China as an economic powerhouse this century. It is the world's seventh-largest country, with the second-largest population. It has borders with six countries (seven if you include Afghanistan). It has 9,000 miles of internal navigable waterways and a water supply flowing from the Himalayas. It also has huge areas of arable land, is a major coal producer and has useful quantities of oil and gas, even if it will always be an importer of all three, and its subsidisation of fuel and heating costs is a drain on its finances.

Despite its natural riches India has not matched China's growth, and because China is now moving out into the world, the two countries may bump up against each other – not along their land border, but at sea.

For thousands of years the regions of what are now modern-day China and India could ignore each other because of their terrain. Expansion into each other's territory through the Himalayas was impossible, and besides, each had more than enough arable land.

Now, though, the rise of technology means each requires vast amounts of energy; geography has not bequeathed them such riches, and so both countries have been forced to expand their horizons and venture out into the oceans, and it is there that they have encountered one another.

Twenty-five years ago India embarked on a 'look east' policy, partially as a block to what it could see would be the imminent rise of China. It has 'taken care of business' by dramatically increasing trade with China (mostly imports) while simultaneously forging strategic relationships in what China regards as its own backyard.

India has strengthened its ties with Myanmar, the Philippines, and Thailand, but more importantly it is working with Vietnam and Japan to check China's increasing domination of the South China Sea.

In this it has a new ally, albeit one it keeps at arm's length – the United States. For decades India was suspicious that the Americans were the new British, but with a different accent and more money. In the twenty-first century a more confident India, in an increasingly multipolar world, has found reason to co-operate with the USA. When President Obama attended the 2015 Indian Republic Day military parade, New Delhi took care to show off its shiny new US-supplied C-130 Hercules and C-17 Globemaster transport aircraft as well as its Russian-supplied tanks. The two giant democracies are slowly moving closer together as demonstrated by the massive bear hug Prime Minister Modi and President Trump gave each other upon their first meeting.

India has a large, well-equipped modern navy which includes an aircraft carrier, but it will not be able to compete with the massive Blue Water navy which China is planning. Instead India is aligning itself with other interested parties so they can together at least shadow, if not dominate, the Chinese navy as it sails the China seas, through the Strait of Malacca, past the Bay of Bengal and around the tip of India into the Arabian Sea towards the friendly port China has built at Gwadar in Pakistan.

With India, it always comes back to Pakistan, and with Pakistan, to India.

CHAPTER 8

KOREA AND JAPAN

'I . . . began to phrase a little pun about Kim Jong-il being the "Oh Dear Leader", but it died on my lips.'

Christopher Hitchens, *Love, Poverty and War: Journeys and Essays*

Kamchatka Peninsula
Sea of Okhotsk
Kuril Islands
Sakhalin
RUSSIA
HOKKAIDO
CHINA
Sea of Japan
Hamgyong Mountains
Yalu River
NORTH KOREA
Pyongyang
Imjin-gang
38th parallel
Demilitarised zone

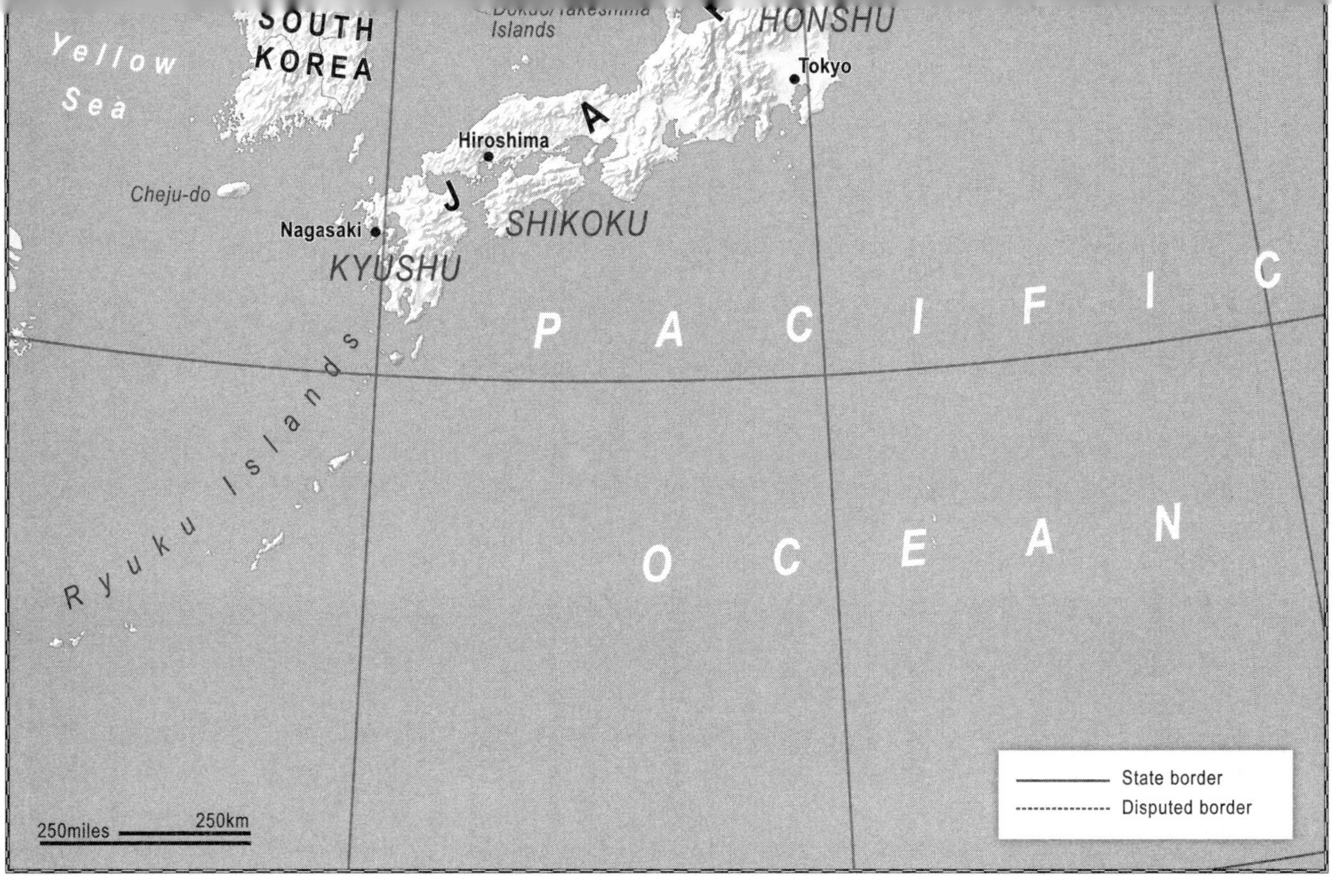

Yellow Sea
SOUTH KOREA
Islands
HONSHU
Tokyo
Hiroshima
Cheju-do
Nagasaki
SHIKOKU
KYUSHU
PACIFIC OCEAN
Ryuku Islands
250miles
250km
State border
Disputed border

HOW DO YOU SOLVE A PROBLEM LIKE KOREA? YOU DON'T, you just manage it – after all, there's a lot of other stuff going on around the world which needs immediate attention.

The whole of the region from Malaysia up to the Russian port of Vladivostok eyes the North/South Korea problem nervously. All the neighbours know it has the potential to blow up in their faces, dragging in other countries and damaging their economies. The Chinese don't want to fight on behalf of North Korea, but nor do they want a united Korea containing American bases close to their border. The Americans don't really want to fight for the South Koreans, but nor can they afford to be seen to be giving up on a friend. The Japanese, with their long history of involvement in the Korean Peninsula, must be seen to tread lightly, knowing that whatever happens will probably involve them.

The solution is compromise, but there is limited appetite for that in South Korea, and none at all displayed by the leadership of the North. The way forward is not at all clear; it seems as if it is always just out of sight over the horizon.

For several years the USA and Cuba danced quietly around each other, dropping hints that they would like to tango without tangling, leading to the breakthrough in re-establishing diplomatic relations in July 2015. North Korea, on the other hand, glares at any requests from would-be suitors to take the floor, occasionally pulling faces.

North Korea is a poverty-stricken country of an estimated 25 million people, led by a basket case of a morally corrupt, bankrupt Communist monarchy, and supported by China, partly out of a fear of millions of refugees flooding north across the Yalu River. The USA, anxious that a military withdrawal would send out the wrong signal and embolden North Korean adventurism, continues to station almost 30,000 troops in South Korea, and the South, with mixed feelings about risking its prosperity, continues to do little to advance reunification.

All the actors in this East Asian drama know that if they try to force an answer to the question at the wrong time, they risk making things worse. A lot worse. It is not unreasonable to fear that you would end up with two capital cities in smoking ruins, a civil war, a humanitarian catastrophe, missiles landing in and around Tokyo and another Chinese/American military face-off on a divided peninsula in which one side has nuclear weapons. If North Korea implodes, it might well also explode, projecting instability across the borders in the form of war, terrorism and/or a flood of refugees, and so the actors are stuck. And so the solution is left to the next generation of leaders, and then the next one.

If world leaders even speak openly about preparing for the day when North Korea collapses, they risk hastening that day; and as no one has planned for it – best keep quiet. Catch-22.

North Korea continues to play the crazed, powerful weakling to good effect. Its foreign policy consists, essentially, of being suspicious of everyone except the Chinese, and even Beijing is not to be fully trusted despite supplying 84.12 per cent of North Korea's imports and buying 84.48 per cent of its exports, according to 2014 figures by the Observatory of Economic Complexity. North Korea puts a lot of effort into playing all outsiders off against each other, including the Chinese, in order to block a united front against it.

To its captive population it says it is a strong, munificent, magnificent state standing up against all the odds and against the evil foreigners, calling itself the Democratic People's Republic of Korea (DPRK). It has a unique political philosophy of '*Juche*', which blends fierce nationalism with Communism and national self-reliance.

In reality, it is the least democratic state in the world: it is not run for the people and it is not a republic. It is a dynasty shared by one family and one party. It also ticks every box in the dictatorship test: arbitrary arrest, torture, show trials, internment camps, censorship, rule of fear, corruption and a litany of horrors on a scale without parallel in the twenty-first century. Satellite images and witness testimony suggest that at least 150,000 political prisoners are held in giant work and 're-education' camps. North Korea is a stain on the world's conscience, and yet few people know the full scale of the horrors taking place there.

News stories about purged members of the elite being executed with an anti-aircraft gun or fed to a pack of starving dogs have never been confirmed. However, true or not, there is little doubt about the litany of horrors perpetrated by the dictatorship upon the people. Total state control has resulted in beatings, torture, prison camps and extrajudicial murder.

Such is the self-imposed isolation of the country, and the state's almost total control of knowledge, that we can only guess at what the people may feel about their country, system and leaders and whether they support the regime. Analysing what is going on politically, and why, is akin to looking through an opaque window whilst wearing sunglasses. A former ambassador to Pyongyang once told me: 'It's like you are on one side of the glass, and you try to prise it open, but there's nothing to get a grip on to peer inside.'

The founding story of Korea is that it was created in 2333 BCE by heavenly design. The Lord of Heaven sent his son Hwanung down to earth, where he descended to the Paektu

(Baekdu) Mountain and married a woman who used to be a bear, and their son Dangun went on to engage in an early example of nation-building.

The earliest recorded version of this creation legend dates from the thirteenth century. It may in some ways explain why a Communist state has a leadership that is passed down through one family and given divine status. For example, Kim Jong-il was described by the Pyongyang propaganda machine as 'Dear Leader, who is a perfect incarnation of the appearance that a leader should have', 'Guiding Sun Ray', 'Shining Star of Paektu Mountain', 'World Leader of the twenty-first century' and 'Great Man who descended from heaven', as well as 'Eternal Bosom of Hot Love'. His father had very similar titles, as does his son.

How does the general population feel about such statements? Even the experts are left guessing. When you look at footage of the mass hysteria of North Koreans mourning Kim Jong-il, who died in 2011, it's interesting to note that after the first few rows of sobbing, shrieking people the level of grief appears to diminish. Is this because those at the front know the camera is on them and thus for their own safety they must do what is required? Or have the Party faithful been put at the front? Or are they ordinary people who are genuinely grief-stricken, a North Korean magnification of the sort of emotional outbursts we saw in the UK after the death of Princess Diana?

Nevertheless, the DPRK is still pulling off the crazy-dangerous, weak-dangerous act. It's quite a trick, and its roots lie partially in Korea's location and history, trapped as it is between the giants of China and Japan.

The name 'The Hermit Kingdom' was earned by Korea

in the eighteenth century after it attempted to isolate itself following centuries of being a target for domination, occupation and plunder, or occasionally simply a route on the way to somewhere else. If you come from the north, then once you are over the Yalu River there are few major natural defensive lines all the way down to the sea, and if you can land from the sea the reverse is true. The Mongols came and went, as did the Chinese Qing dynasty and the Japanese several times. So for a while the country preferred not to engage with the outside world, cutting many of its trade links in the hope that it would be left alone.

It was not successful. In the twentieth century the Japanese were back, annexing the whole country in 1910, and later set about destroying its culture. The Korean language was banned, as was the teaching of Korean history, and worship at Shinto shrines became compulsory. The decades of repression have left a legacy which even today impacts on relations between Japan and both the Korean states.

The defeat of Japan in 1945 left Korea divided along the 38th parallel. North of it was a Communist regime overseen first by the Soviets and later by Communist China, south of the line was a pro-American dictatorship called the Republic of Korea (ROK). This was the very beginning of the Cold War era when every inch of land was contested, with each side looking to establish influence or control around the world, unwilling to let the other maintain a sole presence.

The choice of the 38th parallel as the line of division was unfortunate in many ways and, according to the American historian Don Oberdorfer, arbitrary. He says that Washington was so focused on the Japanese surrender on 10 August 1945 that it had no real strategy for Korea. With Soviet troops on the move in the north of the peninsula and the White House convening an all-night emergency meeting, two junior officers, armed only with a *National Geographic* map, chose the 38th parallel as a place to suggest to the Soviets they halt, on the grounds that it was halfway down the country. One of those officers was Dean Rusk, who would go on to be Secretary of State during the Vietnam War.

No Koreans were present, nor any Korea experts. If they had been they could have told President Truman and his then Secretary of State James Francis Byrnes that the line was the same one as the Russians and Japanese had discussed for spheres of influence half a century earlier, following the Russo–Japanese War of 1904–5. Moscow, not knowing that the Americans were making up policy on the hoof, could be forgiven for thinking this was the USA's de facto recognition of that suggestion and therefore acceptance of division and a Communist north. The deal was done, the nation divided and the die cast.

The Soviets pulled their troops out of the north in 1948 and the Americans followed suit in the south in 1949. In June 1950, an emboldened North Korean military fatally underestimated America's Cold War geopolitical strategy and crossed the 38th parallel, intent on reuniting the peninsula under one Communist government. The Northern forces raced down the country almost to the tip of the southern coast, sounding the alarm bells in Washington.

The North Korean leadership, and its Chinese backers, had correctly worked out that, in a strictly military sense, Korea was not vital to the USA; but what they failed to understand was that the Americans knew that if they didn't stand up for their South Korean ally, their other allies around the world would lose confidence in them. If America's allies, at the height of the Cold War, began to hedge their bets or go over to the Communist side, then its entire global strategy would be in trouble. There are parallels here with the USA's policy in modern East Asia and Eastern Europe. Countries such as Poland, the Baltic States, Japan and the Philippines need to be confident that America has their back when it comes to their relations with Russia and China.

In September 1950 the USA, leading a United Nations force, surged into Korea, pushing the Northern troops back across the 38th parallel and then up almost to the Yalu River and the border with China.

Now it was Beijing's turn to make a decision. It was one thing to have US forces on the peninsula, quite another when they were north of the parallel – indeed north of the mountains above Hamhung – and within striking distance of China itself. Chinese troops poured across the Yalu and thirty-six months of fierce fighting ensued with massive casualties on all sides before they ground to a halt along the current border and agreed a truce, but not a treaty. There they were, stuck on the 38th parallel, and stuck they remain.

The geography of the peninsula is fairly uncomplicated and a reminder of how artificial the division is between North and South. The real (broad-brush) split is west to east. The west of the peninsula is much flatter than the east and is where the majority of people live. The east has the Hamgyong mountain range in the north and lower ranges in the south. The demilitarised zone (DMZ), which cuts the peninsula in half, in parts follows the path of the Imjin-gang River, but this was never a natural barrier between two entities, just a river within a unified geographical space all too frequently entered by foreigners.

The two Koreas are still technically at war, and given the hair-trigger tensions between them a major conflict is never more than a few artillery rounds away.

Japan, the USA and South Korea all worry about North Korea's nuclear weapons, but South Korea in particular has another threat hanging over it. North Korea's ability to successfully miniaturise its nuclear technology and create warheads that could be launched is uncertain, but it is definitely capable, as it already showed in 1950, of a surprise, first-strike, conventional attack.

South Korea's capital, the mega-city of Seoul, lies just 35 miles south of the 38th parallel and the DMZ. Almost half

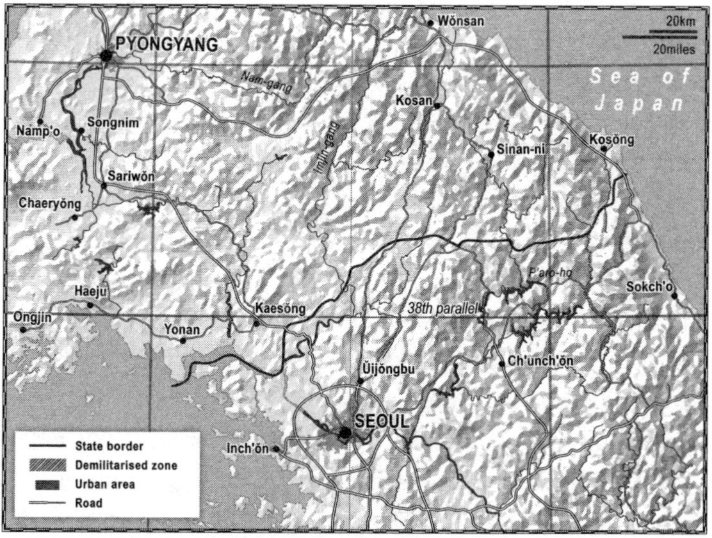

A major concern for South Korea is how close Seoul and the surrounding urban areas are to the border with North Korea. Seoul's position makes it vulnerable to surprise attacks from its neighbour, whose capital is much further away and partially protected by mountainous terrain.

of South Korea's 51 million people live in the greater Seoul region, which is home to much of its industry and financial centres, and it is all within range of North Korean artillery.

In the hills above the 148-mile-long DMZ the North Korean military has an estimated 10,000 artillery pieces. They are well dug in, some in fortified bunkers and caves. Not all of them could reach the centre of Seoul, but some could, and all are able to reach the greater Seoul region. There's little doubt that within two or three days the combined might of the South Korean and US air forces would have destroyed many of them, but by that time Seoul would be in flames. Imagine the effect of just one salvo of shells from 10,000 artillery weapons landing in urban and semi-urban areas, then multiply it dozens of times.

Two experts on North Korea, Victor Cha and David Chang, writing for *Foreign Policy* magazine, estimated that the DPRK forces could fire up to 500,000 rounds towards the city in the first hour of a conflict. That seems a very high estimate, but even if you divide it by five the results would still be devastating. The South Korean government would find itself fighting a major war whilst simultaneously trying to manage the chaos of millions of people fleeing south even as it tried to reinforce the border with troops stationed below the capital.

The hills above the DMZ are not high and there is a lot of flat ground between them and Seoul. In a surprise attack the North Korean army could push forward quite quickly, aided by Special Forces who would enter via underground tunnels which the South Koreans believe have already been built. North Korea's battle plans are thought to include submarines landing shock troops south of Seoul, and the activation of sleeper cells placed in the South's population. It is estimated to have 100,000 personnel it regards as Special Forces.

The North has also already proved it can reach Tokyo with ballistic missiles by firing several of them over the Sea of Japan and into the Pacific, a route which takes them directly over Japanese territory. Its armed forces are more than a million strong, one of the biggest armies in the world, and even if large numbers of them are not highly trained they would be useful to Pyongyang as cannon fodder while it sought to widen the conflict.

The Americans would be fighting alongside the South, the Chinese military would be on full alert and approaching the Yalu, and the Russians and Japanese would be looking on nervously.

These scenarios are – at the time of writing – what has restrained successive American presidents from taking sustained military action to cripple the North's nuclear programme. The 2017 test launches of intercontinental ballistic missiles by North Korea, its potential to miniaturise a nuclear weapon, and its continuing work on submarines all mean we are fast approaching the end game whereby either it becomes a fully fledged nuclear-armed power capable of launching long-range nuclear missiles, or the Americans step in to prevent it.

In the summer of 2018, President Trump brought about what his predecessors had not – a meeting with a North Korean leader, and for this he was widely criticised. Previous presidents had looked at the idea of such a meeting and thought twice, not wanting to 'honour' the dictatorship with a propaganda coup. Trump's opposite number Kim Jong-un bathed in the global limelight. The TV coverage back in North Korea was something to behold, showing the 'great leader' swanning about on equal terms with the US president, while hinting that in fact the stronger figure was Kim.

However, a case can be made that it was not a softer approach but Trump threatening 'fire and fury' that allowed the summit to happen – that and positioning some serious extra US firepower closer to the Korean peninsula. At the beginning of the year, the potential for a US attack was thought to be serious. The summit helped to build a bridge between the two nations, creating a possible route away from confrontation, and for a significant period of time tensions were greatly reduced, leading to a second meeting early in 2019. Even so, little progress was made there. Neither side trusts the other and things may still fall apart. If that happens, it will usher in another dangerous time because if Trump has already tried both sanctions and summit diplomacy without results, he might feel the military option is the only one left.

The situation keeps a lot of people awake at night. The USA's allies in the region fear the military option but also worry that Trump might wake up one morning and decide to pull US troops out of South Korea and even Japan. On the other side of the divide the Chinese don't want a nuclear-armed North Korea, but neither do they want the prospect of the USA going to war to prevent it and sending US troops back up towards the Yalu river on the China–North Korea border as they did in the 1950s. The world worries about the global impact on trade if such a conflict should break out. But the new president has tried something new – it will take some time before we have a clear picture of how successful the change in tactics might be.

It is not in anyone's interest for there to be another major war in Korea, as both sides would be devastated, but that has not prevented wars in the past. In 1950, when North Korea crossed the 38th parallel, it had not foreseen a three-year war with up to four million deaths, ending in stalemate. A full-scale conflict now might be even more catastrophic. The ROK's economy is eighty times stronger than the North's, its population is twice the size and the combined South Korean and US armed forces would almost certainly overwhelm North Korea eventually, assuming China did not decide to join in again.

And then what? There has been limited serious planning for such an eventuality. The South is thought to have done some computer modelling on what might be required, but it is generally accepted that the situation would be chaotic. The problems that would be created by Korea imploding or exploding would be multiplied if it happened as a result of warfare. Many countries would be affected and they would have decisions to make. Even if China did not want to intervene during the fighting, it might decide it had to cross the border and secure the North to retain the buffer zone between it and the US forces. It might decide that a unified Korea, allied to the USA, which is allied to Japan, would be too much of a potential threat to allow.

The USA would have to decide how far across the DMZ it would push and whether it should seek to secure all of North Korea's sites containing nuclear and other weapons of mass destruction material. China would have similar concerns, especially as some of the nuclear facilities are only 35 miles from its border.

On the political front Japan would have to decide if it wanted a powerful, united Korea across the Sea of Japan. Given the brittle relations between Tokyo and Seoul, Japan has reasons to be nervous about such a thing, but as it has far greater concerns about China it would be likely to come down on the side of supporting reunification, despite the probable scenario that it would be asked to assist financially due to its long occupation of the peninsula in the last century. Besides, it knows what Seoul knows: most of the economic costs of reunification will be borne by South Korea, and they will dwarf those of German reunification. East Germany may have been lagging far behind West Germany, but it had a history of development, an industrial base and an educated population. Developing the north of Korea would be building from ground zero and the costs would hold back the economy of a united peninsula for a decade. After that the benefits of the rich natural resources of the north, such as coal, zinc, copper, iron and rare earth elements, and the modernisation programme would be expected to kick in, but there are mixed feelings about risking the prosperity of one of the world's most advanced nations in the meantime.

Those decisions are for the future. For now each side continues to prepare for a war; as with Pakistan and India, they are locked in a mutual embrace of fear and suspicion.

South Korea is now a vibrant, integrated member of the nations of the world, with a foreign policy to match. With open water to its west, east and south, and with few natural resources, it has taken care to build a modern navy in the past three decades, one which is capable of getting out into the Sea of Japan and the East China Sea to safeguard the ROK's interests. Like Japan it is dependent on foreign sources for its energy needs, and so keeps a close eye on the sea lanes of the whole region. It has spent time hedging its bets, investing diplomatic capital in closer relations with Russia and China, much to Pyongyang's annoyance.

A miscalculation by either side could lead to a war which, as well as having devastating effects on the people of the peninsula, could wreck the economies of the region, with massive knock-on effects for the US economy. What started with the USA defending its Cold War stance against Russia has developed into an issue of strategic importance to its economy and that of several other countries.

South Korea still has issues with Tokyo relating back to the Japanese occupation, and even when it is at its best, which is rare, the relationship is only cordial. In early 2015 when the Americans, South Koreans and Japanese got down to the detail of an agreement to share military intelligence they had each gathered on North Korea, Seoul said it would pass only a limited amount of secret information to Tokyo via Washington. It will not deal directly with the Japanese.

The two countries still have a territorial dispute over what South Korea calls the Dokdo (solitary) Islands and the Japanese know as the Takeshima (bamboo) islands. The South Koreans currently control the rocky outcrops, which are in good fishing grounds, and there may be gas reserves in the region. Despite this thorn in their sides, and the still-fresh memories of occupation, both have reasons to co-operate and leave behind their troubled past.

Japan's history is very different to that of Korea, and the reason for this is partly due to its geography.

The Japanese are an island race, with the majority of the 127 million population living mostly on the four large islands that face Korea and Russia across the Sea of Japan, and a minority inhabiting some of the 6,848 smaller islands. The largest of the main islands is Honshu, which includes the biggest mega-city in the world, Tokyo, and its 39 million people.

At its closest point Japan is 120 miles from the Eurasian land mass, which is among the reasons why it has never been successfully invaded. The Chinese are some 500 miles away across the East China Sea; and although there is Russian territory much nearer, the Russian forces are usually far away because of the extremely inhospitable climate and sparse population located across the Sea of Okhotsk.

In the 1300s the Mongols tried to invade Japan after sweeping through China, Manchuria and down through Korea. On the first occasion they were beaten back and on the second a storm wrecked their fleet. The seas in the Korean Strait were whipped up by what the Japanese said was a 'Divine Wind' which they called a '*kamikaze*'.

So the threat from the west and north-west was limited, and to the south-east and east there was nothing but the Pacific. This last perspective is why the Japanese gave themselves the name 'Nippon' or 'sun origin': looking east there was nothing between them and the horizon, and each morning, rising on that horizon, was the sun. Apart from sporadic invasions of Korea they mostly kept themselves to themselves until the modern world arrived, and when it did, after first pushing it away, they went out to meet it.

Opinions differ about when the islands became Japan, but there is a famous letter sent from what we know as Japan to the Emperor of China in 617 CE in which a Japanese leading nobleman writes: 'Here I the emperor of the country where the sun rises send a letter to the emperor of the country where the sun sets. Are you healthy?' History records that the Chinese Emperor took a dim view of such perceived impertinence. His empire was vast, while the main Japanese islands were still only loosely united, a situation which would not change until approximately the sixteenth century.

The territory of the Japanese islands makes up a country

which is bigger than the two Koreas combined, or in European terms bigger than Germany. However, three-quarters of the land is not conducive to human habitation, especially in the mountainous regions, and only 13 per cent is suitable for intensive cultivation. This leaves the Japanese living in close proximity to each other along the coastal plains and in restricted inland areas, where some stepped rice fields can exist in the hills. Its mountains mean that Japan has plenty of water, but the lack of flatland also means that its rivers are unsuited to navigation and therefore trade, a problem exacerbated by the fact that few of the rivers join each other.

So the Japanese became a maritime people, connecting and trading along the coasts of their myriad islands, making forays into Korea, and then after centuries of isolation pushing out to dominate the whole region.

By the beginning of the twentieth century Japan was an industrial power with the third-largest navy in the world, and in 1905 it defeated the Russians in a war fought on land and at sea. However, the very same island-nation geography that had allowed it to remain isolated was now giving it no choice but to engage with the world. The problem was that it chose to engage militarily.

Both the First Sino-Japanese War and the Russo-Japanese War were fought to thwart Chinese and Russian influence in Korea. Japan considered Korea to be, in the words of its Prussian military advisor, Major Klemens Meckel, 'A dagger pointed at the heart of Japan'. Controlling the peninsula removed the threat, and controlling Manchuria made sure the hand of China, and to a lesser extent Russia, could not get near the dagger's handle. Korea's coal and iron ore would also come in handy.

Japan had few of the natural resources required to become an industrialised nation. It had limited and poor-quality supplies of coal, very little oil, scant quantities of natural gas, limited supplies of rubber and a shortage of many metals. This is as true now as it was 100 years ago, although offshore gas fields are being explored along with undersea deposits of precious metals. Nevertheless it remains the world's largest importer of natural gas, and third-largest importer of oil.

It was the thirst for these products that caused Japan to rampage across China in the 1930s and then South-East Asia in the early 1940s. It had already occupied Taiwan in 1895 and followed this up with the annexation of Korea in 1910. Japan occupied Manchuria in 1932, then conducted a full-scale invasion of China in 1937. As each domino fell, the expanding empire and the growing Japanese population required more oil, more coal, more metal, more rubber and more food.

With the European powers preoccupied with war in Europe, Japan went on to invade northern Indo-China. Eventually the Americans, who by then were supplying most of Japan's oil needs, gave them an ultimatum – withdrawal or an oil embargo. The Japanese responded with the attack on Pearl Harbor and then swept on across South-East Asia, taking Myanmar, Singapore and the Philippines, among other territories.

This was a massive overstretch, not just taking on the USA, but grabbing the very resources, rubber for example, which the USA required for its own industry. The giant of the twentieth century mobilised for total war. Japan's geography then played a role in its greatest catastrophe – Hiroshima and Nagasaki.

The Americans had fought their way across the Pacific,

island to island, at great cost. By the time they took Okinawa, which sits in the Ryukyu Island chain between Taiwan and Japan, they were faced with a still-fanatical enemy prepared to defend the approaches and four main islands from amphibious invasion. Massive US losses were predicted. If the terrain had been easier the American choice may have been different – they might have fought their way to Tokyo – but they chose the nuclear option, unleashing upon Japan, and the collective conscience of the world, the terror of a new age.

After the radioactive dust had settled on a complete Japanese surrender, the Americans helped them rebuild, partially as a hedge against Communist China. The new Japan showed its old inventiveness and within three decades became a global economic powerhouse.

However, its previous belligerence and militarism were not entirely gone: they had just been buried beneath the rubble of Hiroshima and Nagasaki and a shattered national psyche. Japan's post-war constitution did not allow for it to have an army, air force or navy, only 'Self-Defence Forces' which for decades were a pale shadow of the pre-war military. The post-war agreement imposed by the USA limited Japan's defence spend to 1 per cent of GDP and left tens of thousands of American forces on Japanese territory, 32,000 of whom are still there.

But by the early 1980s the faint stirrings of nationalism could again be detected. There were sections of the older generation who had never accepted the enormity of Japan's war crimes, and sections of the younger who were not prepared to accept guilt for the sins of their fathers. Many of the children of the Land of the Rising Sun wanted their 'natural' place under the sun of the post-war world.

A flexible view of the constitution became the norm, and slowly the Japanese Self-Defence Forces were turned into a modern fighting unit. This happened as the rise of China was becoming increasingly apparent and so the Americans, realising they were going to need military allies in the Pacific region, were prepared to accept a re-militarised Japan.

In the present century Japan has altered its defence policy to allow its forces to fight alongside allies abroad, and changes to the constitution are expected to follow to put this on a more solid legal footing. Its 2013 Security Strategy document was the first in which it named a potential enemy, saying: 'China has taken actions that can be regarded as attempts to change the status quo by coercion.'

The 2015 defence budget was a record US$42 billion, and it increased again the following year to US$44 billion. Most of this was for naval and air equipment, including six new submarines and six US-made F-35A stealth fighters. In the spring of 2015 Tokyo also unveiled what it called a 'helicopter-carrying destroyer'. It didn't take a military expert to notice that the vessel was as big as the Japanese aircraft carriers of the Second World War, which are forbidden by the surrender terms of 1945. The ship can be adapted for fixed-wing aircraft but the defence minister issued a statement saying that he was 'not thinking of using it as an aircraft carrier'. This is akin to buying a motorbike then saying that because you were not going to use it as a motorbike, it is a pushbike. The Japanese now have an aircraft carrier.

The money spent on that and other shiny new kit is a clear statement of intent, as is much of its positioning. The military infrastructure at Okinawa, which guards the approaches to the main islands, will be upgraded. This will also allow Japan greater flexibility to patrol its Air Defence Zone, part of which overlaps with China's equivalent zone after an expansion was announced by Beijing in 2013.

Both zones cover the islands called the Senkaku or Diaoyu (in Japanese and Chinese respectively), which Japan controls but which are claimed by China too. They also form part of the Ryukyu Island chain, which is particularly sensitive as any hostile power must pass the islands on the way to the Japanese heartlands; they give Japan a lot of territorial sea space and they might contain exploitable underwater gas and oil fields. Thus Tokyo intends to hold on to them by all means necessary.

China's expanded 'Air Defence Identification Zone' in the East China Sea covers territory claimed by China, Japan, Taiwan and South Korea. When Beijing said that any plane flying through the zone must identity itself or 'face defensive measures', Japan, South Korea and the United States responded by flying through it without doing so. There was no hostile response from China, but this is an issue that can be turned into an ultimatum at a time of Beijing's choosing.

Japan also claims sovereignty over the Kuril Islands in its far north, off Hokkaido, which it lost to the Soviet Union in the Second World War and which are still under Russian control. Russia prefers not to discuss the matter, but the debate is not in the same league as Japan's disputes with China. There are only approximately 19,000 inhabitants of the Kuril Islands, and although the islands sit in fertile fishing grounds, the territory is not one of particular strategic importance. The issue ensures that Russia and Japan maintain a frosty relationship, but within that frost they have pretty much frozen the question of the islands.

It is China that keeps Japanese leaders awake at night and

keeps them close to the USA, diplomatically and militarily. Many Japanese, especially on Okinawa, resent the US military presence, but the might of China, added to the decline in the Japanese population, is likely to ensure that the post-war USA–Japan relationship continues, albeit on a more equal basis. Japanese statisticians fear that the population will shrink to under 100 million by the middle of the century. If the current birth rate continues, it is even possible that by 2110 the population will have fallen below the 50 million it was in 1910. Japanese governments are trying a variety of measures to reverse the decline. A recent example is using millions of dollars of tax payers' money to fund a matchmaking service for young couples. Subsidised *konkatsu* parties are arranged for single men and women to meet, eat, drink and – eventually – have babies. Immigration is another possible solution but Japan remains a relatively insular society and immigration is not favoured by the population. Given that an increasingly assertive China has a population of 1.4 billion, Japan, itself a re-militarising power with a quietly hawkish outlook, is going to require friends in the neighbourhood.

So the Americans are staying in both Korea and Japan. There is now a triangular relationship between them, as underlined by the intelligence agreement noted above. Japan and South Korea have plenty to argue about, but will agree that their shared anxiety about China and North Korea will overcome this.

Even if they do go on to solve a problem like Korea, the issue of China will still be there, and this means the US 7th Fleet will remain in the Bay of Tokyo and US Marines will remain in Okinawa, guarding the paths in and out of the Pacific and the China Seas. The waters can be expected to be rough.

CHAPTER 9

LATIN AMERICA

'We like to be called the "continent of hope" . . . This hope is like a promise of heaven, an IOU whose payment is always put off.'

Pablo Neruda, Chilean poet and Nobel laureate

Caribbean Sea
ATLANTIC
OCEAN
Caracas
VENEZUELA
Georgetown
Paramaribo
Cayenne
GUYANA
SURINAM
FRENCH GUIANA
(FRANCE)
Bogotà
COLOMBIA
ANDES
Galapagos Islands
(ECUADOR)
Quito
ECUADOR
Amazon
Amazon Rainforest
BRAZIL
Cerrado
PERU
Lima
Lake Titicaca
La Paz
BOLIVIA
Sucre
Brasília

PACIFIC OCEAN
PARAGUAY
São Paulo
Rio de Janeiro
Asunción
Atacama Dese
CHILE
Aconcagua
Santiago
Paraná
URUGUAY
Buenos Aires
Montevideo
Rio de la Plata
ARGENTINA
Vaca Muerta
ANDES
ATLANTIC OCEAN
Falkland Islands (UK)
Tierra del Fuego
Cape Horn
South Georgia (UK)
State border
Amazon Rainforest
1000miles
1000km

LATIN AMERICA, PARTICULARLY ITS SOUTH, IS PROOF that you can bring the Old World's knowledge and technology to the new, but if geography is against you, then you will have limited success, especially if you get the politics wrong. Just as the geography of the USA helped it become a great power, so that of the twenty countries to the south ensures that none will rise to seriously challenge the North American giant this century nor come together to do so collectively.

The limitations of Latin America's geography were compounded right from the beginning in the formation of its nation states. In the USA, once the land had been taken from its original inhabitants, much of it was sold or given away to small landholders; by contrast, in Latin America the Old World culture of powerful landowners and serfs was imposed, which led to inequality. On top of this, the European settlers introduced another geographical problem that to this day holds many countries back from developing their full potential: they stayed near the coasts, especially (as we saw in Africa) in regions where the interior was infested by mosquitos and disease. Most of the countries' biggest cities, often the capitals, were therefore near the coasts, and all roads from the interior were developed to connect to the capitals but not to each other.

In some cases, for example in Peru and Argentina, the metropolitan area of the capital city contains more than 30 per cent of the country's population. The colonialists concentrated on getting the wealth out of each region, to the coast and on to foreign markets. Even after independence the predominantly European coastal elites failed to invest in the interior, and what population centres there are inland remain poorly connected with each other.

At the beginning of the 2010s it was fashionable among many business leaders, professors and media analysts to argue passionately that we were at the dawn of the 'Latin American decade'. It has not come to pass, and although the region has as yet unfulfilled potential, it will constantly be fighting against the hand it was dealt by nature and history.

Mexico is growing into a regional power, but it will always have the desert wastelands in its north, its mountains to the east and west and its jungles in the south, all physically limiting its economic growth. Brazil has made its appearance on the world stage, but its internal regions will remain isolated from each other; and Argentina and Chile, despite their wealth of natural resources, will still be far further away from New York and Washington than are Paris or London.

Two hundred years after the beginning of the struggle for independence, the Latin American countries lag far behind the North Americans and the Europeans. Their total population (including the Caribbean) is over 600 million, and yet their combined GDP is equivalent to that of France and the UK, which together comprise about 133 million people. They have come a long way since colonialism and slavery. There is still a long way to go.

Latin America begins at the Mexican border with the USA and stretches southwards 7,000 miles through Central America, and then South America, before ending at Tierra del Fuego on Cape Horn where the world's two great oceans, the Pacific and the Atlantic, meet. At its widest point, west to east, from Brazil across to Peru, it is 3,200 miles. On the western side is the Pacific, on the other the Gulf of Mexico, the Caribbean Sea and the Atlantic. None of the coastlines have many natural deep harbours, thus limiting trade.

Central America is hill country with deep valleys and at its narrowest point is only 120 miles across. Then, running parallel to the Pacific for 4,500 miles, is the longest continuous mountain chain in the world – the Andes. They are snow-capped along their entire length and mostly impassable, thus cutting many regions in the west of the continent off from the east. The highest point in the Western Hemisphere is here – the 22,843-foot Aconcagua Mountain – and the waters tumbling down from the mountain range are a source of hydro-electric power for the Andean nations of Chile, Peru, Ecuador, Colombia and Venezuela. Finally the land descends, forests and glaciers appear, we are into the Chilean archipelago and then – land's end. The eastern side of Latin America is dominated by Brazil and the Amazon river, the second-longest in the world after the Nile.

One of the few things the countries have in common is language based on Latin. Spanish is the language of almost all of them, but in Brazil it is Portuguese, and in French Guiana – French. But this linguistic connection disguises the differences in a continent that has five different climatological regions. The relative flatland east of the Andes and temperate climate of the lower third of South America, known as the Southern Cone, are in stark contrast to the mountains and jungle further north and enable agricultural and construction costs to be reduced, thus making them some of the most profitable regions on the entire continent – whereas Brazil, as we shall see, even has difficulty moving goods around its own domestic market.

Academics and journalists are fond of writing that the continent is 'at a crossroads' – as in about to embark at last on its great future. I would argue that, geographically speaking, it is less at a crossroads than at the bottom of the world; there's a lot going on all over this vast space, but the problem is that much of it is going on a long way from anywhere other than itself. That may be considered a Northern Hemispheric view, but it is also a view of where the major economic, military and diplomatic powers are situated.

Despite its remoteness from history's major population centres, there have been people living south of what is now the Mexico–USA border for about 15,000 years. They are thought to have originated from Russia and crossed the Bering Strait on foot at a time when it was still land. The present-day inhabitants are a mixture of Europeans, Africans, indigenous tribes and the Mestizo population, who are of European and native American descent.

This mix can be traced back to the Treaty of Tordesillas between Spain and Portugal in 1494, one of the early examples of European colonialists drawing lines on maps of faraway places about which they knew little – or, in this case, nothing. As they set off westward to explore the oceans, the two great European sea powers agreed that any land discovered outside Europe would be shared between them. The Pope agreed. The rest is a very unfortunate history in which the vast majority of the occupants of the lands now called South America were wiped out.

The independence movements began in the early 1800s, led by Simón Bolívar of Venezuela and José de San Martín of Argentina. Bolivar in particular is etched in the collective consciousness of South America: Bolivia is named in his honour, and the left-leaning countries of the continent are loosely tied in a 'Bolivarian' ideology against the USA. This is a fluctuating set of anti-colonialist/pro-socialist ideas which often stray into nationalism as and when it suits the politicians who espouse them.

In the nineteenth century many of the newly independent countries broke apart, either through civil conflict or cross-border wars, but by the end of that century the borders of the various states were mostly set. The three richest nations – Brazil, Argentina and Chile – then set off on a ruinously expensive naval arms race, which held back the development of all three. There remain border disputes throughout the continent, but the growth of democracy means that most are either frozen or there are attempts to work them out diplomatically.

Particularly bitter is the relationship between Bolivia and Chile, which dates back to the 1879 War of the Pacific in which Bolivia lost a large chunk of its territory, including 250 miles of coastline, and has been landlocked ever since. It has never recovered from this blow, which partially explains why it is among the poorest Latin American countries. This in turn has exacerbated the severe divide between the mostly European lowlands population and the mostly indigenous peoples of the highlands.

Time has not healed the wounds between them, nor those between the two countries. Despite the fact that Bolivia has the third-largest reserves of natural gas in South America it will not sell any to Chile, which is in need of a reliable supplier. Two Bolivian presidents who toyed with the idea were thrown out of office and the current president, Evo Morales, has a 'gas to Chile' policy consisting of a 'gas for coastline' deal, which is dismissed by Chile despite its need for energy. National pride and geographical need on both sides trump diplomatic compromise.

Another border dispute dating back to the nineteenth century is indicated by the borders of the British territory of Belize and neighbouring Guatemala. They are straight lines, such as we have seen in Africa and the Middle East, and they were drawn by the British. Guatemala claims Belize as part of its sovereign territory but, unlike Bolivia, is unwilling to push the issue. Chile and Argentina argue over the Beagle Channel water route, Venezuela claims half of Guyana, and Ecuador has historical claims on Peru. This last example is one of the more serious land disputes on the continent and has led to three border wars over the past seventy-five years, the most recent being in 1995; but again, the growth of democracy has eased tensions.

The second half of the twentieth century saw Central and South America become a proxy battlefield of the Cold War with accompanying coups d'état, military dictatorships and massive human rights abuses, for example in Nicaragua. The end of the Cold War allowed many nations to move towards democracy and, compared to the twentieth century, relations between them are now relatively stable.

The Latin Americans, or at least those south of Panama, mostly reside on, or near, the western and eastern coasts, with the interior and the freezing cold far south very sparsely populated. South America is in effect a demographically hollow continent and its coastline is often referred to as the 'populated rim'. This is less true of Central America and especially Mexico, where the populations are more equally distributed; but Mexico in particular has difficult terrain, which limits its ambitions and foreign policies.

In its far north Mexico has a 2,000-mile-long border with the USA, almost all of which is desert. The land here is so harsh that most of it is uninhabited. This acts as a buffer zone between it and its giant northern neighbour – but a buffer that is more advantageous to the Americans than the Mexicans due to the disparity in their technology. Militarily, only US forces could stage a major invasion across it; any force coming the other way would be destroyed. As a barrier to illegal entry into the USA it is useful, but porous – a problem with which successive US administrations will have to deal. President Trump rode to power partly playing on fears of illegal immigration, with his promise to build a wall along the US–Mexico border. His plans for the wall are flawed; there are usually ways around, under or even through a wall, and there's still the option of bribing your way into the country, or simply crossing over for a holiday and not going back. But not only would a wall help reduce the inward flow, it would stand as an aggressive symbol of intent, with a clear message: 'Don't come'.

All Mexicans know that before the 1846–8 war with the United States the land which is now Texas, California, New Mexico and Arizona was part of Mexico. The conflict led to half of Mexico's territory being ceded to the USA. However, there is no serious political movement to regain the region and no pressing border dispute between the two countries. Throughout most of the twentieth century they squabbled over a small piece of land after the Rio Grande changed course in the 1850s, but in 1967 both sides agreed the area was legally part of Mexico.

By the middle of the twenty-first century Hispanics are likely to be the largest ethnic group in the four US states listed above, and many will be of Mexican origin. There may eventually be Spanish-speaking political movements on both sides of the US–Mexican border calling for reunification, but tempering this would be the fact that many US Latinos will not have Mexican heritage, and that Mexico is unlikely to have anything approaching the living standards of the US. The Mexican government struggles to control even its own territory – it will not be in a position to take on any more in the foreseeable future. Mexico is destined to live in the USA's shadow and as such will always play the subservient role in bilateral relations. It lacks a navy capable of securing the Gulf of Mexico or pushing out into the Atlantic, and so relies on the US navy to ensure the sea lanes remain open and safe.

Private companies from both nations have set up factories just south of the border to cut costs in labour and transport, but the region is hostile to human existence and will remain the buffer land across which many of the poor of Latin America will continue to cross as they seek entry, legal or illegal, to the Promised Land to the north.

Mexico's major mountain ranges, the Sierra Madres, dominate the west and east of the country and between them is a plateau. In the south, in the Valley of Mexico, is the capital – Mexico City – one of the world's mega capital cities with a population of around 21 million people.

On the western slopes of the highlands and in the valleys the soil is poor, and the rivers are of limited assistance in moving goods to market. On the eastern slopes the land is more fertile, but the rugged terrain still prevents Mexico from developing as it would like. To the south lie the borders with Belize and Guatemala. Mexico has little interest in expanding southward because the land quickly rises to become the sort of mountainous terrain it is difficult to conquer or control. Extending into either country would not enlarge the limited amount of profitable land Mexico already has. It has no ideological territorial ambitions and instead concentrates on trying to develop its limited oil-producing industry and attracting more investment into its factories. Besides, Mexico has enough internal problems to cope with, without getting into any foreign adventures – perhaps none greater than its role in satisfying the Americans' voracious appetite for drugs.

The Mexican border has always been a haven for smugglers, but never more so than in the last twenty years. This is a direct result of the US government's policy in Colombia, 1,500 miles away to the south.

It was President Nixon in the 1970s who first declared a 'War on Drugs', which, like a 'War on Terror', is a somewhat nebulous concept in which victory cannot be achieved. However it wasn't until the early 1990s that Washington took the war directly to the Colombian drug cartels with overt assistance to the Colombian government. It also had success in closing down many of the air and sea drug routes from Colombia into the USA.

The cartels responded by creating a land route – up through Central America and Mexico, and into the American Southwest. The route partially follows the Pan-American Highway, which runs south to north up the continent. Originally designed to move goods in each direction to a variety of countries, it is now also used to move drugs north to the USA. This in turn led the Mexican drug gangs to get in on the action by facilitating the routes and manufacturing their own produce. The multibillion-dollar business sparked local turf wars, with the winners using their new power and money to infiltrate and corrupt the Mexican police and military and get inside the political and business elites.

In this there are parallels with the heroin trade in

Afghanistan. Many of the Afghan farmers growing the poppy crop responded to NATO's attempts to destroy their traditional way of making a living by either taking up arms or supporting the Taliban. It may be the government's policy to wage a 'War on Drugs', but this does not mean that the orders are carried out at a regional level, which the Afghan drug lords have penetrated. So it is in Mexico.

Throughout history, successive governments in Mexico City have never had a firm grip on the country. Now its opponents, the drug cartels, have paramilitary wings which are as well armed as the forces of the state, often better paid, more motivated, and in several regions are regarded as a source of employment by some members of the public. The vast sums of money made by the gangs now swill around the country, much of it being washed through what appear on the surface to be legitimate businesses.

Mexico is now in the grip of what is almost a civil war. The cartels try to control territory through intimidation, the government tries to pretend it is in charge of the rule of law, and hundreds of civilians, caught in the middle, are being killed. Among the most horrific manifestations of this was the presumed murder of forty-three student teachers by a cartel in 2014, an act which traumatised the country and galvanised the authorities, but ultimately looks to be 'just' another terrible milestone in what will be a long struggle.

The overland supply route is firmly established, and the demand in the USA shows few signs of diminishing. All Mexican governments try to keep on the right side of their powerful neighbour and have responded to American pressure by waging their own 'War on Drugs'. Here lies a conundrum. Mexico makes its living by supplying consumer goods to

America, and as long as Americans consume drugs, Mexicans will supply them – after all, the idea here is to make things which are cheap to produce and sell them at prices higher than those in legal trade. Without drugs the country would be even poorer than it is, as a vast amount of foreign money would be cut off. With drugs, it is even more violent than it would otherwise be. The same is true of some of the countries to Mexico's south.

Central America has little going for it by way of geography, but for one thing. It is thin. So far the only country to gain advantage from this has been Panama, but with the arrival of new money from China that may be about to change.

Modern technology means the Chinese can see from a glance at a satellite photograph the trade opportunities this thin

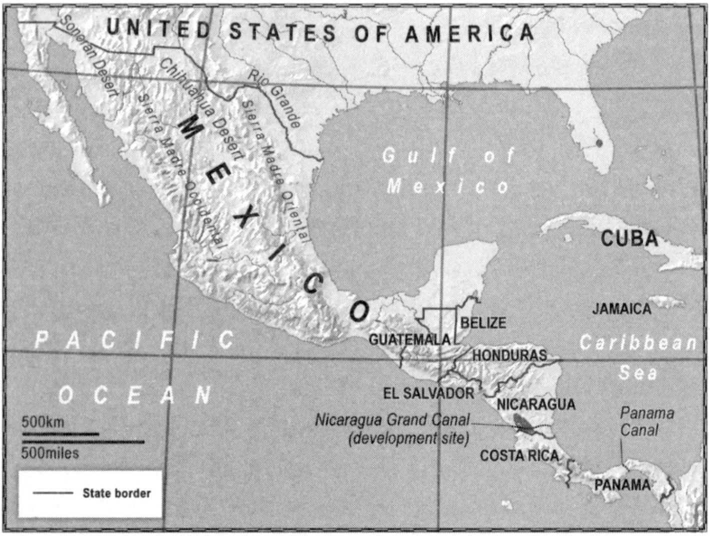

Central America could see many changes in the regions that are receiving Chinese investment, such as the development of the Nicaragua Grand Canal.

stretch of land might bring. In 1513 the Spanish explorer Vasco Núñez de Balboa had to sail across the Atlantic, land in what is now Panama, then trek through jungles and over mountains before seeing before him another vast ocean – the Pacific. The advantages of linking them were obvious, but it was another 401 years before technology caught up with geography. In 1914 the newly built, 50-mile-long, American-controlled Panama Canal opened, thus saving an 8,000-mile journey from the Atlantic to the Pacific oceans and leading to economic growth in the canal region.

Since 1999 the canal has been controlled by Panama, but is regarded as a neutral international waterway which is safeguarded by the US and Panama navies. And therein, for the Chinese, lies a problem.

Panama and the USA are friends – in fact, such good friends that in 2014 Venezuela briefly cut ties with Panama, calling it a 'US lackey'. The effect of the rhetoric of the increasingly embattled country's Bolivarian revolutionary era is tempered by the knowledge that the United States is Venezuela's most important commercial partner and that Venezuela supplies around 10 per cent of US oil imports. Nevertheless, Venezuela's brutal repression of anti-government demonstrations in 2017 did lead the USA to impose sanctions on President Maduro's substantial private assets and those of a number of high-ranking officials whose version of Bolivarian Socialism had led them to redistribute large amounts of money to themselves . In the spring of 2019 the situation came to a head with the opposition attempting to persuade the military to switch sides amid massive anti-government demonstrations.

China, as we saw in Chapter Two, has designs on being a global power and to achieve this aim it will need to keep sea lanes open for its commerce and its navy. The Panama Canal may well be a neutral passageway, but at the end of the day passage through it is dependent on American goodwill. So, why not build your own canal up the road in Nicaragua? After all, what's $50 billion to a growing superpower?

In 2013 the Nicaragua Grand Canal project was announced. It was funded by a Hong Kong businessman named Wang Jing who has made a lot of money in telecommunications but has no experience of engineering, let alone masterminding one of the most ambitious construction projects in the history of the world. Mr Wang is adamant that the Chinese government is not involved in the project. Given the nature of China's business culture and the participation of its government in all aspects of life, this is unusual.

The $50 billion cost estimate for the project, initially due for completion in the early 2020s, is four times the size of the entire Nicaraguan economy and forms part of the substantial investment in Latin America by China, which is slowly but steadily supplanting the USA as the region's main trading partner. Nicaragua's President Daniel Ortega signed up to the plan with alacrity and with scarcely a glance at the 30,000-plus people who may be required to move from their lands because of the project.

The former revolutionary socialist Sandinista firebrand now finds himself accused of being on the side of big business. If ever completed, the canal would split the country in two, and divide six municipalities, with just a single bridge planned to cross the canal along its entire length – although this has not been built because so far there is nothing to build it across.

The project is not going well. Mr Wang lost an estimated 85 per cent of his fortune in the Chinese stock market crash of September 2015. In late 2018 Ortega was still insisting that the project was going ahead, subject to environmental studies, but most construction work had ground to a halt, and the claim looked threadbare.

In the unlikely event of completion, the Nicaraguan canal would be longer than the Panama and, crucially, significantly wider and deeper, thus allowing much bigger tankers and container ships through, not to mention large Chinese naval vessels. However, President Ortega no longer trumpets this 'world-changing plan' and Mr Wang's phone seems to be on silent.

Given that the Panama Canal a few hundred miles to the south is being widened, sceptics ask why the Nicaraguan version was ever thought necessary and if it could ever be profitable, but the whole project appears to have been at least as much about the national interests of China as about commercial profit.

The concept of gouging a link between two oceans out of a nation state was a sign of China's increasing interest and investment in Latin America. We've grown used to seeing the Chinese as major players in Africa, but for twenty years now they have been quietly moving in south of the Rio Grande.

As well as investing in construction projects, China is lending huge sums of money to Latin American governments, notably those in Argentina, Venezuela and Ecuador. In return China will be expecting support in the United Nations for its regional claims back home, including the issue of Taiwan.

Beijing is also buying. The Latin American states have been picked off one by one by the USA, which prefers bilateral trade deals to doing business with the region as a whole, as they have to do with the EU. The Chinese are doing the same thing but at least offer an alternative, thus reducing the region's dependency on the USA as its market. For example, China has now replaced the USA as Brazil's main trading partner, and may do the same with several other Latin American countries.

The Latin American countries do not have a natural affinity with the USA. Relations are dominated by America's starting position, laid out in the Monroe Doctrine of 1823 (as we have seen in Chapter Three) during President Monroe's State of the Union address. The Doctrine warned off the European colonialists and said, in as many words, that Latin America was the USA's backyard and sphere of influence. It has been orchestrating events there ever since and many Latin Americans believe the end results have not always been positive.

Eight decades after Monroe's Doctrine, along came another president with 'Monroe reloaded'. In a speech in 1904 Theodore 'Teddy' Roosevelt said: 'In the Western Hemisphere the adherence of the United States to the Monroe Doctrine may force the United States, however reluctantly, in flagrant cases of [such] wrongdoing or impotence, to the exercise of an international police power.' In other words, the USA could militarily intervene whenever it chose to in the Western Hemisphere. Not including the funding of revolutions, the arming of groups and the provision of military trainers, the USA used force in Latin America almost fifty times between 1890 and the end of the Cold War.

After that, overt interference dropped off rapidly and in 2001 the USA was a signatory to the thirty-four-nation Inter-American Democratic Charter drafted by the Organization of American States, which proclaims that 'The peoples of the Americas have a right to democracy and their governments have an obligation to promote and defend it.' Since then the USA has concentrated on binding the Latin American countries to itself economically by building up existing trade pacts like the North American Free Trade Association, and introducing others such as the Central American Free Trade Agreement.

The lack of warmth thus engendered in south/north historic and economic relationships meant that when the Chinese came knocking, doors quickly opened. Beijing now sells or donates arms to Uruguay, Colombia, Chile, Mexico and Peru, and offers them military exchanges. It is trying to build a military relationship with Venezuela, which it hopes will outlast the Bolivarian revolution if and when it collapses. The arms supplies to Latin America are relatively small-scale but complement China's efforts at soft power. Its sole hospital ship, *Peace Ark*, visited the region in 2011. It is only a 300-bed vessel, dwarfed by the American 1,000-bed versions which also visit, but it was a signal of intent and a reminder that China increasingly 'gets' soft power.

However, with or without Chinese trade, the countries of Latin America are inescapably locked into a geographical region – which means that the USA will always be a major player.

Brazil, which makes up fully one-third of the land of South America, is the best example. It is almost as big as the USA, and its twenty-seven federal states equal an area bigger than the twenty-eight EU countries combined; but unlike them it lacks the infrastructure to be as rich. A third of Brazil is jungle, where it is painfully expensive, and in some areas illegal, to carve out land fit for modern human habitation. The destruction of the Amazon Rainforest is a long-term ecological problem for the whole world, but it is also a medium-term problem for

Brazil: the government allows slash-and-burn farmers to cut down the jungle and then use the land for agriculture. But the soil is so poor that within a few years crop-growing is untenable. The farmers move on to cut down more rainforest, and once the rainforest is cut it does not grow back. The climate and soil work against the development of agriculture.

The River Amazon may be navigable, but its banks are muddy and the surrounding land makes it difficult to build on. This problem, too, seriously limits the amount of profitable land available. Just below the Amazon region, in the highlands, is the savannah and, by contrast, it is a success story. Twenty-five years ago this area was considered unfit for agriculture, but Brazilian technology has turned it into one of the world's largest producer of soybeans, which – together with the growth in grain production – means the country is becoming a major agricultural producer.

To the south of the savannah are the traditional Brazilian agricultural lands. We are now in the Southern Cone of South America, which Brazil shares with Argentina, Uruguay and Chile. The relatively small Brazilian section is where the first Portuguese colonialists lived, and it was to be 300 years before the population could push out from this heartland and significantly populate the rest of the country. To this day most people still live close to the coastal areas, despite the dramatic decision made in the late 1950s to move the capital (previously Rio de Janeiro) several hundred miles inland to the purpose-built city of Brasilia in an attempt to develop the heart of Brazil.

The southern agricultural heartland is about the size of Spain, Portugal and Italy combined and is much flatter than the rest of the country. It is relatively well watered, but most of it is in the interior of the region and lacks properly developed transport routes.

The same is true of most of Brazil. If you look at many of the Brazilian coastal cities from the sea there is usually a massive cliff rising dramatically out of the water either side of the urban area, or directly behind it. Known as the Grand Escarpment, it dominates much of Brazil's coast; it is the end of the plateau called the Brazilian Shield which makes up most of Brazil's interior.

Because the country lacks a coastal plain, to connect its major coastal cities you need to build routes up and over the escarpment, along to the next urban area and then back down. The lack of decent modern roads is compounded by a similar deficiency of rail track. This is not a recipe for profitable trading or for unifying a large space politically.

It gets worse. Brazil does not have direct access to the rivers of the Rio de la Plata region. The River Plate itself empties out into the Atlantic in Argentina, meaning that for centuries traders have moved their goods down the Plate to Buenos Aires rather than carry them up and down the Grand Escarpment to get to Brazil's underdeveloped ports.

Therefore Brazil lacks the volume of trade it would like and, equally importantly, most of its goods are moved along its inadequate roads rather than by river, thus increasing costs. On the plus side Brazil is working on its transport infrastructure, and the newly discovered offshore gas reserves will help pay for this, reduce reliance on Bolivian and Venezuelan energy imports and cushion the inevitable economic dips all nations suffer. Nevertheless, Brazil will require a Herculean effort for it to overcome its geographical disadvantages.

Around 25 per cent of Brazilians are thought to live in the

infamous favela slums. When one in four of a state's population is in abject poverty it is difficult for that state to become rich. This does not mean Brazil is not a rising power, just that its rise will be limited.

A shortcut to growth could be soft power, hence Brazil's efforts to gain a permanent seat on the UN Security Council and its habit of building regional economic alliances such as Mercosur, which loosely ties together Brazil, Argentina, Paraguay, Uruguay and Venezuela. Every few years, often led by Brazil, the South Americans attempt to launch their version of the EU – the latest incarnation being UNASUR, of which twelve South American nations are members. Its headquarters is in Ecuador but Brazil has the loudest voice. In this it resembles the EU, which has an HQ in Belgium and a leading power in Germany. And there the comparison stops. UNASUR has an impressive presence on the internet but it remains more of a website than an economic union. The EU countries have similar political and economic systems and most members share a currency, whereas the Latin Americans differ in their politics, economics, currencies, education levels and labour laws. They also have to overcome the constraints of distance, as well as the heights of the mountains and the density of the jungles which separate them.

But Brazil will keep working to help create a South American powerhouse using its diplomatic and increasing economic strength. The country is by nature non-confrontational, its foreign policy is against intervention in other countries, and war with any of its neighbours seems highly unlikely. It has managed to maintain good relations with all the other eleven South American nations despite having a border with nine of them.

There is a frontier dispute with Uruguay, but it does not

look set to become inflamed; and the rivalry between Brazil and Argentina is unlikely to be played out anywhere more politically significant than a football pitch. In recent years Brazil has moved army units away from its border with Argentina and has seen its Spanish-speaking neighbour reciprocate. An Argentinian navy vessel has been welcomed in a Brazilian port whereas a British Royal Navy ship was denied such access a few years ago, thus pleasing the Argentinians in their ongoing diplomatic battle with the UK over the Falkland Islands.

Brazil is included in the BRICS – a group of major countries said to be on the rise both economically and politically, but, while each one may be rising individually, the concept is more fashion than reality. Brazil, Russia, India, China and South Africa are not a political or geographical grouping in a meaningful way and have very little in common with each other. If the letters had not spelt what sounds like a word then the BRICS theory would not have caught on. The BRICS hold an annual conference and Brazil does sometimes liaise with India and South Africa on international issues in a sort of vague echo of the Cold War Non-Aligned Movement, but it does not join Russia and China in taking a sometimes hostile stance towards the USA.

The North and South American giants did fall out in 2013 over an issue which still rankles in Brazil. The news that the US National Security Agency had spied on the then Brazilian President, Dilma Rousseff, led her to cancel a state visit to Washington. That an apology was not forthcoming from the Obama administration was testament to the fact that the Americans were irritated that China has supplanted them as Brazil's main trading partner. Brazil's subsequent decision to buy Swedish fighter jets for its air force rather than ones from

Boeing is thought to have been informed by the row. However, the state-to-state relationship has mostly now recovered. Confrontation is not Brazil's style, unlike Venezuela under the late President Chavez, and with President Jair Bolsonaro coming to power in 2019, the government is more pro-American than ever before. Bolsonaro is sometimes called the 'Trump of the tropics' and within weeks of assuming the presidency he had aligned himself with the Trump administration's policy on getting rid of Venezuela's President Maduro. The Brazilians know the world thinks they are a coming power, but they also know that their power will never match that of the Americans.

Neither will that of Argentina; however, in some ways it is better placed to become a First World country than is Brazil. It lacks the size and population to become *the* primary regional power in Latin America, which looks to be Brazil's destiny, but it has the quality of land to create a standard of living comparable to that of the European countries. That does not mean it will achieve this potential – simply that, if Argentina gets the economics right, its geography will enable it to become the power it has never been.

The foundations for this potential were laid in the nineteenth century with military victories over Brazil and Paraguay that resulted in control of the flat agricultural regions of the Rio de la Plata, the navigable river system, and therefore the commerce which flows down it towards Buenos Aires and its port. This is among the most valuable pieces of real estate on the whole continent. It immediately gave Argentina an economic and strategic advantage over Brazil, Paraguay and Uruguay – one it holds to this day.

However, Argentina has not always used its advantages to the full. A hundred years ago it was among the ten richest countries in the world – ahead of France and Italy. But a failure to diversify, a stratified and unfair society, a poor education system, a succession of coups d'état and the wildly differing economic policies in the democratic period of the last thirty years have seen a sharp decline in Argentina's status.

The Brazilians have a joke about their snobbish neighbours, as they see them: 'Only people this sophisticated could make a mess this big.' Argentina needs to get it right, and a dead cow may help it.

The Dead Cow, or Vaca Muerta, is a shale formation which, combined with the country's other shale areas, could provide Argentina's energy needs for the next 150 years with excess to export. It is situated halfway down Argentina, in Patagonia, and abuts the western border with Chile. It is the size of Belgium – which might be relatively small for a country, but is large for a shale formation. So far, so good, unless you are against shale-produced energy – but there is a catch. To get the gas and oil out of the shale will require massive foreign investment, and Argentina is not considered a foreign investment-friendly country.

There's more oil and gas further south – in fact, so far south it's offshore in and around islands which are British and have been since 1833. And therein lies a problem, and a news story which never goes away.

What Britain calls the Falkland Islands are known as Las Malvinas by Argentina, and woe befall any Argentine who uses the 'F' word. It is an offence in Argentina to produce a map which describes the islands as anything other than the 'Islas Malvinas' and all primary school children are taught to draw the outlines of the two main islands, west and east. To regain the 'Lost Little Sisters' is a national cause for successive generations of Argentines and one which most of their Latin neighbours support.

In April 1982 the British let their guard down and the Argentinian military dictatorship under General Galtieri ordered an invasion of the islands – which was considered a huge success until the British task force arrived eight weeks later and made short work of the Argentinian army and reclaimed the territory. This in turn led to the fall of the dictatorship.

If the Argentine invasion had happened in the present decade Britain would not have been in a position to retake the islands, as it currently has no functioning aircraft carriers – a situation that will be remedied by 2020, at which time Argentina's window of opportunity closes. However, despite the lure of oil and gas, an Argentinian invasion of the Falklands is unlikely for two reasons.

Firstly, Argentina is now a democracy and knows that the vast majority of Falkland Islanders wish to remain under British control; secondly, the British, once bitten, are twice shy. They may temporarily lack an aircraft carrier to sail the 8,000 miles down to the South Atlantic, but they do now have several hundred combat troops on the islands, along with advanced radar systems, ground-to-air missiles, four Eurofighter jets and probably a nuclear attack submarine lurking nearby most of the time. The British intend to prevent the Argentinians from even thinking they could get onto the beaches, let alone take the islands.

The Argentine air force uses planes which are decades behind the Eurofighter, and British diplomacy has ensured that an attempt by Argentina to buy up-to-date models from Spain was called off. Buying from the USA is a non-starter due to the Special Relationship between the UK and USA, which is indeed, at times, special; so the chances of Argentina being in a position to mount another attack before 2020 are slim.

However, that will not calm the diplomatic war, and Argentina has sharpened its weapons on that front. Buenos Aires has warned that any oil firm which drills in the Falklands/Malvinas cannot bid for a licence to exploit the shale oil and gas in Patagonia's Vaca Muerta field. It has even passed a law threatening fines or imprisonment for individuals who explore the Falklands' continental shelf without its permission. This has put many big oil companies off, but not, of course, the British. However, whoever probes the potential wealth beneath the South Atlantic waters will be operating in one of the most challenging environments in the business. Its gets somewhat cold and windy down there, and the seas are rough.

We have travelled as far south as you can go before you arrive at the frozen wastelands of the Antarctic. While plenty of countries would like to exert control there, a combination of the extremely challenging environment, the Antarctic Treaty and lack of obtainable and valuable resources, together largely prevent overt competition, at least for the present. The same cannot be said of its northern counterpart. Heading straight up from Antarctica to the northernmost part of the globe, you reach a place destined to be a diplomatic battleground in the twenty-first century as countries great and small strive to reach pole position there: the Arctic.

CHAPTER 10

THE ARCTIC

'There are two kinds of Arctic problems,
the imaginary and the real. Of the two,
the imaginary are the most real.'

Vilhjalmur Stefansson, *The Arctic in Fact and Fable*

State border
Ice coverage 26 August 2012
RUS
Siberia
Arctic Circle
Laptev Sea
Novosibirsk Islands
East Siberian Sea
Wrangel Island
Bering Sea
Chukchi Sea
Bering Strait
ARCTI
OCEA
ALASKA (USA)
Prudhoe Bay
Banks Island
Melville Island
Victoria Island
CAN
PACIFIC OCEAN

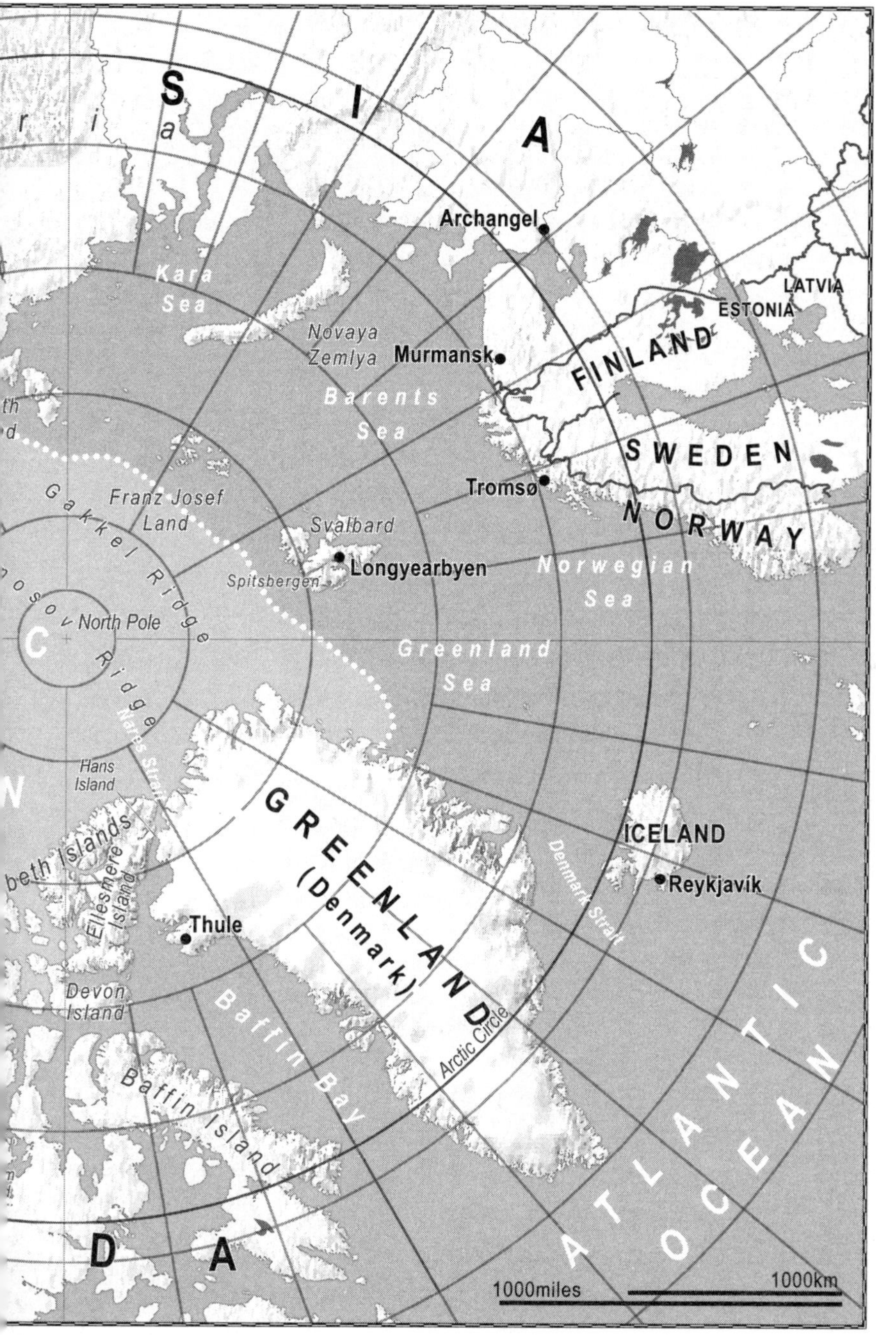
S I A
Archangel
Kara Sea
Novaya Zemlya
Murmansk
LATVIA
ESTONIA
FINLAND
Barents Sea
SWEDEN
Tromsø
NORWAY
Franz Josef Land
Gakkel Ridge
Svalbard
Longyearbyen
Spitsbergen
Norwegian Sea
North Pole
Greenland Sea
Nares Strait
Hans Island
GREENLAND (Denmark)
ICELAND
Reykjavík
Denmark Strait
Ellesmere Island
Thule
Devon Island
Baffin Bay
Arctic Circle
Baffin Island
ATLANTIC OCEAN
D A
1000miles
1000km

WHEN THE ICEMEN COME, THEY WILL COME IN FORCE. Who has the force? The Russians. No one else has such a heavy presence in the region or is as well prepared to tackle the severity of the conditions. All the other nations are lagging behind and, in the case of the USA, do not appear to be even trying to catch up: America is an Arctic nation without an Arctic strategy in a region that is heating up.

The effects of global warming are now showing more than ever in the Arctic: the ice is melting, allowing easier access to the region, coinciding with the discovery of energy deposits and the development of technology to get at them – all of which has focused the Arctic nations' attention on the potential gains and losses to be made in the world's most difficult environment. Many of the countries in the region have competing claims which they haven't bothered to press – until now. But there is a lot to claim, and a lot to argue about.

The word 'arctic' comes from the Greek *arktikos*, which means 'near the bear', and is a reference to the Ursa Major constellation whose last two stars point towards the North Star.

The Arctic Ocean is 5.4 million square miles; this might make it the world's smallest ocean but it is still almost as big as Russia, and one and a half times the size of the USA. The continental shelves on its ocean bed occupy more space proportionally than any other ocean, which is one of the reasons why it can be hard to agree on areas of sovereignty.

The Arctic region includes land in parts of Canada, Finland, Greenland, Iceland, Norway, Russia, Sweden and the USA (Alaska). It is a land of extremes: for brief periods in the summer the temperature can reach 26 degrees Celsius in some places, but for long periods in winter it plunges to below minus 45. There are expanses of rock scoured by the freezing winds, spectacular fjords, polar deserts and even rivers. It is place of great hostility and great beauty that has captivated people for millennia.

The first recorded expedition was in 330 BCE by a Greek mariner called Pytheas of Massilia, who found a strange land called 'Thule'. Back home in the Mediterranean, few believed his startling tales of pure white landscapes, frozen seas and strange creatures including great white bears; but Pytheas was just the first of many people over the centuries to record the wonder of the Arctic and to succumb to the emotions it evokes.

Many also succumbed to its deprivations, especially those voyaging to the edge of the known world in search of what doubters said was the 'mythical' Northwest Passage through the Arctic Ocean, linking the Atlantic to the Pacific Ocean. One example is Henry Hudson. He may have the second-largest bay in the world named after him, but back in 1607 he probably would have preferred to live into old age rather than be cast adrift and almost certainly sent to his death by a mutinous crew sick of his voyages of discovery.

As for the first person to reach the 'North Pole', well, that's a tricky one given that, even though there is a fixed point on the globe denoting its position, below it the ice you are standing on is moving, and without GPS equipment it is hard to tell exactly where you are. Sir Edward Parry, minus a GPS, tried in 1827, but the ice was moving south faster than he could move north and he ended up going backwards; but he did at least survive.

Captain Sir John Franklin had less luck when he attempted to cross the last non-navigated section of the Northwest Passage in 1845. His two ships became stuck in the ice near King William Island in the Canadian archipelago. All 129 members of the expedition perished, some on board the ships, others after they abandoned the vessels and began walking south. Several expeditions were sent to search for survivors but they found only a handful of skeletons, and heard stories from Inuit hunters about dozens of white men who had died walking through the frozen landscape. The ships had vanished completely, but in 2014 technology caught up with geography and a Canadian search team using sonar located one of the vessels, HMS *Erebus*, on the seabed of the Northwest Passage and brought up the ship's bell.

The fate of Franklin's expedition did not deter many more adventurers from trying to find their way through the archipelago, but it wasn't until 1905 that the great Norwegian explorer Roald Amundsen charted his way across in a smaller ship with just five other crew. He passed King William Island, went through the Bering Strait and into the Pacific. He knew he'd made it when he spotted a whaling ship from San Francisco coming from the other direction. In his diary he confessed his emotions got the better of him, an occurrence perhaps almost as rare as his great achievement: 'The Northwest Passage was done. My boyhood dream – at that moment it was accomplished. A strange feeling welled up in my throat; I was somewhat over-strained and worn – it was weakness in me – but I felt tears in my eyes.'

Twenty years later he decided he wanted to be the first man to fly over the North Pole which, although easier than walking across it, is no mean feat. Along with his Italian pilot Umberto Nobile and fourteen crew he flew a semi-rigid airship over the ice and dropped Norwegian, Italian and American flags from a height of 300 feet. A heroic effort this may have been, but in the twenty-first century it was not seen as one giving much legal basis to any claims of ownership of the region by those three countries.

That also applies to the impressive effort of Shinji Kazama of Japan, who in 1987 became the first person to reach the North Pole on a motorbike. Mr Kazama was so intrepid as not to have relied on a shrinking polar ice cap, and is the sort of man who would have ridden through a blizzard in order to get into the history books, but there is no doubt that there is now less ice to cross.

That the ice is receding is not in question – satellite imaging over the past decade clearly shows that the ice has shrunk – only the cause is in doubt. Most scientists are convinced that man is responsible, not merely natural climate cycles, and that the coming exploitation of what is unveiled will quicken the pace.

Already villages along the Bering and Chukchi coasts have been relocated as coastlines are eroded and hunting grounds lost. A biological reshuffle is under way. Polar bears and Arctic foxes are on the move, walruses find themselves competing for space, and fish, unaware of territorial boundaries, are moving northward, depleting stocks for some countries but populating others. Mackerel and Atlantic cod are now being found in Arctic trawler nets.

The effects of the melting ice won't just be felt in the Arctic: countries as far away as the Maldives, Bangladesh and the Netherlands are at risk of increased flooding as the ice melts and sea levels rise. These knock-on effects are why the Arctic is a global, not just a regional, issue.

As the ice melts and the tundra is exposed, two things are likely to happen to accelerate the process of the greying of the ice cap. Residue from the industrial work destined to take place will land on the snow and ice, further reducing the amount of heat-reflecting territory. The darker-coloured land and open water will then absorb more heat than the ice and snow they replace, thus increasing the size of the darker territory. This is known as the Albedo effect, and although there are negative aspects to it there are also positive ones: the warming tundra will allow significantly more natural plant growth and agricultural crops to flourish, helping local populations as they seek new food sources.

There is, though, no getting away from the prospect that

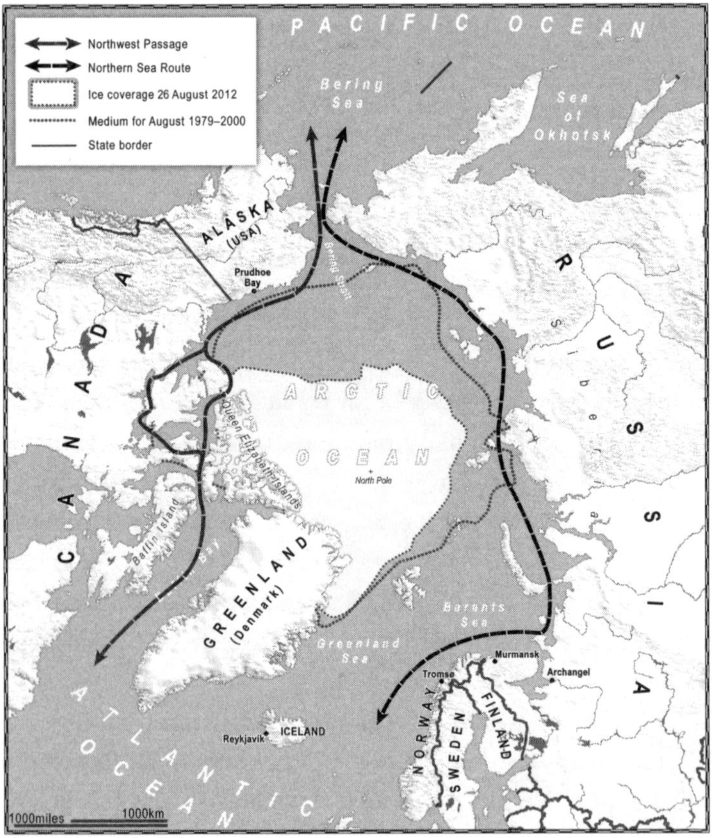

It is clear from satellite images that the ice in the Arctic is receding, making the sea lanes through the region more accessible for longer periods of the year.

one of the world's last great unspoiled regions is about to change. Some climate-prediction models say the Arctic will be ice-free in summer by the end of the century; there are a few which predict it could happen much sooner. What is certain is that, however quickly it happens and dramatic the reduction will be, it has begun.

The melting of the ice cap already allows cargo ships to make the journey through the Northwest Passage in the Canadian archipelago for several summer weeks a year, thus cutting at least a week from the transit time from Europe to China. The first cargo ship not to be escorted by an icebreaker went through in 2014. The *Nunavik* carried 23,000 tons of nickel ore from Canada to China. The polar route was 40 per cent shorter and used deeper waters than if it had gone through the Panama Canal. This allowed the ship to carry more cargo, saved tens of thousands of dollars in fuel costs and reduced the ship's greenhouse emissions by 1,300 metric tons. By 2040 the route is expected to be open for up to two months each year, transforming trade links across the 'High North' and causing knock-on effects as far away as Egypt and Panama in terms of the revenues they enjoy from the Suez and Panama canals.

The north-east route, or Northern Sea Route as the Russians call it, which hugs the Siberian coastline, is also now open for several months a year and is becoming an increasingly popular sea highway.

The melting ice reveals other potential riches. It is thought that vast quantities of undiscovered natural gas and oil reserves may lie in the Arctic region in areas which can now be accessed. In 2008 the United States Geological Survey estimated that 1,670 trillion cubic feet of natural gas, 44 billion barrels of natural gas liquids and 90 billion barrels of oil are in the Arctic, with the vast majority of it offshore. As more territory becomes accessible, extra reserves of the gold, zinc, nickel and iron already found in part of the Arctic may be discovered.

ExxonMobil, Shell and Rosneft are among the energy giants that are applying for licences and beginning exploratory drilling. Countries and companies prepared to make the effort to get at the riches will have to brave a climate where for much of the year the days are endless night, where for the majority of the year the sea freezes to a depth of more than six feet and where, in open water, the waves can reach sixteen feet high.

It is going to be dirty, hard and dangerous work, especially for anyone hoping to run an all-year-round operation. It will also require massive investment. Running gas pipelines will not be possible in many places, and building a complex liquefaction infrastructure at sea, especially in tough conditions, is very expensive. However, the financial and strategic gains to be made mean that the big players will try to stake a claim to the territories and begin drilling, and that the potential environmental consequences are unlikely to stop them.

The claims to sovereignty are not based on the flags of the early explorers but on the United Nations Convention on the Law of the Sea (UNCLOS). This affirms that a signatory to the convention has exclusive economic rights from its shore to a limit of 200 nautical miles (unless this conflicts with another country's limits), and can declare it an Exclusive Economic Zone (EEZ). The oil and gas in the zone is therefore considered to belong to the state. In certain circumstances, and subject to scientific evidence concerning a country's continental shelf, that country can apply to extend its control up to 350 miles from its coast. If accepted, the extension applies only to the seabed and excludes fishing rights.

The melting of the Arctic ice is bringing with it a hardening of attitude from the eight members of the Arctic Council, the forum where geopolitics becomes geopolarctics.

The 'Arctic Five', those states with borders on the Arctic Ocean, are Canada, Russia, the USA, Norway and Denmark (due to its responsibility for Greenland). They are joined by Iceland, Finland and Sweden, which are also full members. There are twelve other nations with Permanent Observer status having recognised the 'Arctic States' sovereignty, sovereign rights and jurisdiction' in the region, among other criteria. For example, at the 2013 Arctic Council, Japan and India, which have sponsored Arctic scientific expeditions, and China, which has a science base on a Norwegian island as well as a modern icebreaker, were granted Observer status.

However, there are countries not in the Council which say they have legitimate interests in the region, and still more which argue that under the theory of the 'common heritage of mankind' the Arctic should be open to everyone.

There currently are at least nine legal disputes and claims over sovereignty in the Arctic Ocean, all legally complicated, and some with the potential to cause serious tensions between the nations. One of the most brazen comes from the Russians: Moscow has already put a marker down – a long way down. In 2007 it sent two manned submersibles 13,980 feet below the waves to the seabed of the North Pole and planted a rust-proof titanium Russian flag as a statement of ambition. As far as is known, it still 'flies' down there today. A Russian think-tank followed this up by suggesting that the Arctic be renamed. After not much thought they came up with an alternative: 'the Russian Ocean'.

Elsewhere Russia argues that the Lomonosov Ridge off its

Siberian coast is an extension of Siberia's continental shelf, and therefore belongs to Russia exclusively. This is problematic for other countries, given that the Ridge extends all the way to the North Pole.

Russia and Norway have particular difficulty in the Barents Sea. Norway claimed the Gakkel Ridge in the Barents Sea as an extension of its EEZ, but the Russians disputed this, and they had a particular dispute over the Svalbard Islands, the northernmost point on Earth with a settled population. They came to an agreement in 2011 to share the area, but it remains a source of tension between them. Most countries and international organisations recognise the islands as being under (limited) Norwegian sovereignty, but the biggest island, Spitsbergen, has a growing population of Russian migrants who have assembled around the coal-mining industry there. The mines are not profitable, but the Russian community serves as a useful tool in furthering Moscow's claims on all of the Svalbard Islands. At a time of Russia's choosing it can raise tensions and justify its actions using geological claims and the 'facts on the ground' of the Russian population. In 2017 Moscow's defence secretary defined Svalbard as a 'potential area for future conflict' with Norway. By extension, that also means a potential area for conflict with NATO. In April 2019 there was a comically serious incident when Norway encountered a beluga whale it suspected of being used by Russia for spying. The whale was wearing a strange Russian-made harness in which, it was claimed, a GoPro camera could fit. On the harness were the words 'Equipment of St Petersburg'. A Russian colonel commented, 'Do you really think we'd attach a mobile phone number with the message "Please call this number"?'

Spy whale or not, Norway knows what might be coming

and has made the High North its foreign policy priority. Its air force regularly intercepts Russian fighter jets approaching its borders; the heightened tensions have caused it to move its centre of military operations from the south of the country to the north, and it is building an Arctic Battalion. Canada is reinforcing its cold-weather military capabilities, and Denmark has also reacted to Moscow's muscle-flexing by creating an Arctic Response Force.

Russia, meanwhile, is building an Arctic Army. Six new military bases are being constructed and several mothballed Cold War installations, such as those on the Novosibirsk Islands, are reopening, and airstrips are being renovated. A force of at least 6,000 combat soldiers is being readied for the Murmansk region and will include two mechanised infantry brigades equipped with snowmobiles and hovercraft.

It is no coincidence that Murmansk is now called 'Russia's northern energy gateway' and that President Putin has said that, in relation to energy supply, 'Offshore fields, especially in the Arctic, are without any exaggeration our strategic reserve for the twenty-first century.'

The Murmansk Brigades will be Moscow's minimum permanent Arctic force, but Russia demonstrated its full cold-weather fighting ability in 2014 with an exercise that involved 155,000 men and thousands of tanks, jets and ships. The Russian Defence Ministry said it was bigger than exercises it had carried out during the Cold War.

During the war games Russian troops were tasked with repelling an invasion by a foreign power named 'Missouri', which clearly signified the USA. The scenario was that 'Missouri' troops had landed in Chukotka, Kamchatka, the Kuril Islands and Sakhalin in support of an unnamed Asian power which had already clashed with Russia. The unnamed power was Japan, and the scenario's conflict was provoked by a territorial dispute said by analysts to be over the South Kuril Islands. The military display of intent was then underlined politically when President Putin for the first time added the Arctic region as a sphere of Russian influence in its official foreign policy doctrine.

Despite Russia's shrinking economic power, resulting in budget cuts in many government departments, its defence budget has increased and this is partially to pay for the boost in Arctic military muscle taking place between now and 2020. Moscow has plans for the future, infrastructure from the past and the advantage of location. As Melissa Bert, a US Coast Guard captain, told the Center for International and Strategic Studies in Washington DC: 'They have cities in the Arctic, we only have villages.'

All this is, in many ways, a continuation, or at least a resurrection, of Russia's Cold War Arctic policies. The Russians know that NATO can bottle up their Baltic Fleet by blockading the Skagerrak Strait. This potential blockade is complicated by the fact that up in the Arctic their Northern Fleet has only 180 miles of open water from the Kola coastline until it hits the Arctic ice pack. From this narrow corridor it must also come down through the Norwegian Sea and then run the potential gauntlet of the GIUK (Greenland, Iceland and the UK) gap to reach the Atlantic Ocean. During the Cold War the area was known by NATO as the 'Kill Zone', as this was where NATO's planes, ships and submarines expected to catch the Soviet fleet.

Fast forward to the New Cold War and the strategies remain the same, even if now the Americans have withdrawn their forces from their NATO ally Iceland. Iceland has no armed forces of its own and the American withdrawal was described by the Icelandic government as 'short-sighted'. In a speech to the Swedish Atlantic Council, Iceland's Justice Minister Björn Bjarnason said: 'A certain military presence should be maintained in the region, sending a signal about a nation's interests and ambitions in a given area, since a military vacuum could be misinterpreted as a lack of national interest and priority.'

However, for more than a decade now it has been clear that the Arctic is a priority for the Russians in a way it is not for the Americans. This is reflected in the degree of attention given to the region by both countries, or in the case of the USA, its relative inattention since the collapse of the Soviet Union.

It takes up to $1 billion and ten years to build an icebreaker. Russia is clearly the leading Arctic power with the largest fleet of icebreakers in the world, forty-four in total, according to the US Coastguard Review of 2013. Five of those are nuclear-powered, the only such versions in the world. In 2018, its most advanced icebreaker to date, the *Ilya Muromets*, arrived on active service in Murmansk. The vessel is capable of breaking ice that is a metre thick. On its first mission it led a nuclear submarine out of harbour and through an ice field. Moscow says that by 2035 it will have thirteen heavy icebreakers, including nine nuclear-powered ones.

By contrast, in 2019 the United States still had only one functioning heavy icebreaker, the USS *Polar Star*, down from the eight it possessed in the 1960s. In February 2019 the forty-three-year-old vessel caught fire while returning from a resupply mission to Antarctica. There were also ship-wide power outages, an evaporator for making drinking water broke and a propeller shaft began leaking. A few days later, Congress and President Trump agreed funding for a new heavy icebreaker. The Polar Star had already been refitted to give it a ten-year service-life extension through to 2023 but it is unlikely the new vessel will be ready in time to take over then. And even when it does come into service, it may still be required to go to Antarctica and not the Arctic. The US coastguard estimates it needs at least six new heavy icebreakers by 2029 to 'adequately' meet its demands. A report to congress suggested the first should be delivered by 2023 and then another each year. Watch this space – it is unlikely to be completely filled as the funds earmarked for the project are being eyed by President Trump for his controversial wall on the Mexican border.

The USA risks being embarrassed about its lack of capability in several ways. In 2012 it had to rely on a Russian ship to resupply its research base in Antarctica, which was a triumph for great power co-operation but simultaneously a demonstration of how far behind the USA has fallen. No other nation presents a challenge either: Canada has seven heavy- and medium-sized icebreakers, Finland has eight, Sweden seven and Denmark four. China, Germany and Norway have one each. But in 2019 China announced plans for a giant nuclear-powered vessel, a move that signals its interests in the energy-rich waters of the Arctic.

In the fall of 2015, then president Obama made a trip to Alaska during which he did call for more US icebreakers to be built. However, this was almost a passing remark on a trip built around the issue of climate change. The security and energy aspects of the Arctic were barely mentioned. Washington remains way behind the curve, something which the election of President Trump has not changed.

The USA has another problem. It has not ratified the UNCLOS treaty, effectively ceding 200,000 square miles of undersea territory in the Arctic as it has not staked a claim for an EEZ.

Nevertheless, it is in dispute with Canada over potential offshore oil rights and access to the waters in the Canadian archipelago. Canada says they are an 'internal waterway', while the USA says they are a strait for international navigation not governed by Canadian law. In 1985 the USA sent an icebreaker through the waters without informing Canada in advance, causing a furious row to break out between the two neighbours, whose relationship is simultaneously friendly and prickly.

The USA is also in dispute with Russia over the Bering Sea, Arctic Ocean and northern Pacific. A 1990 Maritime Boundary Agreement was signed with the then Soviet Union in which Moscow ceded a fishing region. However, following the break-up of the Soviet Union, the Russian parliament refuses to ratify the agreement. The area is treated by both sides as being under US sovereignty, but the Russians reserve the right to return to this issue.

Other disputes include that between Canada and Denmark over Hans Island, located in the Nares Strait, which separates Greenland from Ellesmere Island. Greenland, with its population of 56,000 people, has self-government but remains under Danish sovereignty. A 1953 agreement between Denmark and Canada left the island still in dispute, and since then both countries have taken the trouble to sail to it and plant their national flags on it.

All the sovereignty issues stem from the same desires and fears – the desire to safeguard routes for military and commercial shipping, the desire to own the natural riches of the region, and the fear that others may gain where you lose. Until recently the riches were theoretical, but the melting ice has made the theoretical probable, and in some cases certain.

The melting of the ice changes the geography and the

stakes. The Arctic states and the giant energy firms now have decisions to make about how they deal with these changes and how much attention they pay to the environment and the peoples of the Arctic. The hunger for energy suggests the race is inevitable in what some Arctic specialists have called the 'New Great Game'. There are going to be a lot more ships in the High North, a lot more oil rigs and gas platforms – in fact, a lot more of everything. The Russians not only have their nuclear-powered icebreakers, but are even considering building a floating nuclear power plant capable of withstanding the crushing weight of ten feet of ice.

However, there are differences between this situation and the 'Scramble for Africa' in the nineteenth century or the machinations of the great powers in the Middle East, India and Afghanistan in the original Great Game. This race has rules, a formula and a forum for decision-making. The Arctic Council is composed of mature countries, most of them democratic to a greater or lesser degree. The international laws regulating territorial disputes, environmental pollution, laws of the sea and treatment of minority peoples are in place. Most of the territory in dispute has not been conquered through nineteenth-century imperialism or by nation states at war with each other.

The Arctic states know that theirs is a tough neighbourhood, not so much because of warring factions but because of the challenges presented by its geography. There are five and a half million square miles of ocean up in the Arctic; they can be dark, dangerous and deadly. It is not a good place to be without friends. They know that for anyone to succeed in the region they may need to co-operate, especially on issues such as fishing stocks, smuggling, terrorism, search and rescue and environmental disasters.

It is plausible that a row over fishing rights could escalate into something more serious, given that the UK and Iceland almost came to blows during the 'Cod Wars' of the 1950s and 1970s. Smuggling occurs wherever there are transit routes, and there is no reason to believe the Arctic will be any different; but policing it will be difficult due to the conditions there. And as more commercial vessels and cruise ships head into the area, the search and rescue and anti-terrorism capabilities of the Arctic nations will need to grow accordingly, as will their capacity to react to an environmental disaster in increasingly crowded waters. In 1965 the icebreaker *Lenin* had an accident in its reactor whilst at sea. After its return to shore parts of the reactor were cut out and, along with damaged fuel, placed in a concrete container with a steel liner which was then dumped into the sea. Such incidents are likely to occur more frequently as the Arctic opens up, but they will remain difficult to manage.

Perhaps the Arctic will turn out to be just another battleground for the nation states – after all, wars are started by fear of the other as well as by greed; but the Arctic is different, and so perhaps how it is dealt with will be different. Our history has shown us the rapacious way of the zero-sum game. Arguably, a partial belief in geographic determinism, coupled with human nature, made it difficult for it to have been any other way. However, there are examples of how technology has helped us break out of the prison of geography. For example, we can cross the deserts and seas at speeds previous generations could not have even imagined. We have even broken the shackles of the Earth's gravity. In our newly globalised world we can use that technology to give us all an opportunity in the Arctic. We can overcome the rapacious side of our nature, and get the great game right for the benefit of all.

CONCLUSION

WE FINISHED AT THE TOP OF THE WORLD AND SO THE only way is up.

The final frontier has always called out to our imagination, but ours is the age in which humanity has lived the dream and pushed out into space, a millimetre into infinity, on our way to the future. Humanity's restless spirit ensures that our boundaries are not confined to what Carl Sagan famously called the 'Pale Blue Dot'.

But we must come back down to earth, sometimes with a bump, because we have neither conquered our own geography yet, nor our propensity to compete for it.

Geography has always been a prison of sorts – one that defines what a nation is or can be, and one from which our world leaders have often struggled to break free.

Russia is probably the clearest example, naturally expanding from the small region of flatland it controlled until its heartland covered a huge space ringed mostly by mountains and the sea – with just one vulnerable point across the North European Plain. If the Russian leaders wanted to create a great nation, which they did, then they had little choice as to what to do about that weak spot. Likewise, in Europe no conscious decision was made to become a huge trading area; the long, level networks of rivers made it possible, and to an extent inevitable, over the course of millennia.

As the twenty-first century progresses, the geographical factors that have helped determine our history will mostly continue to determine our future: a century from now, Russia will still be looking anxiously westward across what will remain flatland. India and China will still be separated by the Himalayas. They may eventually come into conflict with each other, but if that does happen, then geography will determine the nature of the fight: either they will need to develop technology to allow a huge military force to cross over the mountains, or, if that remains impossible and neither side wants to descend into nuclear war, to confront each other at sea. Florida will continue to guard the exit of and entrance to the Gulf of Mexico. It is the Gulf's location that is key, not who controls it. To take an extreme and unlikely scenario: imagine a majority Hispanic Florida has seceded from the USA and allied itself with Cuba and Mexico. This would alter only the dynamics of who controlled the Gulf, not the importance of the location.

Of course geography does not dictate the course of all events. Great ideas and great leaders are part of the push and pull of history. But they must all operate within the confines of geography. The leaders of Bangladesh might dream of preventing the waters from flooding up the Bay of Bengal, but they know that 80 per cent of the country is on a flood plain and cannot be moved. It is a point the Scandinavian and English leader King Canute made to his sycophantic courtiers in the eleventh century, when ordering the waves to retreat: nature, or God, was greater than any man. In Bangladesh all that can be done is to react to the realities of nature: build more flood defences, and hope that the computer modelling of rising waters due to global warming is overstated.

New geographical realities such as climate change present new opportunities and challenges. Global warming may well result in the mass movement of people. If the Maldives, and many other islands, really are destined to be lost to the waves, the impact will not just be on those leaving before it is too late but also upon the countries to which they flee. If the flooding of Bangladesh becomes worse, the future of the country and its 164 million people is dire; if the water levels rise much higher, this impoverished country may go under. And if the desertification of the lands just below the Sahel continues, then wars such as the one in Darfur, Sudan (partially caused by the desert encroaching on nomads in the north, which in turn pushed them southwards towards the Fur people), will intensify and spread.

Water wars are another potential problem. Even if stable democracies were to emerge in the Middle East in the coming decades, if the waters of the Murat River, which rises in Turkey before feeding the Euphrates, were to diminish considerably, then the dams Turkey would have to build to protect its own source of life could quite easily be the cause of war with Syria and Iraq downstream.

Looking further ahead, as we continue to break out of the prison of our geography into the universe, the political struggles will persist in space, at least for the foreseeable future.

A human being first burst through the top layer of the stratosphere in 1961 when twenty-seven-year-old Soviet cosmonaut Yuri Gagarin made it into space aboard *Vostok 1*. It is a sad reflection on humanity that the name of a fellow Russian called Kalashnikov is far better known.

Gagarin, Buzz Aldrin and many others are the descendants of Marco Polo and Christopher Columbus, pioneers who pushed the boundaries and who changed the world in ways they could not have imagined in their own lifetimes. Whether for better or worse is not the point; they discovered new opportunities and new spaces in which peoples would compete to make the most of what nature had put there. It will take generations, but in space, too, we will plant our flags, 'conquer' territory, claim ground and overcome the barriers the universe puts in our way.

There are now about 1,100 functioning satellites in space, and at least 2,000 non-functioning ones. The Russians and Americans launched approximately 2,400 of the total, about 100 have come from Japan and a similar number from China, followed by a host of other countries with far fewer. Below them are the space stations, where for the first time people live and work semi-permanently outside the confines of earth's gravity. Further on, at least five American flags are thought to be still standing on the surface of the moon, and further still, much further, our machines have made it out past Mars and Jupiter, some heading way beyond what we can see and are trying to understand.

It is tempting to think of our endeavours in space as linking humanity to a collective and co-operative future. But first there will continue to be competition for supremacy in outer space. The satellites are not just there to beam back our TV pictures, or to predict the weather: they also spy on other countries, to see who is moving where and with what. In addition, America and China are engaged in developing laser technology, which can be used as weapons, and both seek to ensure that they have a missile system that can operate in space and nullify the competition's version. Many of the technologically advanced nations are now making preparations in case they need to fight in space.

When we are reaching for the stars, the challenges ahead are such that we will perhaps have to come together to meet them: to travel the universe not as Russians, Americans or Chinese but as representatives of humanity. But so far, although we have broken free from the shackles of gravity, we are still imprisoned in our own minds, confined by our suspicion of the 'other', and thus our primal competition for resources. There is a long way to go.

BIBLIOGRAPHY

General references

Diamond, Jared, *Guns, Germs, and Steel* (New York: W. W. Norton, 2005)

Dodds, Klaus, *Geopolitics: A Very Short Introduction* (Oxford: Oxford University Press, 2007)

Ikenberry, G. John, 'The Illusion of Geopolitics', *Foreign Affairs* (May/June 2014)

Keegan, John, *Atlas of World War Two* (London: Harper Collins, 2006)

Mackinder, Halford John, 'The Geographical Pivot of History', *The Geographical Society*, Vol. 23, No. 4 (April 1904), 421–37

Mackinder, Halford John, *Democratic Ideals and Reality*, 1919

Mead, Walter Russell, 'The Return of Geopolitics', *Foreign Affairs* (May/June 2014)

Monmonier, M., *How to Lie with Maps* (Chicago: University of Chicago Press, 1996)

Parry, Chris, *Super Highway: Sea Power in the 21st Century* (London: Elliott & Thompson, 2014)

Pickles, John, *A History of Spaces: Cartographic Reason, Mapping and the Geo-Coded World* (London: Routledge, 2004)

Roberts, S., Secor, A., and Sparke, M., 'Neoliberal Geopolitics', *Antipode*, Vol. 35, No. 5 (November 2003), 886–97.

The Times Atlas of World History (London: Times Books, 2000)

The Times Comprehensive Atlas of The World, 12th edition (London: Times Books, 2007)

Weigley, Russell F., *The American Way of War* (Bloomington, IN: Indiana University Press, 1973)

Russia

Eberstadt, Nicholas, 'Russia's Peacetime Demographic Crisis: Dimensions, Causes, Implications' (National Bureau of Asian Research, 2010)

Kennan, George F., 'The Sources of Soviet Conduct', *Foreign Affairs* (July 1947)

'Russia's accusations – setting the record straight', NATO Fact Sheet (April 2014)

China

Beardson, Timothy, *Stumbling Giant: The Threats to China's Future* (New Haven, CT: Yale University Press, 2013)

Boehm, Dana Carver, 'China's Failed War on Terror: Fanning the Flames of Uighur Separatist Violence', *Berkley Journal of Middle Eastern and Islamic Law,* Vol. 2, No. 1:3 (2009)

De Crespigny, Rafe, *China This Century* (Oxford: Oxford University Press, 1992)

Holmes, James, 'When China Rules the Sea', *Foreign Policy* (September 2015)

Kaplan, Robert D., *The Revenge of Geography* (London: Random House, 2012)

Lewis, Martin, 'East Asia', Stanford University Global Geopolitics Lectures, East Asia (15 January 2008)

Shaughnessy, Edward L. (ed.), *China: Empire and Civilization* (London: Duncan Baird Publishers, 2005)

Theroux, Paul, *Riding the Iron Rooster* (London: Hamish Hamilton, 1988)

USA

Commager, S., *Documents of American History Volume 1: to 1898* (10th Edition) (New Jersey: Prentice Hall, 1988)

Kagan, Robert, *Dangerous Nation: America and the World, 1600–1898* (London: Atlantic Books, 2006)

Pei, Minxin, 'How America and China See Each Other', *Foreign Affairs* (March/April 2014)

'The Geopolitics of the United States, Part 1: The Inevitable Empire', Stratfor.com, 4 July 2014 (https://www.stratfor.com/analysis/geopolitics-united-states-part-1-inevitable-empire)

US Department of State, 'Rise to World Power, 1867–1913', A Short History of the Department of State (history.state.gov/departmenthistory/short-history)

Africa

Bloom, David E. and Sachs, Jeffrey D., 'Geography, Demography, and Economic Growth in Africa', Harvard Institute for International Development, Harvard University (October 1998)

Chaves, Isaías, Engerman, Stanley L. and Robinson, James A., 'Reinventing the Wheel: The Economic Benefits of Wheeled Transportation in Early Colonial British West Africa', February 2012 (http://scholar.harvard.edu/files/jrobinson/files/the_wheel_in_africa_february_2012.pdf)

Kasperson, Roger E. and Minghi, Julian V., *The Structure of Political Geography* (New Brunswick, NJ: Transaction Publishers, 2011)

Western Europe

Kagan, Robert, *Of Paradise and Power* (New York: Random House, 2003)

Ottens, Nick, '"Too Big for Europe": The Recurring German Problem', *Atlantic Sentinel*, 28 April 2014

Speck, Ulrich, 'Power and Purpose: German Foreign Policy at a Crossroads', 3 November 2014 (http://carnegieeurope.eu/publications/?fa=57167)

Simon, Luis and Rogers, James, 'The Return of European Geopolitics? All roads run through London', *The RUSI Journal*, Vol. 155, No. 3 (2010), 57–63

Turchin, Peter, *War and Peace and War* (London: Plume Books, 2007)

Middle East

Fisher, Max, '40 Maps Which Explain The Middle East', Vox.com, 5 May 2014 (http://www.vox.com/a/maps-explain-the-middle-east)

Malinowski, Jon C. (ed.), 'Iraq: A Geography', United States Military Academy, West Point, New York, 2004 (http://www.usma.edu/gene/SiteAssets/SitePages/Publications/Iraq%20A%20Geography.pdf?Mobile=1)

India and Pakistan

French, Patrick, *India: A Portrait* (London: Allen Lane, 2011)

'Geography of India', MapsofIndia.com, 12 November 2014 (http://www.mapsofindia.com/geography/)

Institute for the Study of War, 'Pakistan and Afghanistan' (2009)

Kreft, Dr. Heinrich, 'The Geopolitical Importance of Pakistan', Institut für Strategie- Politik- Sicherheits- und Wirtschaftsberatung (ISPSW), 15 February 2008

Musharraf, Pervez, *In The Line Of Fire: A Memoir* (New York: Free Press, 2008)

Latin America

Keen, Benjamin and Haynes, Keith, *A History of Latin America, Volume 1* (Wadsworth: Cengage Learning, 2012)

World Economic Forum on Latin America 2011 (http://www.weforum.org/events/world-economic-forum-latin-america-2011)

Zovatto, Daniel, 'Elections in the Southern Cone: Citizens Chose Continuity', Brookings, 30 October 2014 (http://www.brookings.edu/research/opinions/2014/10/30-democracy-alternation-latin-america-zovatto)

Korea and Japan

Chang, Gordon G., *Nuclear Showdown: North Korea Takes On The World* (London: Hutchinson, 2006)

Kim, Seung-Young, *American Diplomacy and Strategy Toward Korea and Northeast Asia 1882–1950 and After* (London: Palgrave Macmillan, 2009)

Oberdorfer, Don, *The Two Koreas* (New York: Basic Books, 2001)

Arctic

Bjarnason, Björn, 'Climate Change and Iceland's Role in North Atlantic Security' (speech), Belfer Center, John F. Kennedy School of Government, Harvard, 26 November 2007

Conant, Eve, 'Breaking the Ice: Russian Nuclear-Powered Ice-Breakers', Scientific American blog, 8 September 2012 (http://blogs.scientificamerican.com/guest-blog/2012/09/08/breaking-the-ice/)

Grydehøj, Anne, Grydehøj, Adam and Akrén, Maria, 'The Globalization of the Arctic: Negotiating Sovereignty and Building Communities in Svalbard, Norway', *Island Studies Journal* Vol. 7, No. 1 (2012), 99–119

United Nations, 'Part V: Exclusive Economic Zone', UNCLOS Treaty (http://www.un.org/depts/los/convention_agreements/texts/unclos/part5.htm)

Woods Hole Oceanographic Institution, 'The Arctic: Exploration Timeline, Polar Discovery', 2009 (http://polardiscovery.whoi.edu/arctic/330.html)

ACKNOWLEDGEMENTS

Many thanks to all those who freely gave of their time, advice and encouragement.

I would like to thank my wife Joanna for her patience and natural spellcheck abilities, Pippa Crane and Jennie Condell at Elliott and Thompson for giving shape and direction to my geographic wanderings, and Ollie Dewis for her encouragement and ideas.

I am grateful to the following for casting their experienced eyes over sections of the book and would like to reiterate that any errors contained therein are my doing and responsibility: James Richards (former official Chinese interpreter to the UK government, Chairman of China Association), Professor James D. Boys (Visiting Senior Research Fellow, Kings College London), David Slinn (former UK Ambassador to North Korea), Joel Richards MA (South American specialist), Kelvin O'Shea (Sky News), Tim Miller (Sky News), Jaksa Scekic (Reuters Belgrade) and Aleksander Vasca (Reuters Belgrade).

Also, thanks to those serving members of governments and the civil service who kindly gave me their expertise, but preferred it to be used without attribution.

INDEX

A

Abdullah, King 157
Abe of Japan, Prime Minister 61
Abkhazia 115
Adams, Henry 70
Adams, John Quincy 71
Addis Ababa 133
Aegean Sea 16, 99, 183
Afghanistan 9, 11–12, 23, 44, 48, 79, 80, 88, 109, 175, 177–8, 195–6, 199, 201, 202, 203–5, 206–211, 214, 253, 286
Africa
- agriculture 122, 136
- China and 61, 129, 133, 136, 135–8, 140
- climate and terrain 121–3, 124–5, 141
- diseases 122–3, 125, 130, 141
- early empires 124
- energy resources/oil 131, 134–5, 136, 137–8, 140, 141, 143
- European influence 124–5
- human rights 140
- internal conflicts 126–136, 143
- mineral resources 127, 128–9, 139, 140, 141, 143
- North 30, 88, 97, 121
- rivers 120, 123, 131–3, 137, 143
- size and population 120–1, 128, 131–2, 134, 139, 141, 144
- slavery 125
- Southern 122, 137, 140–3
- trading links 120–1, 123, 124–5, 127, 140, 143
- *see also* individual countries by name

African National Congress (ANC) 141–2
Aksai Chin 44
al-Bashir, Omar 140
Al Qaeda x–xi, 50, 161–2, 167–8, 204–6, 208, 210–11
al-Qaradawi, Yusuf 187–8
Alaska 10, 54, 74, 121, 196, 272, 284
Alawites 152, 159, 173
Albania 7, 14, 103
Algeria 149
Alps Mountains 26, 46, 92, 95
Amazon River 246, 260
Amazon Rainforest 128, 259–260
American Revolutionary War 68
Amundsen, Roald 274
Andes Mountains 246
Angola 61, 122, 126, 128, 129, 130, 136–7
Antarctica 267, 283–4
Appalachian Mountains 66, 68, 69
Arab-Israeli War 157
Arab Spring 41, 185
Arabian Desert 149
Arabian Peninsula 156
Arabian Sea 148, 192–3, 201, 216
Arctic xii, xiii, 8, 9, 12, 31, 54, 111, 267, 269–287
- Arctic Council 279, 286
- claims to sovereignty xiii, 278, 279, 280, 285
- expeditions 273–5, 279
- extent of region 272–3
- global warming 272, 275–8
- icebreakers 279, 283–4, 285, 286
- natural resources 272, 277–8, 281, 284–6
- Northern Sea Route 277
- Northwest Passage 273–4, 277
- Russia and the 279–282

United Nations Convention on the Law of the Sea 278, 284
Argentina 244, 245, 247, 248, 249, 257, 260, 262, 263, 264–7
Armenia 13–14, 27, 175
Armitage, Richard 205
Arunachal Pradesh 44, 213
Asia vi, 4–6, 10–11, 39, 41, 59, 81–2, 164, 180, 182, 184, 200, 201, 221, 226, 236, 281–2
see also individual countries by name
Assad, Bashar al- 155, 159, 160–1, 182
Assam 200, 214
Atatürk 181, 185
Atlantic Ocean 6, 16, 17, 29, 37, 60, 68, 75, 78, 79, 95, 97–8, 105, 109, 111, 120, 124, 136, 142, 183, 245, 251, 255, 261, 266, 267, 273, 282–3
Australia xii, 75, 78, 82
Austria 28, 40
Austro-Hungarian Empire 96
Azerbaijan 12, 13

B

Bahrain 81, 86, 180
Balbek, Ruslan 22
Balboa, Vasco Núñez de 255
Balkans x, 28–9, 103, 184
Baltic Sea 5, 9, 17, 24, 28, 29, 79, 115–6
Baltic States 7, 9, 22–4, 27–8, 115–6, 226
Baluchistan 61, 193, 197, 198–9, 210
Bangladesh 48, 60, 167, 193, 195, 196, 275, 289–290
Bay of Bengal 61, 192–3, 216, 289–290
Belarus 12, 13–14, 28
Belgium 5, 19, 111, 130, 262
Belize 249, 251
Berlin Wall 6
Bert, Melissa 282
Bessarabia *see* Moldova
Bhutan 193, 212–3
Bhutto, Benazir 205–6
Bild newspaper 116
bin Laden, Osama 208, 210–211
Bjarnason, Björn 283
Black Sea 8, 9, 15, 16, 17, 21–2, 26, 27, 28–9, 79, 95, 148–9, 182–3
Boko Haram 135–6
Bolívar, Simón 247–8
Bolivia 247–8, 255, 259, 261
Bolsonaro, Jair 264
Bosporus Strait 16, 17
Brahmaputra River 194
Brazil 75, 87, 245, 248, 258, 259–265
BRICS 263
Britain 28, 42, 99, 102, 109–112, 134, 164, 193–5
Afghanistan and 206–7
Belize and 249
Brexit 101, 108, 111–12
Falkland Islands 263, 265–6, 267
Israel/Palestine and 169
Libya and 78–9
Middle East and 150, 153, 156, 167
military forces 36, 60, 76–7, 78–9, 105, 108, 164, 167, 168, 206–7
USA and 68–9, 76–7
Brunei 58
Bulgaria 7, 14, 28–9, 95, 103
Burkina Faso 57
Burma *see* Myanmar
Burundi 129–130, 142

C

California, USA 73, 90
Cameron, David 79
Cameroon 135–6
Canada xii, 67, 272, 273–4, 277, 279, 281, 284, 285
Canadian Shield 67
Cape of Good Hope 120–1, 142
Caribbean 75, 245
Caribbean Sea 60, 87, 245
Catalonia 95, 112
Catherine the Great 8–9, 20
Caucasus 8, 9, 11, 27, 167, 184
Central African Republic 122, 129
Chad 121, 126, 136
Charles XII of Sweden, King 6
Chechnya, Caucasus 8, 11
Chile 75, 245, 246, 248, 249, 259, 260, 265
China viii–ix, xii, xiv, 9, 11, 30, 31–2, 33–62, 75, 76, 78, 80, 81, 82, 83–5, 87, 89, 123, 129, 133, 136, 137–140, 141, 188, 193, 198–9, 200, 211–13, 214–16, 220–1, 223–4, 225–6, 230, 231–2, 234, 235, 236, 237, 238, 239–240, 254–8, 259, 263, 277, 279, 284, 289, 291–2
Africa and 61, 129, 133, 136, 135–8, 140

China (continued)
Air Defence Identification Zone 56, 57–8, 83–4, 239
Arctic and 53, 279, 284
Bhutan 212–13
Communism 40–2, 44, 45–6, 51, 84–5, 237
early history 37–40
energy resources 85, 137–8, 139
Han Chinese 37–40, 43, 45–7, 48–9, 50
human rights 45–6, 51, 140
India and viii–ix, 44–5, 47–8, 61, 200, 201, 211–13
Japan and 55–6
Korea and 220, 224, 225–6, 229, 230
Latin America/Central and 254–8, 259, 263
Middle East and 188
military forces 47–8, 229 (*see also* Navy)
Mongol invasions 39
Navy 36–7, 52–6, 57–8, 59–61
North China Plain 'the heartland' 37–8
Pakistan and 198–9, 200, 201
Russia and 43, 48
Taiwan and 41, 54, 56–8, 85, 257
Tibet and 38, 41, 44–7, 48, 200, 211–12
USA and 36, 57–8, 59, 61, 62, 78, 80, 81, 82, 83–5, 220–1, 225–6, 237, 238, 255–6
Vietnam and 43–4, 58
Xinjiang 46, 47, 48–50
Churchill, Winston 4–5
Collective Security Treaty Organization (CSTO) 14
Colombia 246, 252, 259
colonialism xiii, xiv, 11, 126, 128, 130, 131, 134, 141, 152, 161, 185, 193–4, 203, 244, 247, 258, 260
Communism 6, 9, 12, 31, 32, 87, 137, 185–6
China 40–2, 44, 45–6, 51, 84–5, 237
Korea 220, 222, 223, 225–6
see also Russia/Soviet Union (USSR)
concrete 77, 80–1, 86, 136
Congo 120, 122
see also Democratic Republic of the Congo
Congo River 123
Crimea 14, 16–22, 26, 29, 32, 109, 115
Crimean War 6, 26
Croatia 95, 103
Cuba 60, 74–5, 83, 87–8, 137, 220, 289
Cuban Missile Crisis 74
Cyprus 183
Cyrenaica 126–7
Czech Republic 7, 14, 28, 30

D

Dagestan, Caucasus 12
Dalai Lama 45, 49, 200, 212
Danube River 26, 94, 95–6, 123
Democratic Republic of the Congo (DRC) 126, 127–130, 131, 136, 138, 141, 143, 140
Deng Xiaoping 42
Denmark 17, 104, 107, 113, 279, 281, 284, 285
Destroyers for Bases Agreement 76–7, 80–1
Diamond, Jared 120, 122
Dnieper river 7, 20, 24
Dodko/Takeshima Islands 233
Dominican Republic 74
dos Santos, José Eduardo 139–140
drones 136, 163–4, 205, 209–210
drug trafficking 252–4
Durand, Mortimer 203

E

East African Community 136
East China Sea 36, 43, 56, 77, 232, 234, 239
East Coast Plain 66
East Turkestan 48, 49
Ecuador 246, 249, 257, 262
Egypt 37, 75, 127, 131–4, 149, 160–1, 164, 168, 169–170, 172, 174, 177, 178, 180, 182, 183, 187, 277
Elburz Mountains 175
Erdoğan, Recep Tayyib 160, 182, 184–5
Eritrea 121, 129, 131
Estonia 7, 9, 12, 14, 24, 28
Ethiopia 61, 131, 132–4
Eurasian Economic Union 14
Europe xii, 4, 5, 6, 8–9, 10–11, 12, 18, 19, 22–3, 28–30, 31, 40, 46, 47, 66, 68, 71, 72, 76–7, 78–9, 80, 81–2, 86, 88, 89, 94–116, 120, 121, 123, 124–6, 127, 130, 132, 137–8, 141, 143, 148, 149, 150, 152, 164, 167, 169, 180–2, 183–4, 185–6, 206, 207, 226, 236, 244, 247, 248, 258, 264, 277, 288–9

see also European Union; Western Europe; individual countries by name
European Union (EU) xiii, 7, 14–15, 19–20, 27–8, 29, 30, 66, 78–9, 98, 99–101, 106–8, 111–12, 257, 259, 262
eurozone 99–100, 107

F
Falkland Islands 263, 265–6, 267
Fezzan 127
Finland 27, 28, 104, 272–3, 279, 284
First World War 6, 76, 130, 148, 150, 154, 156, 157, 169, 181
Florida 67, 71, 74, 87, 289
Florida Straits 74, 75
France 5, 6, 66, 69–70, 71, 77, 78–9, 95, 97–8, 102, 104, 105, 106, 107, 111, 114–5, 128, 136, 150, 157, 159, 164, 181, 246, 265
Franco, Francisco 98
Franco-Prussian War 105
Franklin, John 273–4
Free Tibet movement 45–6, 47

G
Gaddafi, Muammar 79
Gagarin, Yuri 290–1
Gakkel Ridge 280
Ganges River 194, 195
Gaza 169, 171, 172–3
Georges-Picot, François 150
Georgia 12, 14, 22, 27, 80
Georgia (USA) 68
Georgia–Russian war (2008) 22, 27, 115
Germany 5, 6, 10, 15, 19, 28, 40, 49, 74, 77, 90, 95, 97, 100, 102, 104–6, 108–110, 113, 114–5, 116, 130, 165, 232, 262, 284
Gibraltar Straits 16
GIUK gap 17, 111, 282
global warming/climate change 90, 201–2, 272, 275–8, 290
Gobi Desert 37, 42–3
Golan Heights 172, 174
Gorbachev, Mikhail 6–7
Grand Canal, China 39
Great Wall of China 39, 44
Great Zimbabwe 124
Greece 28, 32, 97, 99–101, 107, 126–7, 183
Greenland 17, 31, 111, 121, 272, 279, 282, 285
Guam 74–5, 77
Guatemala 249, 251–2
Gujarat 194–5
Gulf of Mexico 67, 69, 70, 74, 245, 251, 289
Gulf States 178
Gulf Stream 94
Guyana 249
Gwadar 49, 61, 198–9, 216

H
Hanbal, Ahmad ibn 151
Hanbali Islam 151
Hans Island 285
Hashemites 156–7, 168
Hawaii 75
Helmand Province 206–7
Herodotus 131
Hezbollah 158, 161, 174, 178
Himalayas viii–ix, 37, 44, 47–8, 193, 194, 201, 211, 214, 215, 289
Hindu Kush ix, 12, 193
Hindus 194, 195, 198
Hitler, Adolf 5, 100, 116
Hokkaido 55–6, 239
Holy Roman Empire 104–5
Hong Kong 42, 53, 57, 256
Honshu 233
Houthi rebels 179
Hu Jintao 46
Hudson, Henry 273
Hungary x, 7, 14, 28, 94–5
Hussein, Saddam 151, 154, 161, 178
Hutchison, Kay Bailey 21–2
Hutu people 129–131

I
Iberian Peninsula 95
Iceland 17, 77–8, 111, 272–3, 279, 282–3, 287
Imjin-gang River 226
India xiii, 13, 82, 121, 178, 188, 193–216, 232, 263, 279, 286, 289
  Afghanistan and 202–3
  China and viii–ix, 44–5, 47–8, 61, 200, 201, 211–13
  Kashmir 197, 198, 200–2
India–China war (1962) 200
Indian Defence Review 192
Indian Ocean 12, 16, 37, 43, 52, 58, 61, 120, 123–4, 142, 149, 192–3, 199

Indo-China 40, 236
Indonesia xii, 52, 58, 81, 84, 167
Indus River 194, 195, 201
Inner Mongolia 37, 41, 42, 47
Interahamwe 129
Iran 85–7, 89–90, 148, 149, 155, 158, 160, 161, 163, 164, 174, 175–180, 182, 185, 188, 198
Iran–Iraq War (1980) 176
Iraq xiv, 50, 79, 88, 114, 149–150, 152, 153–5, 157, 158–9, 160–1, 162, 165–6, 167, 168, 175, 176, 177–8, 180, 186, 188, 290
Islam
  militants/jihadists 50, 87, 127, 132, 135–6, 151, 161–6, 179, 193
  see also India; Islamic State; Middle East; Pakistan; Shia tribes; Sunni tribes
Islamic State 50, 113, 145, 148, 155, 161–5, 211
Israel 87, 114, 132, 149, 150, 156, 157, 167, 168, 169, 170–4, 176–7, 179, 183, 184
Italy 28, 70, 74, 75, 77–8, 98, 265, 274
Ivan the Great 8
Ivan the Terrible 7–8, 32

J

Japan xiii, 9, 12, 36, 41, 56, 61, 62, 75, 76, 77, 81, 82, 84, 215, 217–240, 275, 279, 282, 291
  Arctic and 275, 279, 282
  China and 55–6
  Korea and 224
  military forces 238–9
  Russia and 12, 225, 226, 232, 233–4, 239
  Second World War 224, 235–6, 238
  USA and 75, 76, 77, 81, 82, 84, 236–7, 240
Jefferson, Thomas 69, 87
Jerusalem 167, 169, 171–2
Jews *see* Israel
Jinnah 196
Jordan 149, 150, 156–7, 167, 168, 169–170, 173, 177

K

Kagan, Robert 116
Kaliningrad 115
Kaplan, Robert 60, 106
Karakoram Range 44, 193
Kashmir 197, 198, 200–2, 210
Kazakhstan 9, 13–14, 32, 48, 80
Kazama, Shinji 275
Kemal, Mustafa *see* Atatürk
Kenya 52, 61, 126, 131, 138, 139, 142
Khartoum, Sudan 132
Khrushchev, Nikita 17
Kiev, Ukraine 7, 14, 15–16, 17, 19, 20
Kim Jong-il 217, 223
Kim Jong-un 229–230
Kissinger, Henry 103
Klitschko, Vitaly 15
Kohl, Helmut 116
Korea xiii, 55, 217–240
  China and 220, 224, 225–6, 229, 230
  Korean War (1950–3) 78, 225–6
  North Korea 9, 82, 89, 220–2, 223, 225–6, 227–231, 233, 240
  nuclear weapons 221, 227, 229, 230, 231
  Russia and 225, 226, 229, 232–3
  South Korea 81, 82, 220–1, 225–8, 230, 231–2, 233, 239, 240
  USA and 220–1, 224–6, 227, 229–230, 231, 233
Kosovo ix, 103, 109
Kublai Khan 39
Kunlun Range 46
Kurds/Kurdistan 88, 149–150, 152–5, 160, 164, 165, 166, 176, 180
Kuril Islands 56, 239, 281–2
Kuwait 86, 149, 150, 154, 163
Kyrgyzstan 13–14, 48

L

Laos 43, 44
Latin America xiii, 31, 74, 87–8, 241–267
  agriculture 259–260, 264
  China and 254–8, 259, 263
  climate and terrain 245–6, 251–2
  drug trafficking 252–4
  energy resources 248, 261, 265, 267
  UNASUR 262
  USA and 244, 249–251, 252–4, 255, 257–9 (*see also* Mexico)
  see also individual names by country
Latvia 7, 9, 12, 14, 24, 28
Lebanon 132, 150, 157–8, 161, 167, 174, 178
Leopold of Belgium, King 128–9
Lhasa, Tibet 46, 47

Liberia 138
Libya 78–9, 109, 126–7, 149, 164, 186, 188
Lithuania 7, 9, 14, 24, 28, 29–30
Little Diomede Island 10
Louisiana Purchase (1803) 70
Luanda 137, 139

M

Macau 42
Macron, Emmanuel 107–8
Maduro, Nicolás 31, 255, 264
Magna Carta (1215) 110
Malaysia 58, 81, 84, 220
Maldives 275, 290
Mali Empire 124
Manchuria 32, 37, 41, 43, 47, 234, 235
Mao Zedong 41–2
Margvelashvili, Giorgi 27
Marshall Plan 77
Massachusetts 68
Meckel, Klemens 235
Mediterranean/Mediterranean Sea 16, 32, 78, 79, 97–8, 99, 121–2, 124, 132, 148, 150, 155, 169, 183, 273
Mekong River 45
Mercator maps 120–1
Merkel, Angela 100
Meseta Central 98
Mexican War (1846–48) 73
Mexico 67, 71–3, 75, 245, 247, 249–254, 259, 284, 289
Middle East xii–xiii, 30, 31, 77, 85–7, 89–90, 112, 113, 122, 124, 145–188, 249, 286, 290
  see also individual countries by name
migrants 112–3, 240
Ming dynasty, Chinese 39–40
Minneapolis 70
Mischief Islands 58
Mississippi Basin/River 66–7, 69–71, 73
Modi, Narendra 216
Moldova (Bessarabia) 14, 22, 24–6
Mongolia 9, 11, 37, 38, 41, 42–3, 47, 48
Monroe Doctrine 72, 258
Montreux Convention (1936) 16
Morales, Evo 248
Mozambique 123, 141
Mubarak, Hosni 187–8
Murmansk Brigades 281
Musharraf, Pervez 205–6
Muslim Brotherhood 159, 182, 187
Muslims *see* India; Islam; Middle East; Pakistan; Shia tribes; Sunni tribes
Myanmar 40, 43, 60, 61, 81, 193, 213, 215, 236

N

Nagaland 214
Namibia 120, 130
Napoleon Bonaparte 5, 6, 71, 98, 116
National Geographic 120, 225
NATO (North Atlantic Treaty Organization) ix–x, 6, 7, 14–17, 19, 20–3, 24–5, 26, 27, 32, 77–8, 80, 89, 102–4, 106, 108, 109, 114–5, 183, 202, 205–8, 210, 253, 280, 282
Nepal 193, 212
Netanyahu, Benjamin 87
Netherlands 5, 40, 111, 275
New Orleans 69, 71, 72–3, 74, 261
New Zealand 75, 78
Nicaragua 249
Nicaraguan Grand Canal project 87, 256–7
Niger River 123, 134
Nigeria 9, 124, 126, 134–6, 141, 143
Nile River 37, 123, 131–3, 246
Nixon, Richard 51, 252
North China Plain 37
North European Plain vii, 5, 6, 12–13, 14, 26, 32, 77, 96, 101–2, 104, 105, 116, 288–9
North Korea *see under* Korea
North Pole 273–5, 279–280
North Sea 17, 79, 105, 111, 116
Northwest Passage 273–4, 277
Norway 17, 77–8, 272–3, 274, 279, 280–1, 284
Nubian Desert 132

O

Obama, Barack 45, 61, 79, 81, 87–8, 89, 131, 160, 171, 210, 215, 263–4, 284
Oberdorfer, Don 224–5
Ohio River 69
Okinawa 56, 77, 84, 237, 238–9, 240
Oman 138, 148, 149
Ortega, Daniel 256–7
Ottoman Empire ix, 8, 20, 26, 96, 123, 149–150, 152, 156, 169, 182, 196
Özal, Turgut 181–2

P

Pacific Ocean 4, 8, 9, 12, 37, 43, 54, 55–6, 58, 59–60, 67, 69, 71, 73, 75, 77, 78, 82, 83, 84, 87, 229, 234, 236–7, 238, 240, 245–6, 255, 273, 274, 285
Pakistan xiii, 44, 48, 49, 60, 177, 189–216
  China and 198–9, 200, 201
  internal conflict 197–8, 199–200, 208–9
  Kashmir and 197, 198, 200–2
  see also Bangladesh
Palestine 114, 149, 156–7, 168–173
Palin, Sarah 9–10
Panama 249, 254–6, 257, 277
Panama Canal 75, 87, 255, 256, 257, 277
Papoulias, Karolos 100
Paracel Islands 60
Paraguay 262, 264
Parry, Edward 273
Pashtuns 197–8, 203–4, 206–7, 209–211
Pearl Harbor 236
Persian Empire 8, 153, 178
Peru 244, 246, 249, 259
Peshawar 204
Peter the Great 8, 13, 32
Philippines 58, 74–5, 84, 215, 226, 236
Poland 5, 7, 14, 16, 22, 23, 26, 28, 101–3, 226
Portugal 40, 42, 95, 97, 136, 137, 141–2, 246, 247, 260
Powell, Colin 205
Provisions of Oxford (1258) 110
Puerto Rico 74–5
Punjab 194–5, 197–8, 202–3, 209, 210, 213–4
Putin, Vladimir vii, 5, 6–7, 15–20, 23, 29, 30, 32, 79–80, 103, 160–1, 281, 282
Pyongyang 222, 223, 229, 231
Pyrenees Mountains 95, 97, 98
Pytheas of Massilia 273

Q

Qatar 151, 161, 180, 188
Qin dynasty, Chinese 39

R

refugees 112–3, 157, 169, 171, 195, 220
  see also migrants
Reid, John 206–7
Rhine River 95, 106, 123
Rhône River 98
Rio Grande 73, 250
Rocky Mountains 66–7, 70
Rojava 155
Roman Empire 95–6
Romania 7, 14, 17, 95, 103
Roosevelt, Theodore 75, 83, 258
Rousseff, Dilma 263–4
Russia/Soviet Union (USSR) vii, xii, 1–32, 38, 56, 67, 74, 79–80, 97, 102–4, 105, 114–5, 123, 137, 160–1, 182–3, 198–9, 203, 215–6, 225, 226, 229, 232, 233, 239, 247, 263, 272, 279–283, 284, 287–9, 290–1
  Afghanistan and 12–13, 203
  Arctic and 272, 279–283
  Baltic States and 7, 9, 22–4 (*see also* individual countries by name)
  China and 43, 48
  Empire established 9
  energy resources 24, 28–31, 109
  Georgia and 12, 14, 22, 27
  invasions of 6
  Ivan the Terrible 7–8, 32
  Japan and 12, 225, 226, 232, 233–4, 239
  Korea and 225, 226, 229, 232
  military forces 31, 32, 161, 164, 280–2
  Moldova and 14, 22, 24–6
  NATO and EU 6–7, 14–15, 19–24, 102–4
  Nord Stream 2 project 29
  naval forces 16–17, 111, 183, 282
  Poland and 5, 7, 14, 22
  ports and trade 12–13, 15, 16–17, 43
  Syria 159, 160
  Ukraine and 13–22, 24, 25–6, 29, 43
  USA and 21–2, 25, 31, 77, 78, 79–80, 89, 281–3, 285
Russo-Japanese War (1904–5) 225, 235
Rwanda 129–130, 131, 138, 142, 143
Ryukyu Islands 56, 237, 239

S

Saakashvili, Mikheil 27
Sadat, Anwar 160
Sahara Desert 120, 121–2, 124, 136
Sahel region, Africa 121–2, 125, 136, 290
Salafi Islam 151, 167
San Martín, José de 247
Sargasso Sea 78

satellites xi, 165, 213, 222, 254–5, 275, 291
Saudi Arabia 86, 136, 149, 150, 156, 161, 167–8, 177, 178–180, 188, 203
Scandinavia 74, 103–4
Schäuble, Wolfgang 100
Scotland 111–12
Sea of Japan 12, 43, 55–6, 229, 231
Second World War 6, 9, 41, 76–7, 98, 100, 106, 109, 116, 130, 169, 238, 239
Seminole Indian nation 71
Serbia ix–x, 28, 95, 103
Sevastopol 14, 16, 17
Seward, William 74
Shang dynasty, Chinese 38
Shanghai 40, 46, 56
Shia tribes 88, 150–3, 155, 157, 158, 165, 167, 174, 177, 178, 179–180, 198
Siachen Glacier 200
Siberia 4, 8, 10–11, 277, 280
Sierra Madres Mountains 251
Sierra Nevada Mountains 67
Sikhs 194, 195, 213–14
Sindhs 197–8, 210
Singapore 58, 81, 34, 236
Singh, Amarjit 192
Sino-Japanese War, First 235
Six-Day War (1967) 171
Skagerrak Strait 17, 282
slavery 39, 125, 245
Slovakia 7, 14, 28, 95
Slovenia 103
Southern African Development Community (SADC) 142
South African National Defence Force 143
South America *see* Latin America; individual countries by name
South China Sea 39, 53–5, 58–60, 84, 215
South Korea *see under* Korea
South Ossetia 27, 115
Soviet Union (USSR) *see* Russia/Soviet Union (USSR)
space programmes 290–2
Spain 40, 60, 69, 71, 74–5, 95, 97, 98, 112, 121, 128, 181, 246, 247, 266
Spratly Islands 58, 59, 84
Sri Lanka 60–1
Stalin, Joseph 13, 26, 32
Strait of Hormuz 111, 175, 177
Strait of Malacca 58, 61, 84, 111, 199, 216
Sudan 125, 126, 131, 132, 138, 140, 143, 290
Suez Canal 16, 121, 132, 277
Suez Crisis (1956) 77
Sui dynasty, Chinese 39
Sunni tribes 87, 88, 150–3, 157, 158–9, 161, 163, 165–7, 178, 179–180, 182, 198
Svalbard Islands 280
Sweden 6, 104, 113, 263–4, 272, 279, 283, 284
Sykes, Mark 150
Sykes–Picot 150
Syria xi–xii, xiv, 16, 32, 50, 81, 89, 148, 149–150, 152, 155, 157, 158–161, 162, 163–4, 166, 169–170, 174, 180, 182–3, 188, 290

T

Taiwan (Republic of China) 36, 41, 54–5, 56–8, 85, 236, 237, 239, 257
Tajikstan x, 13–14, 44, 48, 50
Taliban x–xi, 203–211, 253
Tanzania 122, 124, 129, 130, 131, 138–9, 141, 142
Tehran 86–7, 173
Texas 69, 72–3, 250
Thailand 52, 81, 215
Theroux, Paul 46
Tibet xiv, 38–9, 41, 44–7, 48, 50, 200, 201, 211–12, 213
Tibetan Plateau 37, 45
Transcontinental Treaty (1819) 71
Transnistria, Moldova 26, 115
Treaty of Tordesillas 247
Triple Entente (1907) 105, 150
Tripolitania 126–7
Trump, Donald 22–3, 25, 61, 80, 81–2, 86–7, 89–90, 171–2, 207, 211, 216, 229–230, 250, 264, 283–4
Turkey 13, 16, 17, 26, 28–9, 49, 50, 83, 99, 103, 125, 127, 152, 155, 160, 164, 175, 177, 180–5, 290
Turkmenistan 13, 175, 183
Tutsi people 129–131

U

Uganda 122, 129–130, 131, 142
Uighur people 47, 48, 49–50

Ukraine vii, xii, 7, 9, 12, 13–22, 24, 25–6, 27, 28, 43, 53, 79–80, 102, 109, 115
Umayyad Caliphate 194
United Arab Emirates (UAE) 86, 163, 180
United Nations 129, 134, 140, 143, 169, 179, 226, 257
  Convention on the Law of the Sea 278, 284
  Human Development Index 129
  Security Council 20–1, 140, 262
United States of America xii, 9–10, 17, 18, 21, 23, 27, 29, 31, 36, 57–8, 59, 61, 62, 63–90, 99, 102–3, 106, 109, 128, 132, 136, 137–8, 154, 167, 171–2, 176, 183, 188, 196, 200, 201, 203, 204–5, 206, 207–211, 215–16, 289
  Afghanistan 211
  American Revolutionary War 68
  Arctic and 281, 283–5
  Britain and 68–9, 76–7
  California Gold Rush 73–4
  Caribbean and 75
  China and 36, 57–8, 59, 61, 62, 78, 80, 81, 82, 83–5, 220–1, 225–6, 237, 238, 255–6
  Cuba and 74–5, 83, 87–8
  Declaration of Independence (1776) 68–9
  Destroyers for Bases Agreement 76–7, 80–1
  early settlers and explorers 68
  energy resources 85–6, 255
  French territory 69–70
  Homestead Act (1862) 73–4
  Iran and 86–7, 89–90, 176, 177–8
  Israel and 87, 171–2
  Japan and 75, 76, 77, 81, 82, 84, 236–7, 240
  Korea and 82, 89, 220–1, 224–6, 227, 229–230, 231, 233
  Latin America and 244, 247, 249–254, 255, 256, 257–9, 263–4, 266–7 (*see also under* Mexico)
  military forces 67, 72, 76–7, 81, 82, 86, 106, 136, 163, 164–5, 209–211, 230 (*see also* NATO; Navy and naval bases)
  Monroe doctrine 72, 258
  native Americans 247
  Navy and naval bases 53, 74, 75, 76–7, 80–1, 82, 86, 163, 255
  Russia/Soviet Union and 21–2, 25, 31, 77, 78, 79–80, 89, 281–3, 285
  space programme 291–2
Ural Mountains 4–6, 8–10, 24, 97
Uruguay 259, 260, 262–3, 264
USS *Kitty Hawk* 36
USSR *see* Russia/Soviet Union
Uzbekistan 13

V

Vaca Muerta 'Dead Cow' 265, 267
Venezuela 31, 246, 249, 255, 257, 259, 261, 262, 264
Vietnam 43–4, 58, 78, 81, 84, 215
von Bismarck, Otto 90, 103

W

War of Independence 69
War on Drugs 252–4
War on Terror/Afghanistan 205, 252
  see also NATO; individual states by name
Wang Jing 256–7
War of the Pacific (1879) 248
Warsaw Pact 6, 7, 13, 14, 102–3
Washington, George 76
West Bank 156, 169–170, 171, 172–3
Western Europe 17, 26, 28–9, 91–116, 120, 121, 181
  see also European Union (EU); individual countries by name
Williamson, Gavin 60

X, Y

Xinjiang 40, 46, 47, 48–50, 199
Yangtze River 37, 39, 45
Yanukovych, Viktor 15, 109
Yellow River 37, 39, 45
Yellow Sea 43, 55
Yemen 149, 168, 178–9, 188
Yuan dynasty, Mongol 39

Z

Zagros Mountains 175, 176
Zambezi River 123, 124
Zambia 129, 136, 138, 141
Zheng He 52
Zhirinovsky, Vladimir 12
Zhou Enlai 51
Zimbabwe 124, 126, 130, 141